D0207076

Reconceptualizing Qualitative Research

SAGE was founded in 1965 by Sara Miller McCune to support the dissemination of usable knowledge by publishing innovative and high-quality research and teaching content. Today, we publish more than 750 journals, including those of more than 300 learned societies, more than 800 new books per year, and a growing range of library products including archives, data, case studies, reports, conference highlights, and video. SAGE remains majority-owned by our founder, and after Sara's lifetime will become owned by a charitable trust that secures our continued independence.

Los Angeles | London | Washington DC | New Delhi | Singapore | Boston

Reconceptualizing Qualitative Research

Methodologies without Methodology

Mirka Koro-Ljungberg

Arizona State University

Los Angeles | London | New Delhi
Singapore | Washington DC | Boston

Los Angeles | London | New Delhi
Singapore | Washington DC | Boston

FOR INFORMATION:

SAGE Publications, Inc.
2455 Teller Road
Thousand Oaks, California 91320
E-mail: order@sagepub.com

SAGE Publications Ltd.
1 Oliver's Yard
55 City Road
London EC1Y 1SP
United Kingdom

SAGE Publications India Pvt. Ltd.
B 1/I 1 Mohan Cooperative Industrial Area
Mathura Road, New Delhi 110 044
India

SAGE Publications Asia-Pacific Pte. Ltd.
3 Church Street
#10-04 Samsung Hub
Singapore 049483

Acquisitions Editor: Helen Salmon
Associate Digital Content Editor: Katie Bierach
Editorial Assistant: Anna Villarruel
Production Editor: Kelly DeRosa
Copy Editor: Rachel Keith
Typesetter: C&M Digitals (P) Ltd.
Proofreader: Caryne Brown
Indexer: Maria Sosnowski
Cover Designer: Rose Storey
Marketing Manager: Nicole Elliott

Copyright © 2016 by SAGE Publications, Inc.

All rights reserved. No part of this book may be reproduced or utilized in any form or by any means, electronic or mechanical, including photocopying, recording, or by any information storage and retrieval system, without permission in writing from the publisher.

Printed in the United States of America

Cataloging-in-Publication Data is available for this title from the Library of Congress.

ISBN 978-1-4833-5171-1

This book is printed on acid-free paper.

15 16 17 18 19 10 9 8 7 6 5 4 3 2 1

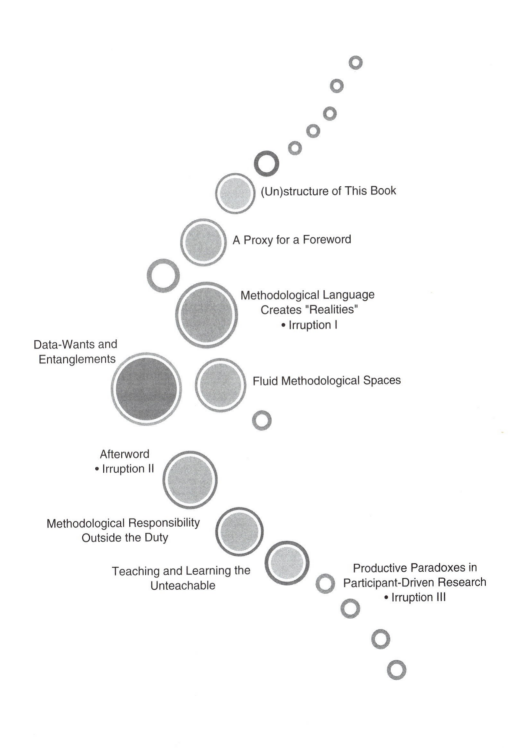

(Un)structure of This Book

A Proxy for a Foreword

Methodological Language
Creates "Realities"
• Irruption I

Data-Wants and
Entanglements

Fluid Methodological Spaces

Afterword
• Irruption II

Methodological Responsibility
Outside the Duty

Teaching and Learning the
Unteachable

Productive Paradoxes in
Participant-Driven Research
• Irruption III

Brief Table of Contents

Detailed Table of Contents

About the Author

Mirka Koro-Ljungberg (PhD, University of Helsinki) is a Professor of qualitative research at the Arizona State University. Her research and publications focus on various conceptual and theoretical aspects of qualitative inquiry and participant-driven methodologies. In particular, Koro-Ljungberg's scholarship brings together theory and practice, the promotion of epistemology, and the development of situated and experimental methodologies.

Random yet Necessary Appreciation Notes

This book has many different authors (material, spiritual, cognitive, experiential, national, international authors), and there are far too many people to thank. This book is about qualitative research methodology but also about my life as a teacher, scholar, student, learner, collaborator, reader, writer, woman, immigrant, wife, and mother. Therefore, I want to acknowledge my dear family—my husband Jonas and sweet and active kids Emil, Rasmus, and Jonathan. I am sorry I have missed far too many soccer practices and ball games to write these pages. And without Jonas—his household help, cooking skills, and impeccable sense of when to take our boys for a hike or bike ride or to the soccer field—finishing this writing task would have been very close to impossible. Furthermore, my parents Ulla and Markku have been faithful and endless supporters throughout my career. They have followed my career with (ignorant) bliss.

I take full responsibility for all text in this book, even though I had many lovely opportunities to collaborate and work with many doctoral students at the University of Florida. For example, Chandra Bowden and Kristi Cheyney helped me conceptualize and co-author chapters on participant-driven research and pedagogy. I also utilized an advisory board consisting of 12 graduate students to shape the content and development of this book. I met with the advisory board biannually to solicit their feedback, comments, and questions. To all these students and future colleagues, I express deep appreciation and gratitude. You inspire, challenge, friend, and move me. Melanie Acosta, Amber Benedict, Kathryn Comerford, Jessica Gouldthorpe, Cliff Haynes, Ann Hayslip, Justin Hendricks, Cheryl McLaughlin, Jason Schnipper, Darby Shannon, Jasmine Ulmer, and Becky Williams—you rock, and you are my rock stars! Thanks for writing this book with me!

I also want to thank Robert Ulmer and Jim Benedict for allowing me to use their inspiring photography. I owe a big hug to my SAGE editor Helen Salmon, who encouraged me to write, and to express sometimes overly complex thoughts through simpler sentences—and who simply and graciously guided me through the writing of my first book. I could not have hoped for more supportive publication relationship. In addition, many thanks to my constructively critical peer reviewers Ruth Ban, Jori Hall, Cassie Quigley, and Jenni F. Wolgemuth.

In addition, I would like to thank Hanna Guttorm for inspiring me to add more poetic elements and writing to this project. I did not aim for "poetic" in the sense of strict structures or poetic forms, but poetic in the sense of becoming more expressive and effective—poetic texts to add more personal, intimate, and risky elements to the text.

Last, but definitely not least, I need to acknowledge my muscles, blood cells, neurons, and other organs for fueling and nurturing me. After long early morning runs through Florida swamps and parks, you pumped blood, activated new connections between neurons, and made me physically exhausted. During these misty early morning hours, creative ideas were born and this text was written.

The (Un)Structure of This Book

This book does not provide an introduction to normative qualitative research. I do not describe the most common processes of qualitative research, strictly define many terms, or discuss in detail why I believe qualitative research is rigorous and scientific. From my perspective, all these tasks have been carried out successfully in the past (see, e.g., Creswell, 2007; Denzin & Lincoln, 2011; Flick, 2009; Freeman, deMarrais, Preissle, Roulston, & Elizabeth, 2007; Schwandt, 2007). This book does not repeat step-by-step approaches or provide easy answers. It does not offer a readily available methodological manual to be uncritically copied and implemented. Maybe it does not even refer to qualitative research as many of us have come to know it.

Some introductory textbooks describe qualitative research as a simplified and sometimes (overly) technical process. These types of introductions might offer some pedagogical value through their easily accessible texts. At the same time, they may perpetuate notions of the methodological immaturity, randomness, atheoreticalness, or insufficiency of qualitative research. To counter this potential immaturity and absence of theory, I intend to provide more complex and theoretically situated discussions about qualitative research practices and processes. I will discuss the complexity, multiplicity, and methodological uncertainty embedded in different methodological configurations and entanglements. These configurations and entanglements blur the boundaries between doing research, theorizing, thinking, and reflecting.

What can I expect from this book?

This book has a structure in its "un-structuredness" (note: I do not refer to randomness but to a structure that works against structure). These texts represent my commitment to thinking about qualitative research differently, often in creative ways, continually questioning existing grand narratives and dogmas. Furthermore, I may provide only few "answers" to complex methodological and theoretical questions in the form of examples or critical reflections, but, more important, these texts focus on asking for "more": more "appropriate," critical, provocative, and different questions about theories, methodology, research designs, and practices.

This book includes eight discrete but linked sections. Each section deals with one area of methodological puzzlement (i.e., nagging interest and conceptual investment) that I find important for emerging and more senior scholars interested in qualitative research to address. In addition, qualitative research spreads across diverse fields and disciplines, and thus writing a book to cover all methodological territory or even all personal puzzlements is impossible. As a result, I have carefully selected methodological sticky points and ongoing questions that have the potential to debunk certain methodological grand narratives and simplified notions often associated with methodology.

I must begin somewhere. The following "Proxy for a Foreword" addresses multiplicity and complexity in research methodologies. Toward the end of the book, I chronicle a discussion by novice and senior researchers about how to translate the proposed methodological ideas into learning, pedagogy, and teaching practice, and I envision collaborative scholarship that engages individuals outside academia. And then there is the middle of the book: a middle embedded with ideas, musings, questions, and rebuttals, all in an effort to encourage comfort with the discomfort of conducting research without methodology.

I would also like to note that the sections of this book do not need to be read in a specific order. Some co-readings or parallel readings may also be helpful.

How do I read this book?

At the end of each section I have created a beginning list of potential co-reading and parallel materials, which I call the "reading list of life." These readings (outside academic prose) may help readers move away from simplified notions of text, reductionist readings, and linguistic authority. Co-reading may also create openness and exposure to alternative means of expression, such as films and other visual and bodily forms of art and experimentation.

Robert Ulmer

How might the irruptions work?

To disrupt the linear logic and topical flow often associated with traditional scientific reporting and introductory texts to qualitative research, I have created some "irruptions" that will provide provocative extensions to the discussed topics. Irruptions also serve as examples of uncertainty and "unthinkable" energy. For example, some irruptions simultaneously exemplify and question linearity and normativity embedded in current research practices and "knowing," whereas others have been conceived as breaks from potentially disturbing and challenging discourses. In addition, the sections including more poetic text serve as a form of irruption: a change of textual and linguistic pace that, it is hoped, will promote and stimulate a different affect and reaction in readers. Images are also aimed at providing transitional irruptions, shifting attention and focus between different objects and textual dimensions.

The first section ("A Proxy for a Foreword") serves as a distant substitute for a formal introduction or foreword, since "introduction" as a concept is problematic and implies a fixed beginning. The texts in this book are not designed to flow from "beginning" to "end," but operate in the "middle" (middle of writings, ideas, classes, readings, research projects, and life). Furthermore, the narration and ideas shared here have multiple unrelated tiny beginnings, and the writing as well as thinking presented here has happened in various physical, conceptual, and theoretical places. An original outline was crafted for the editor and reviewers to provide a conceptual space where thinking and writing would happen. I also used the preliminary outline as a constellation of a few raw and unfinished textual dots that could be used to link different pieces of narration together if readers so desired. In time-ordered space, "foreword" signifies "before-ness"—standing before the other words—whereas outside the sequential time-space metaphor a foreword is just another word beside and alongside the other words. Here I subscribe to the latter perspective. **I wrote here and there, everywhere, and sometimes nowhere**. (Note: Here and in the sections to come, bolded text is referenced in the students' comments presented in the boxes alongside the main text.) In other words, the first section does not reflect an overview per se or any kind of solid theoretical grounding for various methodological extensions I present later. Instead, I use the space traditionally reserved for introduction to provide conceptual clues and hints of theoretical styles and of how I interact with methodology and stay attentive to thinking and practices as a qualitative researcher.

> *Writing as an inquiry. We each (un)learned while reading, writing, reflecting, and discussing. There is no end or beginning, only being.*
>
> —Chandra

The second section of this book, "Methodological Language Creates 'Realities': Labels and Language Matter," focuses on language and ways in which some (qualitative) researchers use labels and signifiers. More specifically, the purpose of this section is to draw attention to the various ways methodological language and labels are used in qualitative research to create diverse and continually changing "realities." Language can serve as an epistemological strategy or device, and it cannot be taken for granted. Instead, this section prompts more creative and innovative uses of methodological labels and research-centered language/discourse across traditions and disciplines.

Data should not be taken for granted. In the third section, titled "Data-Wants and Entanglements: Data Matter," my intention is to stimulate scholars to re/un/consider the "definitions" and role of data, hoping that this move might lead to different practices/processes/thoughts/questions outside the realm of certainty and knowing. This section pays attention to data and the various layered and complex ways scholars can generate and interact with data without taking data for granted. What we (researchers, scholars, students, teachers, etc.) do with "data" once we have/gain/doubt/seek "access" to it often happens in unexpected, unpredictable, and entangled ways. I suggest that, instead of capturing or gathering the data, we could begin by investigating/rethinking/releasing data's positioning and relationships—the "role of data." I also wonder how we come to know the relationship between data and researchers as one-directional but ultimately controlled by the researcher. In what ways does this position of researcher-as-knower bind and limit us as well as the data? I propose that without ever really knowing what "data wants," researchers are bound to consider data amorphous, uncertain, and shifting instead of reductionist, fixed, and "knowable."

The fourth section, "Fluid Methodological Spaces: Methodologies Matter," questions the linearity of research designs and provides possible alternatives to the linear logic often associated with methodologies. More specifically, I work against given, stable, rigid, and predetermined methodological structures. Instead, I discuss fluid methodological spaces where multiple things and methods occur simultaneously and where frameworks and methodological foci are diverse and continuously changing. I also provide examples of research designs and methodological flows, including varied research objects, practices, enactments, and ways of representing realities. In these spaces that could be called incorporeal (i.e., where reality is abstract) and in fluid spaces, methods are conceptualized as temporary structures that are being regenerated again and again. Following this line of thought, methodological flows and approaches do not collapse or disappoint. Instead, they melt, transform, circumvent, infiltrate, appear, and disappear while opening up new directions for qualitative research.

The "Afterword" of this book, "This Project (and Other Projects Alike) May Be Productively 'Failing,'" is located in the middle of other sections to follow my notion of "after," which is not about "past" or "last" per se—not confined to anticipation or historical linearity—but refers to an always present past or an already past present. I propose that "before," "present," and "after" do not signify fixed notions of time, but form temporary conceptual linkages between events that are overturned or questioned by the next emerging or established linkage/event. In this section, I also refer to productive failures as unfinished and unceasingly emergent research and writing that pose ongoing challenges to scholars due to their emergent and surprising character. When one approaches methodologies without methodology, from the perspective of productive failures, one commits to reinventing, revising, and reenvisioning methodologies today and in the future. The methodological work needs to stay in motion and under constant inquiry and questioning. Scholars should not be satisfied with existing methodological practices, since these practices often need modification to be suitable for new contexts and projects. Furthermore, I use questions as a tool or a technique to think about the past/present/future of qualitative research and inquiry.

Methodological work and research designs are not neutral or value free. Rather, methodology calls for responsible decision making in the face of the unknown. I have dedicated the sixth section, named "Methodological Responsibility Outside Duty: Responsibility Matters," to ethical discussions in order to remind qualitative scholars about their responsibilities beyond their duty. I problematize the decontextualized, widely generalizable, and "readily applicable" uses of methodology and methods across all disciplines and research traditions. I aim to resist structures that force scholars to view their duty as researchers as being that of creators of readily applicable and widely generalizable research to advance humankind or contribute to scientific progress. I also encourage scholars to shy away from easy methodological practices, decontextualized methodological decision making, and the uncomplicated use of methodology. Instead, I direct attention to responsibility, cultural values, troublesome questions, multiple viewpoints, and ideological and methodological impossibilities.

Resistance to qualitative research practices comes in different forms. In addition to resistance that is politically influenced, many forms of resistance relate to pedagogy, teaching, and learning. I have found teaching methodology (i.e., methodology as exemplified in this book) very hard and challenging. Thus, my chapter co-authors and I saw the importance of dedicating a section to teaching, and we have titled it "Teaching and Learning the Unteachable: Pedagogies Matter." Like many qualitative researchers and methodologists, we see qualitative inquiry as nuanced and complicated, and this diversity and complexity are also reflected in the ways in which qualitative research is being taught. In this section, we propose that the phenomenon "teaching–learning–research–methodology" forms complex relationships and entanglements among theory, teaching, learning, living, practices, and so on. These entanglements are always enacted differently each time we attend a class, talk about research, or carry out research or teaching activities. This section is also about pedagogies of uncertainty and multiplicity, and about our struggles with teaching content and experiences that are mostly unteachable. We utilize three main thinking devices—ghosts, events, and erasure—to process thoughts, materials, experiences, and memories associated with learning and teaching qualitative research in potentially less normative ways. More specifically, we think with ghosts (Marx and Derrida) and through events (Deleuze), and we resist institutional structures by placing writing and one potential curriculum for qualitative methodology "under erasure" (Derrida). These thinking devices come in the form of demonstrations, or pedagogical experimentations, if you will— experimentations as we have experienced them, as influenced by others, lived events and moments, and institutional structures and expectations.

The collaboratively written section, "Productive Paradoxes in Participant-Driven Research, or Stop Research for Research's Sake! Communities and Audiences Matter," speaks to research practices and processes that are driven by participants. We explore what might happen if social science researchers were to reconceptualize the reasons and ways in which they engage in research, more collectively making research not only more accessible but increasingly more collaborative between scholars and individuals outside academia. We promote research that is always directly linked to practice, not only the form of practice that scholars claim to know or address but also practice as experienced or described by the public, laymen, participants, and our friends, neighbors, fellow residents, and so on. At the same time, we acknowledge the challenges of this type of work. Thus, we provide insights into potential paradoxes accompanying such research and previously mentioned propositions. We draw our examples from research studies, students' body maps, and a dialogue across our colleagues and collaborators.

It is my hope that this book will prompt current and future qualitative researchers to reconceptualize research and counter the normativity of methodologies and research approaches by moving toward theories and practices that are culturally responsive, ethical, and methodologically flexible. Maybe this material can be used as a resource to promote and valorize the diversity, cultural situatedness, and uniqueness of critical social science inquiries, offering one testimony to the engaging and powerful analytical and inventive potential of critical social science and qualitative research.

Everything is possible. At some point you, my dear reader, may feel confused, irritated, lost, and frustrated, and you might even stop reading. This book text may also haunt you by hailing your return and stimulating reinteractions even after you finish the grant, design the method course, prepare the conference presentation, or complete the research project. Maybe some ideas will nurture your inner creativity and ongoing questioning and foster your movement toward innovative sciences and research practices. Let these and other examples and theories take you in unexpected directions!

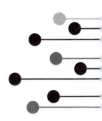

The notion of methodologies without methodology represents methodologies without strict boundaries or normative structures— methodologies that may begin anywhere, anytime, but by doing so can create a sense of uncertainty and loss (or mourning of stable, fixed, preconceptualized, or historical knowledge). Methodologies without methodology bring about methodological challenges and examples that may push current research practices and question rigid methodological traditions. They can begin anywhere, stay (at least temporarily) lost and uncertain, and still promote change in onto-episte-methodological practices.

Robert Ulmer

Lather and St. Pierre (2013), in their QSE special issue on post-qualitative research, put forward engaging ideas regarding the presence and "future" of qualitative research in the wake of "after" and "posts." Scholars such as Lather and St. Pierre have questioned various neopositivist tenets in qualitative research practice, and they have envisioned qualitative research beyond positivism, after interpretive and linguistic turns. Similar to Lather and St. Pierre, many post-qualitative scholars focus on ontological turn, especially rethinking and moving beyond humanist ontology. Representation, voice, "I," analysis, data, binary logic, and many other central concepts of neopositivist and interpretive frameworks are put under erasure and sometimes even completely avoided or found irrelevant. In addition, many recent developments of qualitative inquiry have had to do with new materialism and bringing individuals and their materials worlds closer. For example, some post-qualitative scholars, including new materialists, find it refreshing and important to study entanglements between humans and matter, spirit/mind and particles. Braidotti (2006) argued that Haraway's and Deleuze's theories share two key features of posthuman and *new process ontology*: neofoundational materialism and theory of relationality. Cyborgs and body-machines are connection-making entities that deliberately blend and mix categories and binaries. MacLure (2013), in turn, promoted practices that could engage the materiality of language itself through nonrepresentational or post-representational thoughts and methodologies, paying attention to the materiality embedded in social and cultural practices. From these perspectives, material relations matter and impact the ways in which individuals perceive and experience their lives.

Lather (2013) proposed that post-qualitative research examples utilize multidirectionality, post-human bodies, networks, othernesses, and disparities. In some ways, this book also builds from post-qualitative research practices, and Lather's (2013) description of QUAL 4.0 reassembles many approaches and thoughts highlighted in this book. For instance, inquiries and methodological approaches in this book cannot be tidily described, and many instrumental methodologies may not apply to these ideas or may seem insufficient. *Methodologies without methodology* (as well as *qualitative, methodology, ethics*, etc.) is a label without stable identity and identifiers, and thus these methodologies are always, at least partially, becoming. In addition, I am not quite sure what can be gained by the presence or absence of labels such as *qualitative, methodology, post-qualitative, post-methodology*, and *post-methods*. However, I encourage scholars to consider what kind of work the labels do, what kind of discourses and practices they are associated with, and how different labels constitute scholars. In addition, it might be important to move beyond qualitative research 1.0 or 2.0 toward more complex understandings and practices. However, at the same time, I am not willing to give up, surrender, or replace labels such as *data, qualitative, subjectivity*, and *data analysis* quite yet. I use and problematize them simultaneously. I also desire to think about labels differently and use them in untraditional or unconventional ways. Drawing from Spivak (1997), many labels associated with qualitative research and inquiry are inaccurate (i.e., they do not create stable signifier–signified links) yet necessary (to engage in a dialogue about research with other scholars and those outside academia).

Methodologies without methodology generates a "messy" qualitative research process that may involve continuous decision making in the face of uncertainty, and this process of deciding is not linear or even circular. Instead, decisions might be sketched on a map and thus they can be traveled across, backward or forward, or scholars might stay still and sit on a decision for a while.

Figure 1.1   Traveling Methodologies Without Methodology

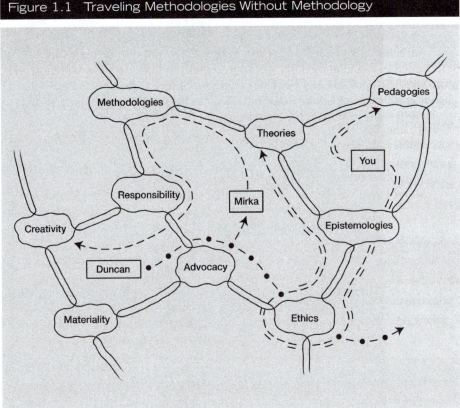

However, decisions have to be made. For example, researchers are expected to make (potentially informed) decisions about theories, methods, representation, emergent questions, interactions with other scholars, peer reviews, and so on. Methodology is a kind of journey—a journey without a clear beginning or ending point and a journey with multiple paths to be taken. Different scholars travel different paths (e.g., Mirka; Duncan, a colleague who shares my interest in questions addressing teaching qualitative research; and you, my readers, who face different decisions and responsibilities). Different projects and research plans call for exploration and expansion of existing and new methodological spaces. Life, contexts, interactions, and data are likely to prompt scholars to deviate from the planned methodological path to visit other methodological places and theoretical spaces. No two methodological journeys are alike! Once all existing roads have been traveled and explored (if that is possible and if one lives by that kind of map) and all research questions have been answered, scholarship is finished and complete. Academia can be de-occupied. Alternatively, one can imagine qualitative research that does not include "answers" per se but temporary breathing pauses, halts, and energy voids that initiate new series of moments and extensions of thought. For example, I cannot image research and projects without voids, empty spaces, and unanswered questions, and without a sense of continuation. The promise and potential embedded in a void and empty space are energizing. Similarly, every section of this book includes an empty page for readers to interact with, fill in, tear out, use as construction material, fold, unfold, or to do anything or nothing with. I challenge you to play with the emptiness!

Methodologies without methodology could also refer to positions where researchers are simultaneously working within and against existing methodological structures, ideas, and established methodological literature. The notion of methodologies without methodology builds from Derrida's (1993) concept of community without community. Derrida discussed a community that is so open and wide that community cannot recognize itself anymore. Similarly, a methodology without methodology is open to other methodologies that are not themselves or their Other. The lines between a methodology and other methodologies blur, and stable methodological identities are no longer desirable. Research and scholarship that build from Derrida's notions stay open-ended and conceptually/theoretically flexible to the extent that it is hard to recognize methodology in its "standard, typical, or socially accepted" form, type, or representation. In other words, methodology without methodology builds on and utilizes methodologies that may not be identified as methodologies in the traditional sense or use. Despite this potential lack of recognition of such methodologies as methodologically acceptable, they do the work of (recognized and validated) methodologies, and they may operate in ways similar to more standardized and normative processes, simultaneously both confirming and resisting normativity. In addition, methodologies without methodology can never be completely known ahead of time, since they can be read and understood as aporetic concepts without strict unity or borders. *Aporia*, Greek for *difficulty*, *puzzle*, or *impassable*, informs Derrida's (1993) conceptualization of ethical responsibility and decision making. Also viewed as "a momentary paralysis in the face of the impasse, it is the 'testing out of the undecidable; only in this testing can a decision come about'" (Derrida, 2005, p. 154). Methodologies without methodology may resemble but not copy. Methodologies without methodology can simultaneously appear as methodologies, but they also escape meanings and signifiers commonly associated with notions of methodology (e.g., *systematic*, *linearly logical*, *auditable*). This paradox and continuous movement within and against methodologies can be generative and inspiring—maybe even provocative.

Diverse and methodologically constantly moving qualitative research might not present itself in clear and familiar ways. Too many books have been written that offer familiar tales and easily digestible overviews of complex qualitative inquiries. To avoid repeating "the same" and forcing one structure to fit all circumstances, scholars ought to get surprised, confused, disoriented, and uncomfortable. Following Deleuze (1995), one might find it debilitating to become a foreigner in one's own language, in one's field, and within oneself. Familiarity becomes strange and attractive. Texts and research projects have been written, rewritten, and erased numerous times. Subjects are lost. Work becomes messy (see also Lather, 2010).

However, messy work can be dangerous. Over the past decade, scholars have argued that the academic marketplace has limited tolerance for epistemological diversity and methodological flexibility, especially since epistemological

How do methodologies without methodology operate and function?

diversification can disrupt existing power structures and the epistemological-ontological dominance of neopositivist research (see, e.g., Lather, 2010; St. Pierre & Roulston, 2006; Torrance, 2011). It appears that the more research institutions are moving toward financial independence, entrepreneurship, and epistemological conservatism, the narrower their mission, tools, and openness to (cultural, epistemological, methodological) diversity are becoming. To crack open narrow scientism, methodologies without methodology can serve as a useful metaphor for thinking about research approaches that deviate from the normative and reductionist notions of research and also as an example of a material and actualized push toward "scientism's" own limits. Methodology and science may no longer be recognizable, at least in the ways scholars seem to know them.

Furthermore, during these times of economically driven decision making, the role of critical social science and qualitative research has often been viewed as **insignificant and less important, since these inquiries are viewed by some scholars as epistemologically and ontologically insufficient and disabled.** (A reminder: Bolded text is referenced in the students' comments presented in the boxes beside the main text.) Some of the most alarming and persistent problems and misconceptions associated with critical social science and qualitative research relate to its perceived value (i.e., what research or qualitative researchers can and should do) and lingering misbeliefs characterizing and portraying qualitative research as less valid, rigorous, scientific, or meaningful than other (mostly neopositivist) forms of research. Many of these misconceptions are guided by simplified and uninformed notions of critical social science and qualitative research. Methodologies are being reduced to technologies, research is seen to benefit only the privileged, and textbooks are mass-producing recipes for valid and trustworthy qualitative research. **Students interested in qualitative research are caught between the expectations of academic conformity, linearity, audit culture, and external control.**

Critical social science and qualitative research can be more than the sum of their perceived intuitive or random parts. Qualitative research can make a difference without defaulting into linear or causal logic. Qualitative research can be meaningful and collaborative, but it is important to pay attention to diverse interaction theories, since they shape practice and the ways in which methodologies and research practices are carried out (see, e.g., Jackson & Mazzei, 2012). Thus, it is impossible to think about qualitative research without considering (1) power, privilege, and assumed legitimacy as impacting lives and

Doctor of Science and Doctor of Psychology degrees are replacing the Doctor of Philosophy. This political move signals the end of science as a philosophy, transforming it instead into a technology (and therefore a technology of power). It also reifies science as a foolproof means of producing knowledge and empirico-rationalism as the ultimate epistemology.

—Justin

Yes! Pressures to conform have been a surprising element of graduate studies. Methodologies, citations, discourses, specific language . . .

—Jasmine

research practices; and (2) methodological knowledge, theoretical awareness, and creativity as productive forces in critical scholarship. Power and legitimacy, knowledge and theories cannot be bypassed or simplified, but they need to be addressed and dealt with. Onto-episte-methodological frames and theories and philosophy can be effectively used to "think with" (Brown & Stenner, 2009; Jackson & Mazzei, 2012) and to process challenging issues of methods, participation, writing, and representation. Theorizing methodologies is a productive onto-epistemological and political move.

Theorizing methodologies is also a creative move. Once qualitative researchers integrate (creative and maybe artistic) experimentation as a part of their everyday scholarship, they can also be more likely to become comfortable with uncertainty and partially unfinished thought and practice. When "normative perfection" (based on externally established criteria) is put aside, impartiality, raw text, and unfinished practices may generate new methodological possibilities and experimentation. Experimentation, in turn, calls for emotions and affect in response to the movement found in energy, relationality, and reactions. Maybe the search for "true" and valid answers to methodological questions could become less important, and the interest would lie in generating more provocative questions of various kinds. We could borrow from Deleuze (1995) and how he describes his relationship to Foucault's work:

> You have to take the work as a whole, to try and follow
> rather than judge it, see where it branches out in different
> directions, where it gets bogged down, moves forward, makes
> a breakthrough; you have to accept it, welcome it, as a whole.
> Otherwise you just won't understand it at all. (p. 85)

Qualitative research is important, and methodology matters! Critical social sciences and qualitative research can play a crucial role in exploring, investigating, and responding to complex social words and phenomena. As a part of studying and investigating complex social worlds, scholars ought to draw attention to multifaceted and interrelated dilemmas of methodology-ontology and methodology-epistemology, as well as scholars' desire to use simplified notions of research and methodology to study complex social problems. I call for scholarship that could work against simplified notions of research, avoiding the trap of methodological reductionism, political pressure, and external expectations of "goodness" and validity often coming from various (methodological) grand narratives. Critical social science research and qualitative work in particular needs more rejoinders to scientific reductionism and the ever-increasing lack of onto-epistemological diversity and methodological creativity in higher education.

Methodology, Methods, Methodology, Metho—

oh

Me

Together, apart, flowing, away

You make me, you consume me, you taunt me, you become

Me (or you, or me-you)

Leaping into the unknown

What will happen?

READING LIST OF LIFE

Carroll, L. (2007). *Alice in wonderland.* Scituate, MA: Digital Scanning.

Härkönen, A.-L. (1998). *Avoimien ovien päivä.* Keuruu, Finland: Otavan Kirjapaino Oy.

Kafka, F. (2003). *The metamorphosis and other stories* (D. Freed, Trans.). New York, NY: Barnes & Noble.

BPTU/Shutterstock

2 Methodological Language Creates "Realities"

Labels and Language Matter

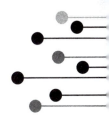

Why Do Labels Matter?

The purpose of this section is to draw attention to the various ways in which methodological language and labels are used in qualitative research to create "realities" ("reality" in this context refers to onto-epistemological spaces that have been created, and I do not use the label "reality" in an objectivist, positivist, or neopositivist sense, but quite possibly in opposite ways). It is important to emphasize that I am especially interested in diverse and changing realities that labels can provoke and set in motion.

Section key points:

- Labels reflect power, legitimacy, and historical markers
- Labels should not be taken for granted
- Labels are creations, and scholars can create new labels to represent new material and linguistic connections
- **Labels and their uses cannot be separated from their contexts**
- Labels and concepts carry diverse and possibly continuously changing meanings, and they guide practice in particular and specific ways
- The informed use of labels calls for theoretical and methodological awareness
- More flexible and critical use of labels could add to methodological conversations and discourses

Why do you choose to rely on a particular linguistic or theoretical tradition in your research?

I disagree. This happens all the time where the meaning of the words evolves to mean new things when adopted and carried across contexts. Maybe I am misunderstanding?

—Darby

Methodological language and labels are presented and located within a particular time, space, and cultural context. Additionally, different uses of language and labels are often historical

How are you using different labels, and for what purposes?

and ideological, building from and referring to traditions, intertextual connections, and values and beliefs of the users. Methodological labels are stances and indications of linguistic and material connections. Labels matter, since they serve as epistemological markers, ontological reference points, and personal preferences, and they are often used as means to legitimize one's scholarship. However, the connections and realities language and labels create may not always be easily identified, readily available, or direct. From this perspective, uncertainty associated with linguistic signifiers and the impact of this uncertainty on methodology is one of my main dilemmas in this section. I also question the directly decodable nature of methodological labels, and thus I approach language and labels from a questioning, wondering point of view, possibly devalidating established ways of reasoning by creating a type of humble and unfinished paralogy, a staggering movement against established way of reasoning.

What do I wonder

    Where do I want to go, not sure

Do I wonder?   or

    Am I expected to know?

Am I afraid of dismissal

of me, this text,

these not/un/finished ideas

Purposefully not arriving

    just puzzled

What kinds of onto-epistemological connections are being created and repeated through your use of methodological labels?

When thinking about methodologies without methodology, a part of the potential rethinking has to do with the ways in which qualitative researchers buy into different traditions of doing and believing that are enacted through and explained by the labels. Labels and methodological language guide scholars' methodological activities, and thus I begin this section by looking more deeply into different ways scholars use labels. A part of my goal in this chapter is to enable students and those new to qualitative inquiry to begin to detect differences in the ways in which linguistic grand narratives produce methodological language and generate normative labels and signifiers used in research discourses.

GLOSSARY

Label. Way of making social discriminations and distinctions in human interaction (Gochman, 1982, p. 167).

Label. Form of social control (Gochman, 1982, p. 167).

Paralogy. A conversation that tries to break out of old systems of thought by not relying on experts and meta-narratives to legitimate ideas (Shawver, 2001, p. 246).

Paralogy. Promotes dissensus rather than consensus, heterogeneity and plurality rather than homogeneity and universality, on the grounds that new knowledge comes about by dissent, by questioning what is consensually assented to (Nola & Irzik, 2003, p. 419).

Signifier. A word or related symbol that refers to a class of objects (Jacques, 2010).

Signifier. Everyday language we take for granted: science, method, validity, truth, power, rationality, objectivity, identity, sexuality, culture, history, democracy, and so forth (St. Pierre, 1997, p. 175).

Signified. The object referred to (Jacques, 2010).

Intertextuality. Occurs at levels higher than merely interacting with texts. Is socially constructed during the discussion of texts (Bloome & Egan-Robertson, 1993, p. 304).

Intertextuality. Does not occur with questioning author's intent. Only occurs with the comparison of other "texts" (including cultures, social systems). It's impossible to comprehend a text without the network of additional texts (Kristeva, as translated by Freiherr von der Goltz, 2011, p. 42).

Different Uses of Labels

Throughout history, established names, labels, and categories have been used to gain legitimacy and power. For example, Gubrium and Holstein (1997) believed that language use, terminology, and labels are vital for qualitative methods and for the process of social science research. Language-in-use is everywhere and always political according to Gee (2005). Foucault (1995), in turn, proposed that knowledge and power are inseparable and that the corpus of knowledge and techniques of scientific discourses are formed and entangled with the practices of power.

> Power produces knowledge . . . power and knowledge directly imply one another; . . . there is no power relation without the correlative constitution of a field of knowledge, nor any knowledge that does not presuppose and constitute at the same time power relations. (Foucault, 1995, p. 27)

Knowledge is defined by the discourse rather than by the researcher or by the method. According to Foucault (1972), knowledge is formed within discursive practices, and those practices further guide future knowledge production

Political choices and epistemological decisions characterize the method selection of many qualitative researchers who desire to gain legitimacy and acceptance in the field. However, scholars' awareness of the connection between labels and power, between labels and history, and between labels and cultural values vary considerably. Some scholars are attentive, informed, and careful about the ways in which they label, cite, and connect labels with material, whereas others never think about these questions or connections. (Here is where I think you place the first sentence with the people who know and purposefully resist being classified by the label.) Labels, including methodological labels, are dispelled by informed researchers, who place labels in a particular epistemological and empirical context. Questions will arise, for these scholars, about specific disciplinary practices, such as "Who has the right label?" or "Who uses the right term?"
—Darby

and power associated with knowledge. **Labels, including methodological labels, are dispelled by researchers, who place labels in a particular epistemological and empirical context. Political choices and epistemological conclusions and preferences characterize the method selection of many qualitative researchers who desire to gain legitimacy and acceptance in the field.** However, scholars' awareness of the connection between labels and power, between labels and history, and between labels and cultural values can vary considerably.

The question of labels, legitimizing language, or perceived inappropriate uses of labels can challenge the positions of power vested in epistemological or knowledge authority— the authority that is "accepted" to produce taken-for-granted definitions and regulate normative research practices. In the past, those scholars working against normative research practices have raised many questions about the "ownership" or "policing" associated with methods, about the assumed context and functions of particular labels, and about the overall "justifications" for different methodological practices (see, e.g., Lather, 2010; St. Pierre, 2002; Torrance, 2011). The concerns emerging in these discussions have been and still are very important. Researchers should ask themselves why they prefer to use particular labels or make specific discursive connections in their work. Why are they drawn to a particular set of beliefs? What are labels such as "paradigms," "reflexivity," or "triangulation" expected to signify? What do particular labels do? How do they operate? Who might gain from the use of these methods?

What can challenging the norms of labels do to/for the researcher?

Qualitative Researchers' Romance With *the* Meaning

What is the connection between "labels" and "meaning"?

For the longest time

in my own successful and unsuccessful research

I wanted to know what labels, experiences, connections, comparisons, and theories

mean

endless search   for meaning

purposefully   shaping   my   interactions

talk, listening, thinking, not thinking,

doing something

with participants and me and participants and others

Forming my analytical approaches with data

I worried   endlessly

about the right ways to represent the meanings

I

had

found

or created.

I've been reading Baudrillard this week and was reminded of this fragment: "The world does not exist so that we may know it. It is not in any way predestined for knowledge. However, knowledge itself is part of the world, but of the world in its profound illusoriness, which consists in bearing no necessary relation to knowledge" (Baudrillard, 2003, p. 104).
—Jasmine

I am not an exception. I also have had a love affair with meaning. For a long time, I wanted to find participants' meaning and be "true" to their meanings when (re)presenting the research and findings. Many aspects of my research seemed to relate to the concept of meaning in different ways. It has not been until quite recently that I have been able (at least temporarily) to see beyond the meaning and have allowed myself to conceptualize research and data without being bounded by restrictive notions of meaning or an exclusive focus on meaning making. Giving up my search for meaning—that is, meaning as a thing or state—has changed my views on data, the research process, and research outcomes. As a result, I have also

Robert Ulmer

changed my view on meaning. Instead of restricting meaning to signifying an intentional core or cognitive center that may lie at the heart of a knowable object, I propose that qualitative researchers could allow meaning to reestablish itself in a flux, in the liminal space, at the limit of words and things, as what is said of a thing (not its attribute or the thing in itself) and as something that happens (not its process or its state; see also Foucault & Faubion, 1998).

This is not to say that meaning and searching for meaning cannot be important, epistemologically consistent, and culturally appropriate, especially for many scholars operating from interpretivist traditions and humanistic perspectives. For example, Polkinghorne (2005) discussed his purpose of locating core meanings, and he explained how data triangulation can assist researchers in recognizing variations in participants' experiences and in "locating its core meaning by approaching it through different accounts" (p. 140). Polkinghorne also emphasized the role of meaning in storytelling by stating how interviewers can support interviewees in recalling an experience and its meaning. He noted that by remembering past events, interviewees can reflect on the meaning of the events and their impact on the lives of the participants.

When can searching for meaning be useful?

Furthermore, meanings can be significant, illuminative, or an essential concept and approach within one's qualitative research. For example, in phenomenology, scholars might study meanings through the manifestations, presence, and appearance of different experiences and phenomena (see, e.g., Heidegger, 1996, 2010; Merleau-Ponty, 1974, 2004). Similarly, in constructivist studies, the investigations of participants and community members' meaning-making processes, collaborative meanings created within particular social interactions, and meanings associated with key educational concepts can enhance understanding, empathy, and information about the needs and desires of particular individuals or cultural groups (see, e.g., Crotty, 1998; Fosnot, 2005). In these examples, a focus on meaning is aligned with theories, scholarly interests, and theoretical perspectives. **However, some scholars might associate qualitative research exclusively with meaning making. It is possible that for these qualitative researchers, locating and describing *the meaning* is *the ultimate task*** in every qualitative project, and all qualitative research is or should be about the meaning. This kind of theoretical narrowing may be dangerous and counterproductive at the time of theoretical dispersion. Thus, I worry about this imperative and the exclusive meaning-making task sometimes associated with qualitative research and qualitative studies. Instead, I would like to think about meaning as something one might think to do with data, or it could be a way to theoretically guide one's research, but it cannot possibly represent everything qualitative researchers can do with their research, projects, or theories.

> *That is a very interesting point. Meaning is the purpose behind qualitative research methods in general, but the method of constructing it or surfacing it varies depending on the epistemological orientation to knowledge that the theoretical framework holds. Hmm.*
> —Kathryn

> *I wonder how you are defining meaning. It seems like to you it may not be a thing but a verb or a process of doing.*
> —Darby

Some qualitative and critical scholars have also expressed concerns about epistemologically and theoretically blinded searches for meaning. For example, St. Pierre (2009) wrote that she no longer believes in meaning as a portable property or that language can transport meaning in some unmediated way. She also explained that in her work, signifiers and meanings do not emerge miraculously or spontaneously. Jackson and Mazzei (2012) referred to the representational trap associated with meaning seeking and finding during the analysis, and insisted that they try to avoid the desire to reduce participants' words and stories into coherent narratives and pure meaning. Derrida (1997) also worried about readers' and writers' desire to think through meanings:

> From the moment that there is meaning, there are nothing but signs. We *think only in signs*. Which amounts to ruining the notion of sign at the very moment when, as in Nietzsche, its exigency is recognized in the absoluteness of its right. (p. 50)

However, meanings could also be thought of through plurality. For example, meaning does not necessarily need to close down dialogue, and meanings can, indeed, be multiple. Once meanings begin to multiply and happen more spontaneously, the "nature" of research and research activities changes. Knowledge is no longer tied to the search for (right, true, singular, or universal) meaning (in meaning's strict or objectified sense), but knowledge can be found in living, experiencing, material interactions, intuition, and subject–object relations without clear or direct signifier–signified links. These interactions and experiences might generate references or linkages to meaning, but they do not capture it. **Research and findings can be more about meaning-making processes than outcomes, more about questions than answers,** more about connecting and living than arriving, and more about exploration than delivery.

Giving up objectified notions of meaning also has implications for the ways in which we approach labels. When one is dedicated to finding stable and potentially generalizable meaning, this dedication usually implies an unquestionable and direct connection between the signifier and the signified. The question of what labels, language, or data mean is not necessarily driven by anticipated outcomes and consequences of one's research, but may be related to the researcher's individual desire to square off the data, locate the meaning to provide closure, and put an end to the project. Finding meaning may be viewed as a simplified task linked with all qualitative research practices, especially by those less familiar with diverse qualitative research traditions.

> *The idea of focusing more on processes rather than outcomes really resonates with me. To me, qualitative research involves a complex process in which authors "find out" about themselves as well as the subjects/objects being studied.*
>
> —Cheryl

You

my dear colleague, collaborator, my grant sugar-daddy

you want an answer

reason(s) to engage in

qualitative   inquiry

How about this   or that?

I need to know the meaning

meaning of the world,   you,   life,   text

I need to know the meaning of all there is

   to be studied   empirically

I am committed

to answer   you

through, by, side-by-side with the meaning   or was it meanings (sorry)

> *This poem is great. It challenges the dominant positivist perspective in a powerful way.*
>
> —Kathryn

> *I feel some resistance here within myself, because labels can exclude, and I have found that providing artifacts or narratives of the context can be a tool for inviting others into the conversation. I am not sure if this is advocating discovery or unintentional alienation or exclusion. I am feeling challenged to rethink my practices.*
>
> —Darby

You mention the constant comparative method. This is a common label, and I think it represents more of a power move to legitimate the research methodology rather than a representation of what was done (not to say they didn't do anything like it, but mentioning it is strategic). This is especially apparent when someone says they are doing grounded theory and then cites Glaser and Strauss, mid-1990s Glaser, Charmaz, and Clarke. These all represent different approaches with different underlying assumptions. I have seen this done (my own adviser did something akin to this in his first grounded theory paper), and it seems to be more of a need to justify the method and the authors' knowledge of it (or lack thereof) than an attempt to explain how the research was performed.

—Justin

BUT

I am not sure   if my meaning

is your meaning

or meaning at all

but I have a meaning to offer

to answer   your question

OR have I?

Labels Create, Act, Provoke, and Do Other Things

Labels can create meaning, but they can also act, provoke, and do many other things. For example, labels shape individuals' interactions with their environment, and labels guide and generate conversations. Labels can silence and move. Labels also categorize. However, a label does not create or dispel anything outside its context (e.g., the label's theoretical context, processes it is associated with, or other conceptual connections it generates) **unless labels are intentionally decontextualized and overgeneralized**. Every label also forms an indefinite number of connections, orderings, and traces, which are always political and theoretical. Additionally, this infinite intertextuality and interconnectivity of labels calls for critical reflection by scholars who desire to work against normative practices and taken-for-granted assumptions.

I see three main areas of critical reflection and possible dilemmas with the (un)critical use of labels in qualitative research. The first is about legitimization. For example, certain terms such as *saturation*, *triangulation*, *emergent themes*, and *interrater reliability* are sometimes used merely to indicate quasi-connections, or what I would call "shallow conceptual links" to "socially accepted" qualitative research practices used mainly to gain reviewers' trust and create a sense of expertise. In this case, the researcher's goal is to demonstrate and reproduce acceptable knowledge that can lead to acknowledgment, further acceptance, and belonging. For example, by using labels this way, researchers can gain membership in the qualitative research community, which in turn can legitimize scholars' claims and validate their studies and findings.

Another type of dilemma has to do with ambiguity, the potential overgeneralization of labels, and the lack of contextual grounding or understandings of historical discourses shaping different language uses (see also Gürtler & Huber, 2006). For example, it is also possible to use **the constant comparative method** to describe *any* type of data analysis or with interview study as a proxy for all qualitative research traditions. Sometimes these unintentional or uninformed uses of labels may not only lead to overgeneralization, but may also exemplify undesirable decontextualization and limited knowledge about diverse traditions associated with qualitative research. Decontextualization can also lead to what I call "conceptual immunity." For example, **when labels and their uses are not situated in discursive, epistemological, and theoretical contexts**, proposed meanings, uses of labels, or things that labels do cannot easily be dismantled or questioned on epistemological and theoretical grounds by other discourses or language users. In this case, researchers may establish an illusion of a generalizable label that can be used uncritically across contexts. By doing this, researchers grant a sort of conceptual immunity to the labels—**a view from nowhere**—as if a label associated with nothing is possible.

A third dilemma relates to the acknowledged insufficiency of language to describe or represent realities (see, e.g., MacLure, 2013). This dilemma is practical but also ontological, and it is often faced by postmodernist and poststructuralist scholars alike. From this perspective, labels are always inaccurate in describing meanings, realities, relationships, or thinking. Words do not signify, and labels are never fixed but escaping (Derrida), becoming (Deleuze), or only reproductions (Baudrillard). In the following section, I briefly discuss Dilemmas 1 and 2, but my main argument has to do with productive, critical, and informed ways of using labels, acknowledging that labels are always insufficient and inaccurate but necessary (Dilemma 3). For me, the insufficiency of language and labels is a productive and stimulating dilemma that makes me reconsider the ways in which I am accustomed to approaching labels and signifiers.

Scholars may situate their uses of labels in various moving, shifting, and overlapping networks of discourses where assigning a single and stable connection or privileged/preferred purpose is impossible and undesirable. In this case, labels, their connections, and their doings/actions are situated in epistemological temporality, conceptual emergence, and linguistic movement.

The awareness of contextualized linkages, traces, and potentially different discursive uses of labels can make researchers more sensitive to language games

> *This makes me so anxious. I find the politically nuanced language of specific discourse/ theoretical communities very challenging sometimes. When I write, I write alongside the fear of committing epistemological sins.*
>
> —Jasmine

> *As a young scholar trying to join the field, this is a daily challenge. Few mentors and veterans want to engage in these conversations when I am constructing my understanding.*
>
> —Darby

and power embedded in these games. More specifically, different uses of labels can be seen as a part of language games that are shaped by language users and their resistance toward normativity and structured rules of language (see also Browning, 2000; Lyotard, 1997). For Lyotard (1999), "postmodern knowledge is not simply a tool of the authorities; it refines our sensitivity to differences and reinforces our ability to tolerate the incommensurable. Its principle is not the expert's homology, but the inventor's paralogy" (p. xxv). By working against established ways of reasoning and linguistic structures, scholars are able to dissent from normative language, which in turn can lead to linguistic creation and conceptual movement.

In your own research, you could:

- Be conscious and conceptually aware of the ways in which you tend to use labels

- Articulate how you intend to use particular labels and why

- Try to stay uncertain about the labels and their function and see what might happen

- Allow your labels to change, morph, and disappear

The labels one uses are only as accurate as the individuals that designate them. What does a novice researcher do when those who designate them have differences in opinion? How do we navigate the potentially confusing world of labels?
—Cheryl

Even though this section critically examines normative uses of labels and calls for experimentation in terms of diverse uses of labels, it is hard and sometimes even impossible to give up labels altogether. Spivak (1997) wrote that labels are necessary **yet inaccurate**. They are necessary for engaging in various forms of dialogue, producing text, and showing intertextual connections between discourses and within texts, but at the same time labels never truly capture or represent what they signify.

To make myself more clear   or not

I provide   I look closer

various inaccuracies, problems, inaccuracies, problems, inaccuracies

Maybe I find possibilities

Maybe I find different uses of labels   or l-abels or la-bels or lab-els

Two common ones, negotiated, agreed upon

Yet I wonder

what is common, negotiated, agreed upon   for whom with whom?

Labels in qualitative research?

Reflexivity, ref-lexivity, reflex-ivity, reflexiv-i-t-y   and

triangulation as stuttered mislabels   inaccuracies

KEEP READING

Using Labels of Reflexivity and Triangulation

In the following paragraphs, I elaborate in more detail two common labels used in qualitative research discourses and introductory textbooks. Both reflexivity and triangulation are methodological labels that can be understood differently in different discourse communities. These labels may also be new to students in qualitative research courses and thus need introduction and explanation. Drawing from the *Oxford English Dictionary*, we can see that both of these labels have a long and diverse history. For example, *reflexivity* was used in the mid-1600s in philosophy to indicate the quality or condition of being reflexive and in the 1950s in sociology as an opposite of automatism. Additionally, reflexivity has been linked to logic and math discourses since the 1930s (as the fact of being a reflexive relation). For qualitative researchers, reflexivity might indicate a stance of being reflective, a disposition of qualitative researchers, or maybe a characteristic of a thoughtful scholar. Schwandt (2007) defines reflexivity as critical self-reflection focusing on biases, theoretical orientation, and preferences. Reflexivity can also be used to critically evaluate and inspect the entire research process.

Triangulation, in turn, was used in the early 1800s to trace and measure series of triangles to map our territory or regions in geography and medicine. Later, namely in the mid and late 1900s, triangulation was used in math and political discourses to describe the process of positioning oneself between left and right ideologies. In the context of qualitative research, triangulation can be seen as one validation strategy, a means of studying and representing various perspectives simultaneously. For example, triangulation can be conceptualized as a means of checking the validity or the integrity of inference utilizing multiple data sources, researchers, theoretical perspectives, and methods—that is, checking arguments and conclusions against a variety of viewpoints (see Schwandt, 2007).

The Label of Reflexivity

I was curious how different authors utilize the labels *triangulation* and *reflexivity* in their work. To locate article examples, I reviewed all articles that met the following criteria: (1) appeared in Academic Search Premier, (2) included the keyword "qualitative research," and (3) included the article title term "triangulation" or "reflexivity." By using these criteria, I hoped to eliminate articles that were not directly associated with qualitative inquiry. Based on these criteria, I found 14 articles related to reflexivity that had been published between 1998 and 2013. Thirty-six percent of them were in method-focused journals such as *Qualitative Social Work, Qualitative Research, and Qualitative Health Research.* Eighty-six percent of these articles were conceptual papers, and 14% were research papers.

Overall, when the authors of these 14 papers wrote about reflexivity, they used the label as a reference to data contamination and a description of the impact of the researcher's presence on the findings. However, the authors who published in health-related journals and who took a postmodern or hermeneutical perspective emphasized less the concept of reflexivity in relation to the validity questions. Instead, they paid more attention to the possible connections between empowerment and reflexivity and between critical self-reflection and reflexivity. Similarly, those authors who situated their work more deeply in epistemological and theoretical contexts also seemed to extend the traditional uses of reflexivity. Rather than recycling existing discourses and relying on the documented practices commonly associated with the label, these authors connected reflexivity with other concepts and practices.

In the following paragraphs, I point to some ways in which the authors put the labels to "work" and what kinds of actions these labels created. Thus, rather than focusing on the definitions per se, I center my attention on the verbs associated with the labels. First, I share a figure that highlights actions associated with reflexivity among all authors of the reviewed articles. Then I discuss some examples in more detail. The verbs that I use to summarize or synthesize authors' ways of operationalizing the labels in the articles are marked in brackets in my narration.

When I thought not only about the linguistic connections associated with the label but also about the ways in which this particular label functioned to guide researchers' and writers' actions, various conceptual and practical connections became visible and possible. For example, the label of reflexivity was enacted in ways that promoted self-awareness but also self-critique. Being reflexive was often connected with interviewing and validating interview data rather than thinking about reflexivity as a more central activity within any qualitative research project. Reflexivity was also seen as a skill that needs to be taught. Interestingly, some authors linked reflexivity with an ability to think not just critically but as a solely cognitive activity without the involvement of and relation to the body, affect, and so on. Not surprisingly, for many authors, to "do" reflexivity was to write about oneself and one's thinking while interviewing or to be aware of one's assumptions

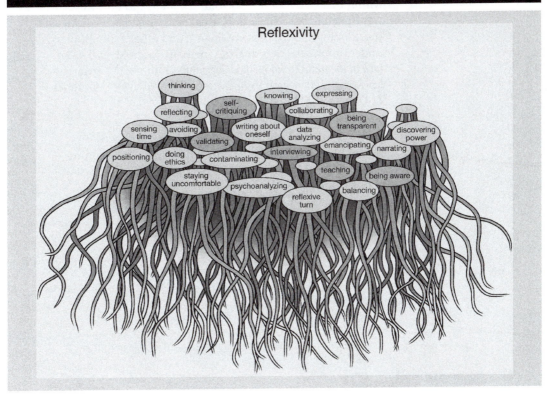

and epistemologies in order to increase the validity of one's qualitative study. Alternatively, some authors proposed that emancipating and being responsible for one's choices (i.e., Foucault's care of self) exemplified practices they associated with reflexivity. Thus, doing reflexivity was seen as an ethical act: an ethical act turned toward oneself, seen as responsive and methodologically the "right thing" to do.

When reviewing the authors' text more carefully, I also located less direct connections and conceptual linkages. For example, a feminist article (citing, e.g., Benhabib, Butler, Brown & Gilligan, Haraway, Lather, and Olesen) published in *Sociology* described the authors' conceptual linkages as follows (emphasis and action linkages added, here and in quotes throughout chapter):

> Our interest in reflexivity generally, and as it relates to data analysis in particular, is *more recent* [sensing time]. It has

developed largely in response to our increasing awareness of how *limited our reflexive processes were at the time* [reflecting within reflexivity] of our doctoral research, and how this was linked to *our ambivalence about our role in the research* [positioning], to the epistemological and other assumptions underpinning the data analysis methods we used, and *to our lack of theoretical and methodological tools* [methodological knowing] with which to operationalize reflexivity (Mauthner & Doucet, 2003, p. 414).

- **These authors link the following "doings" and activities: Sensing time + reflecting within reflexivity + positioning + methodological knowing +   + (possible other things that I did not come to think about)**

There are days when time comes   closer

time seems   as if it has stopped,

Research has momentarily   ended

to begin again

in immediacy

offering a moment

to reflect

if   when   how

I know   methodologically

These authors also made multiple links between reflexivity and other concepts. For example, the **authors proposed that it is possible that when qualitative researchers become more experienced, they also become more reflexive**. Learning experiences, an increased awareness of the complexities of data analysis, and multifaceted roles of researchers in the analysis process may also prompt reflexivity. Alternatively, more sophisticated and nuanced knowledge about theoretical and methodological tools can assist scholars in integrating and using reflexivity in their scholarship. Or it could also be that reflexivity always takes a long time and that reflexivity is about gaining methodological expertise over time through practice and methodological and theoretical exposure.

Could it also be possible that over time scholars become less reflexive (i.e., they fall into a certain pattern of doing research and they don't question it)?

—Kathryn

In the second postmodern example (citing Foucault), published in the *Journal of Advanced Nursing*, reflexivity was enacted through self-discovery and gaining awareness of power and social norms. Instead of focusing solely on the reflexivity of researchers, these authors proposed that interview participants "use reflexivity to *discover dominating* discourses and power structures [discovering power] with the *assistance* of the researcher [collaborating]" (McCabe & Holmes, 2009, p. 1523). Reflexivity was also about becoming aware of power relations and later readjusting one's actions based on newly acquired knowledge. This use of reflexivity was more collaborative, collective, and action oriented, and it emphasized the goals of emancipation.

- **These authors link the following "doings" and activities: Discovering power + collaborating + + (possible other things that I did not come to think about)**

The last example, situated in psychoanalytic theory (Bion), was published in *Qualitative Health Research*. In this example, the author portrayed reflexivity as thinking in the present. In other words, rather than conceptualizing reflexivity as a past or retrospective activity, this author introduced a notion of reflexivity that required individuals to be active in the moment-to-moment research interactions. Additionally, the author proposed that reflexivity calls for researchers to acknowledge and follow their epistemological frameworks. The author also suggested that

> the reflexive ability to share the feeling [expressing feelings] is revealed to be essential but not enough [needs to be accompanied by other activity]. It must be accompanied by the capacity to think [thinking], so that the experience can be thought about (Doyle, 2013, p. 251) . . . This surely requires that the researcher maintain awareness [being aware] of the context, purpose, and focus of the research, which should mitigate risks of excessive focus on self [balancing risks + avoiding self-centeredness]. Last example also emphasized the need for thinking about, rather than simply revealing [avoiding simple revealing], aspects of self. (p. 253)

Reflexivity during the interviews could lead to momentary failure—not being able to share feelings and thoughts with the study participants. As a temporary halt or situated expressions, reflexivity cannot be decontextualized or separated from the sense of self.

- **This author links the following "doings" and activities: Expressing feelings + needs to be accompanied by other activity + thinking + being aware + balancing risks + avoiding self-centeredness + avoiding simple revealing + + (possible other things that I did not come to think about).**

These examples illustrate that the label of reflexivity is used in various connected yet disconnected ways. Each time the authors use the term, they situate their examples in different contexts, connect with other uses of the same label, and create different understandings or purposes for the label. These examples also show that it is impossible to take for granted one assumed or normative notion associated with a label. Even though all authors used the same label, they put the label to work in considerably different ways, and the labels prompted and stimulated different actions and outcomes in these research reports and conceptualizations. Thus, rather than debating the label itself, it might be more illuminative and important to look at the conceptual, material, but also activating connections that the authors put forward in their texts and practices.

In your own research, you could:

- Trace back your conceptual development throughout the years. How have you used similar labels, and how have your connections between the label and cited literature possibly changed?

- Consider the following questions: What does your use of reflexivity do to you? How does your reflexivity label function, and what does that label generate?

The Label of Triangulation

Based on the reviewed articles, reflexivity appears to have been used earlier than the more recent methodological label of **triangulation**. Eight articles discussing triangulation (published between 2002 and 2012) reflected more recent discourses, potentially following the expansion of mixed-methods research. Sixty-three percent of these articles appeared in methodological journals and came from health disciplines. Unsurprisingly, most of the triangulation papers (62%) reported research findings rather than advanced a methodological argument per se, even though these articles were published in the journals focusing on methodology. Interestingly, the opposite happened with the reflexivity articles. The articles that focused on reflexivity had more of a conceptual or methodological focus, but they were published in content journals. Additionally, more than half of the authors writing about reflexivity mentioned their epistemology and theoretical perspective, whereas only 25% of the authors writing about triangulation did the same. Thus, it could be argued that reflexivity was by and large a more theoretically situated label, while triangulation appeared to be used more mechanically and possibly in decontextualized ways.

When I picture triangulation and the sharp edges of a triangle, the rigidity you are describing fits perfectly, yet when I picture reflexivity, it is far more chaotic and cyclical.

—Darby

Why do you think that the label of triangulation is less "theoretically situated" than the label of reflexivity?

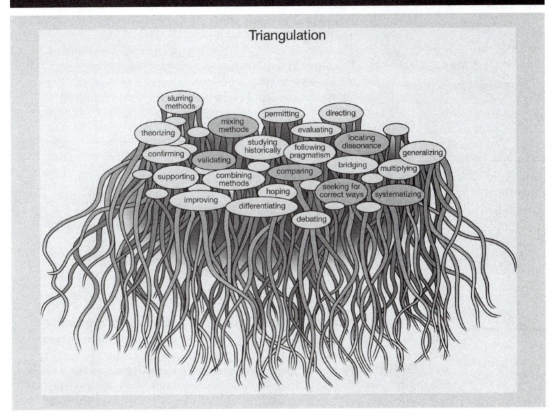

Some authors of the reviewed articles (especially those scholars who took a pragmatist or unidentified epistemological stance) seemed to approach triangulation as a response to and potential cure for dissonant and discrepant data. Some authors across different disciplines adopted a somewhat technical approach to triangulation. For example, these authors developed matrices, frameworks, or "systematic" tools and techniques to carry out triangulation processes. The triangulation label prompted methodological "doings" and activities, often in objectivist, epistemologically neutral, or assumingly "correct" ways.

In the reviewed articles, "doing triangulation" happened mostly in the mixed-methods context, and it was seen as an analytical activity involving comparing, systemizing, or validating data and findings. **Doing triangulation** was also viewed as a mechanical task that called for systems, rules, steps, and **protocols**.

According to the authors of reviewed articles, without triangulation, scholars would slur methods and conduct invalid studies, and they would not know what to do with inconsistent or divergent findings. Thus, "doing triangulation" was seen as "purifying" and verifying.

An author in the *International Journal of Social Research Methodology* offering a pragmatist perspective (citing Creswell, Onwuegbuzie, and Leech) conceptualized triangulation as a way of validating combined and mixed perspectives. This author stated,

> In *permitting a variety of perspectives* [permitting multiplicity], triangulation offers *explorat*ory possibilities for all those scholars looking to *bridge disciplinary divides* [bridging paradigms] or paradigm borders and *enjoy new, or each other's,* expertise to solve [supporting new perspectives + solving problems] the issue. (Vikström, 2010, p. 220)

> *I was impressed with Richardson's (2000) view that one should "crystallize" rather than "triangulate," because there are far more than three sides from which the data can be approached.*
> —Cheryl

> *It feels natural here to say this is not surprising, given that the etymology of the word implies systematic, legitimate, or legal proof of ownership.*
> —Darby

For this author, triangulation may have more to do with "permitting"—providing permission—and "allowing" scholars to use and mix different perspectives and methods than accumulating findings to ensure validity or rigor. Alternatively, the author saw triangulation as an opportunity to explore possibilities, to bridge paradigms and paradigmatic debates, and to support new perspectives and collaborations. It is possible that triangulation offered a solution to problems that required expert knowledge. In this context, the label of triangulation also put forward future-oriented and optimistic activities related to blending paradigms and engaging in exploratory and collaborative work. In some ways, this author used triangulation as a proxy or justification for interdisciplinary collaboration and theoretically hybrid perspectives.

- **This author links the following "doings" and activities: permitting multiplicity + bridging paradigms + supporting new perspectives + solving problems + + (possible other things that I did not come to think about).**

Whereas the previous article connected the label "triangulation" with permission to conduct mixed-methods research, another example from *Qualitative Health Research* (no theoretical perspective identified) put forward notions of triangulation that implied completeness and procedures that can ultimately enhance validity. Both ways to operationalize triangulation (permit/allow/call for mixed-methods work and support validity) are common in qualitative research literature, yet scholars rarely specify which way they use the term in their particular context.

> By triangulating the findings from different methodological approaches, we were able to tap *into different elements of the issue* [differentiating], *providing complementary findings that contributed to achieving a more complete picture* [achieving holistic Truth] of the issue under study. It is our *hope* [hoping] that by sharing and *debating* [debating] the methodological processes and challenges of triangulation, qualitative researchers *will not have to rely on intuitively "feeling our way"* [gaining legitimacy] but, rather, can be *guided by a set of basic triangulation procedures* [following procedures] *that aim to enhance the validity* [validating] of research results. (Farmer et al., 2006, p. 378)

This conceptualization emphasized triangulation as a process to bring together complementary findings from different sources in order to achieve a more complete picture and "True" findings while simultaneously working against intuitive, emotional, or unconscious ways of carrying out research. According to this author, feelings and intuition should be replaced by a guided set of procedures, since the ultimate goal of triangulation is to enhance validity and gain legitimacy.

- **These authors link the following "doings" and activities: differentiating + achieving holistic Truth + hoping + debating + gaining legitimacy + following procedures + validating +   + (possible other things that I did not come to think about)**

I love to differentiate

locate difference   to build   to reflect   to move on

but

I fail   to find Truth in   difference

truths escape

Truths do not   follow   procedures

or other predetermined structures

I find this sometimes challenging, because the audience (often faculty or editors) seem to have more power to decide what is valid. Do you think a certain amount of time in the field or specific references would be needed for your scholars to deviate from normative research trajectories?

—Darby

Just differences to differentiate

me from you, us from us, from from froms

Differentiated "validity"

is

that

possible

Is that legitimate

Who decides?

The last example comes from the *International Journal of Medical Informatics* (no theoretical perspective identified). This article used triangulation in the context of evaluation and argued that triangulation can be beneficial for evaluation studies. In this example, the authors situated the discussion of triangulation in a particular disciplinary context (evaluation research). At the same time, the authors made generalizations within evaluation studies, implying that there might be one (generalizable) way to triangulate within these types of studies. In some ways, the authors mixed local and generalizable discourses and ways to use the label. By generalizing the practice, the authors created a vision of a standardized practice and legitimization through standardization. The authors explained:

> The *theory of triangulation* [theorizing] deals with the integration of methods and approaches so as to *conduct better* [improving] evaluation studies. In evaluation research, triangulation *in general* [generalizing] means the multiple employments of various sources of data, observers, methods, and/or theories in investigations of the same phenomenon. Triangulation has *two main objectives* [directing action]: to *confirm results* [confirming] with data from other sources (validation of results [validating]), and to *find new data* [finding new data] to get a more *complete picture* [achieving a complete picture] (completeness of results). (Ammenwerth et al., 2003, p. 237)

Here, the authors also referred to the theory of triangulation, a set of related arguments associated with triangulation, or an argumentation system of triangulation. The integration of methods was seen as a form of abstracting and exemplifying how nature works (i.e., through theorizing). Similar to other authors, these authors linked triangulation to overall improvement of research practice and quality control. In addition, the act of triangulation was positioned as a somewhat limited and narrow activity, since it aimed only to confirm results and find additional data to achieve completeness and potential Truth.

- **These authors link the following "doings" and activities: Theorizing + improving + generalizing + directing action + confirming + validating + finding new data + achieving a complete picture +   + (possible other things that I did not come to think about).**

In your own research, you could:

- Discuss with a colleague why you are drawn to particular ways to carry out the label of triangulation and what could explain the differences between your views and your colleague's views.

- Locate 5 to 10 citations outside your discipline and social and geographical context. Investigate and review how these authors put the label of triangulation to work and what kinds of discourses and practices the label generates and promotes.

The Label of "Triangulaxivity"

Based on the previous examples, we see that the ways in which labels operate can vary considerably, and each function or action prompted by the label is contextual, historical, and in some ways intentional yet also irrational. Labels and their conceptual connections can come together in unlimited ways and through infinite connections. This infinite connectivity does not diminish the value of these labels or make this type of language use less scholarly, especially when notions of scholarship and knowledge extend beyond positivism and empiricism. It is also likely that some connections appear to readers to be more familiar than others. However, this unfamiliarity should not lead to rejection or dismissal. I wonder whether rejection of some labels or distancing oneself from specific uses of labels based solely on unfamiliarity or normativity is productive or desirable when one attempts to work through dilemmas and problems associated with unstable signifiers. Maybe the more important question is: Can the new label or function work for me?

What happens if one desires to move away from the normative meanings and existing labels to create a new label that implies alternative conceptual connections? What happens when scholars enter into language games without clear norms or social expectations? What happens to language when it no longer identifies or confirms? What if language moves and provokes? What becomes possible, and what are some risks associated with these practices?

That's interesting. Like the inverse of positivism.

—Kathryn

Or is it to mean we all arrive at individual acceptance of answers for the moment?

—Darby

Answers to the previous questions vary or may not exist at all, at least in general or generalizable ways. **Alternatively, only temporary answers may lie in particulars that will stay always partially unknown.** We may not know what labels can do, not even after we have interacted with labels or have encountered the events where we are affected by new irrational labels. It is also possible that at the moment when we thought we knew the impact of the label on our practices, the label and its affect have shifted, moved on, and escaped our attention. In this case we might be better off to become less concerned about the label itself. Instead, we might want to process and analyze the affect and effect any labels have on our practices.

We also know that context matters. For example, in the context of qualitative research, it matters whether the person who is being affected by the labels is a tenured, accepted, and known member of a scholarly community (power); whether this person is seen as knowledgeable (knowledge); and how this person views himself or herself in relation to other individuals and matter (self-reflection and situatedness). Similarly, the context—when, why, and how new labels are introduced—matters, for example, in the context of a textbook, casual conversation, policy brief, call for proposals, image, or movie.

Alternative uses of labels may come with a cost. Regardless of the context, any move away from normative uses of labels can be risky, since alternative or new conceptual connections may create new linguistic extensions, understandings, or actions that other individuals might not recognize. Newly created labels may fail to produce the intended impact or anticipated outcome—but maybe they accomplish something else, something unanticipated. Since the path is not given, the only way to find out is to take the risk and make the leap of faith.

Second, it is interesting to consider what changes when qualitative researchers develop their own concepts (as they have done in the past; consider, for example, double[d] science [Lather], autoethnography [Ellis], intersubjectivity [Mead], and how a label becomes recognized and accepted). There seem to be at least two main areas of consideration: (1) disciplinary gatekeeping and (2) the goals and purposes of scholarly communication. First, let us consider the issue of recognition and acceptance by peer qualitative researchers and other scientists. Who is to decide the legitimized use of a label? Who is required or privileged to recognize it? Who cannot know the label or who should not know? When exactly does something become a label, and when is the signifier–signified link established?

Recognition and acceptance are, of course, emphasized in the context of peer reviews, collegial support, funding decisions, national and international reputation, tenure, and promotion, among other things. All these tasks and activities represent normative ways in which academia and higher education operate, identify, and mark their community and exercise power. Presence is shaped by the past, and innovation is linked to the tradition. However, this leaves little room for innovation or creativity outside normativity, especially when a tradition or existing practice is used as a measuring stick for success. Innovative and creative uses of labels may go unrecognized and sometimes rejected by peer reviewers, since these reviewers cannot identify or locate existing traditions that can legitimize proposed uses or practices. There may exist no predefined criteria, and therefore reviewers cannot rely on existing authority and cannot delegate the responsibility to make a decision to others or other things (see also Section 7). One can wonder whether this discursive and authoritative problem and lack of citational authority is a valid reason to make a new label or an innovative use of a label less important, purposeful, or meaningful. What about paradigm shifts (Kuhn, 1996) and less paradigmatic ways to use labels and language?

Another issue relates to the goals and purposes of scholarly communication. Why do qualitative researchers communicate and share their thoughts? For example, are our communications based on technical, communicative, or other types of interests (Habermas, 1971), or is something else at stake? For Habermas (1990), communicative action builds on mutual understanding and reaching a type of consensus related to shared language. Certainly, many researchers communicate to create mutual understanding, but sometimes shared understanding may be impossible to achieve or is an undesirable goal to begin with. This might especially be the case when scholars have considerably different standpoints and/or epistemologies, or when power dictates communication practices. Alternatively, mutual understanding may be both desired and resisted. At the same time, the notion of different communicative interests is not new for qualitative researchers. For example, some qualitative researchers communicate to share self-expression, to deliver information, to describe and understand, to engage in cultural critique, to emancipate or persuade, and to provoke. If a mutual or agreed-upon understanding is not one's goal, the lack of shared language might be less problematic, and communicative persuasion might ultimately be even more effective when alternative language or new labels have been introduced. Do we need to rely on known labels in order to achieve effective communication, or is "effective" communication even desirable? (Especially if effectiveness is being defined by narrow policy discourses.) Maybe unclear, less directed or directive, less coherent and logical communication can create more productive dialogue—inviting space to think differently.

To think without normative labels could imply thinking about language in deterritorialized ways (breaking free from existing paths, lines of inquiry, and practices to generate new connection and possibilities). Deleuze encouraged us to deviate from the normativity of language, since this helps to deterritorialize meanings and subvert linguistic structures (see, e.g., Bogue, 2005; Deleuze &

To be honest, I am not sure I understand this. . . . is it to mean if I think I have a case, someone labeled that thing I have a case, and therefore I can have a case, but if I do not have one I may still have the thing but not the label of case, and therefore it has been taken away? Maybe a footnote to help people like me who are confused.

—Darby

If it was really "nonsense," why draw on known words? Are you feeling bound to this topic based on your anticipated audience?

—Darby

Guattari, 1987). Deleuze (1990) drew a subversion example from a Zen master: **"If you have a case," says the Zen master, "I am giving you one; if you do not have one, I am taking it away" (p. 136).** Language games are infinitive in number, and diverse events make these games and subversion possible. Nonsense, absurdity, and paradox are Deleuze's preferred expressions of language, since these forms of events can free language from its referential and normative functions. Deleuze asks, what happens to systems and normativity when language becomes nonrepresentational?

Additionally, "concepts [or labels] are not waiting for us ready-made, like heavenly bodies. There is no heaven for concepts. They must be invented, fabricated, or rather created and would be nothing without their creator's signature" (Deleuze & Guattari, 1994, p. 5). Concepts are also becoming and always regenerating and recreating themselves through their interactions and relationships with other concepts. In the next two examples I create two different forms of "triangulaxivity," **a "nonsense"** and possibly unrecognizable label that combines distinct functions of both reflexivity and triangulation. My purpose is not to argue for the use or adaptation of this particular concept (triangulaxivity) per se, but I use this example to illustrate my point about infinite iterations. I also chose to use concepts closely associated with the initial concepts instead of using concepts outside methodological discourses (which of itself is a limitation, of course). For example, I could have put forward conceptual connections to history, the arts, literature, and pop culture rather than creating relations to other scholarly discourses. In addition, there could be an indefinite number of examples and forms of intertextuality, but for the sake of the argument I present only a few here.

> *Let's play*
>
> *even though you   might*
>
> *not want to*
>
> *You don't have time*
>
> *to play   not in my space*
>
> *Not according to my rules   but   wait*
>
> *There are no rules*

we can just pretend   maybe

we like to play   crazy games

We like to respond to oneself and otherness

within and outside   ourselves   us and over ourselves (and labels)

done   again and again

In the following examples, I engage both preexisting versions of the concepts (reflexivity and triangulation) and attempt to create a new space where concepts respond to otherness outside and within themselves. This experiment is also meant to illustrate how "nonsense" activity like this and untraditional function of a label can be both nonsensical and sensical at the same time.

From Deleuze's (1990) perspective, concepts speak to events, not meanings. So, think about an event where the acts of triangulating and being reflexive come together in their singularity within the same study. For example, Scholar A (see Form IA, IB) desires to use multiple techniques of data collection or analysis, and she is also committed to self-inspection, including different ways to gather and handle one's thoughts and activities. Neither multiple techniques nor self-inspection can take place without the other (so this particular way of engaging and doing differs, e.g., from the event where triangulation is followed by being reflexive). The acts and practices of triangulation and being reflexive are also simultaneous. Furthermore, this event is not a pure triangulation event, since being reflexive blends with and bleeds into triangulation activity. A new event is created that also carries another label. In addition, triangulaxivity is more than a unifying act of triangulation and reflexivity. Since we do not know this conceptual space beforehand, something unanticipated is likely to take place. Doing multiple techniques and engaging in self-inspection simultaneously are likely to bring along other concepts and new forms of intertextuality and "inter-doing." Maybe triangulaxivity involves a choice (regarding methods, a choice between dichotomies, a choice to continue or stop), resolutions between conflicting thoughts and methods, methodological conflicts that may stay unsolved, stops and pauses to think or practice methods, and comparisons (self and others, past, present, and future), and triangulaxivity might be used as an approach that aims to create change and promote action. Think about these options as possibilities, events to come—not just any possibility but possibilities that will work for you.

Form I:

Triangulation is the use of multiple techniques for gathering and/or handling data within a single study.

Reflexivity is the commitment to self-inspection based on the researchers' own thoughts and activities.

IA. Triangulaxivity is the use of multiple techniques and a commitment to self-inspection for gathering and /or handling researchers' own thoughts and activities within a single study.

IB. Triangulaxivity is pausing and stopping during research activities to consider the choice regarding multiple methodological techniques and commitment to action-oriented self-inspection for gathering and /or handling researchers' own thoughts and activities within a single study.

Form II:

Triangulation is a methodological approach that contributes to the validity of research results when multiple methods, sources, theories, and/or investigators are employed.

Reflexivity is the personal, interpersonal, institutional, pragmatic, emotional, theoretical, epistemological, and ontological influences on our research and data analysis processes.

IIA. Triangulaxivity is a methodological approach that contributes to the validity of personal, interpersonal, institutional, pragmatic, emotional, theoretical, epistemological, and ontological influences when multiple methods, sources, theories, and/or investigators are employed during research and data analysis processes.

IIB. Triangulaxivity is an analysis of the validity of personal, interpersonal, institutional, pragmatic, emotional, theoretical, epistemological and ontological influences when multiple methods, sources, theories, and/or investigators are employed during the research and data analysis processes. This analysis can be used to externally evaluate the rigor of the research process and study findings.

An infinite number of combinations and events are possible. For example, another form of "triangulaxivity" might be more appropriate or needed for other qualitative researchers. In this second form of "triangulaxivity," the label itself stays the same but the signifier–signified connection changes. For instance, Scholar B (see Form IIA and IIB) has thought about a relationship between triangulation, validity, and reflexivity for some time now. For Scholar B, triangulating always happens in the context of validation, and he also believes that triangulating and validation take place outside their narrowly defined methodological contexts. Triangulation connects not only methods, investigators, and theories, but also power, institutional influences, pragmatic desires, and epistemologies in reflective ways.

Maybe

triangulaxivity is the outcome of rigorous   Did I say rigorous?

research,

A process

you may use for your purposes

Maybe your purpose is   to carry out external evaluation

But what is external and what is evaluation   Mirka asks

Alternatively

triangulaxivity is an analysis;   analysis of analysis, analysis of oneself

not the other

Alternatively

analysis of the impact   did I say impact?

of multiple methods

Impact on individual choices the researcher makes

Are there any?

Alternatively

concepts come together   maybe more randomly than expected

to help you   and the world

to think with triangulation and reflexivity

In the previous examples, the body of triangulaxivity could be seen as a virtual label—a label without stable conceptual origins, linguistic limbs, or methodological structures. Multiple heads thinking the thought, committed eyes searching for references, thoughtful facial muscles exercising discipline, and epistemological fingertips crafting solid claims—all becoming everything and nothing. Fingers and words fold into each other to form praying hands. Fingers, words, prayers, and labels. Or do fingers and words pray? Intermingled energy, messy wordiness, puzzling connection. Are we there yet? A triangulaxivity yawn or a tringulaxivity prayer? Not sure.

Huh, that is a fascinating way to convey that idea.

—Kathryn

In its becoming, triangulaxivity brings together multiple techniques and self-inspection; doing and thinking (Form I); the (im)possibility of validity of the personal, the institutional, and the emotional; a multiplicity of methods, theories, and investigators (Form II); and many other connections to come. These paradoxical and somewhat absurd connections can create new lines of thought, practices, and application (e.g., the multiplicity of the researcher self, a continuum of theorizing and practicing theory, multiple validities of the personal or institutional). Concepts and labels become more promiscuous but not too palatable or too illegible (Childers, Rhee, & Daza, 2013). And maybe one's researcher self or selves become a dog in training, and theorizing and practicing appear on same side of the coin; and institutional validity creates an institution. Think about these options as possibilities, events to come—not just any possibility but the possibilities that will work for you (return of possibility).

How does the concept of privilege influence label use and meaning making?

These examples also illustrate how triangulaxivity could change and vary based on activities and perspectives that are used to construct or enact it. Meaning is harder to capture and normativity is more challenging to sustain if there are no preferred or privileged uses or users. Different forms of triangulaxivity bring together unexpected relations to other concepts, and they do not honor disciplinary or socially accepted uses of signifiers. However, this disturbance can be productive and even liberating, thus leading to other unconventional uses or labels. Triangulaxivity is a playful creation that could prompt other conceptual interchanges and linkages, such as trianography (forms of cultural triangulation), unsubjectivity (forms of subjectivity working against themselves), samplexivity (forms of reflexive sampling), and **themaxivity (forms of synthesized reflexivity)**.

How about crystalaxivity?

—Cheryl

But why care? Who would care about these different forms of triangulaxivity? Maybe those scholars who have been searching for ways to share what they have been doing that is "not this or that" care. Those scholars who think that the tasks of triangulation or reflexivity cannot be decontextualized but that these tasks take different, simultaneous, and overlapping forms might also care. Those scholars who believe that triangulation is always a reflexive task might care. Some other scholars might care for other reasons.

In your own research, you could:

1. Discuss with a colleague why you are drawn to particular ways to carry the label of triangulation and what could explain, express, use, transfer, or transplant the differences between your views and your colleague's views.

2. Consider what happens when the same label has vastly different actions and activities associated with it. Who needs to control different uses of labels? Why do the ways in which we use labels need to be guarded and socially accepted?

3. **E-mail me your thoughts and reactions to "triangulaxivity."**

Possibilities of Linguistic Creativity and Innovation in Research: Living With Words Without Stable Meaning

LOL. Readers e-mailing you their thoughts and reactions— that might be the best book assignment I've ever seen! What would you do with these thoughts and reactions?
—Jasmine

Some of the possibilities of (linguistic) creativity and innovation in research are endless, inspiring, freeing, and still to come. It is fascinating to think about methodology and its vocabulary that is always becoming and never a finished project. From this perspective, qualitative researchers cannot rest their cases, finish their learning, or close their glossaries. Similar to the social and material worlds at large, methodology, its labels, and its concepts are in constant flux. There is work to do and new expressions and "formalizations" to be created. Deleuze and Guattari (1987) explained that language becomes the new form of expression and a set of formal traits defining this new expression. "Signs are not signs of a thing; they are signs of deterritorialization and reterritorialization, they mark a certain threshold crossed in the course of these movements . . . signs designate only a certain formalization of expression" (Deleuze & Guattari, 1987, pp. 67–68).

Living with words without stable and fixed meaning can create a space to think about scholarship and our lives differently. We will have more time to experience, live, and do scholarship and life rather than seeking for meanings that may or may not confirm the norm. In addition, we may be able to give up notions of finality of knowledge or findings and approach ending and "conclusions" as temporary and unstable. Instead of rigidly studying methodological techniques or worrying about right ways to carry out scholarship, we could try to live research. Different notions of *living research* present interesting intellectual and material challenges, especially related to expertise, time, resources, and peer evaluations. Who will fund living research? Will living research serve as justification for a faculty member's sabbatical or a student's request to have one summer funded without completing any traditional course credits?

Words without meaning could be contrasted to Massumi's (2002) concept of the body without an image. Both words without meaning and bodies without an image are accumulative spaces and intersections of perspectives and, as Massumi put it, "passages between" and "a gap in space that is also a suspension of the normal unfolding of time" (p. 57). Massumi also suggested that we should rethink bodies, subjectivities, and social change through movement, affect, and force instead of code, text, and signification.

Words without meaning create anticipation that can produce and inspire. "Subject and object are embedded in the situational relation in a way that cannot be fully determined in advance. As long as the event is ongoing, its outcome even slightly uncertain, their contextual identity is open to amendment" (Massumi, 2002, p. 231).

> *I understand.*
>
> —Jasmine

Here, today

I follow Deleuze and Guattari

I think with them about   maps

>   *zones of proximity*

>   *you, me, texts, labels   and our temporary meeting, rapid encounter*

>   *us coming together*

Copresence and the impossible

Difficult to say where one

word   and

particle ends   Think with triangulation!

and other begins   Think with reflexivity!

Triangulaxivity is becoming   neither triangulation nor reflexivity

has a privileged position

in that becoming   Think privilege! Not!

What would happen to the labels associated with qualitative research if one thought similarly to Deleuze and Guattari (1987), who proposed that "form itself became *a great form in continuous development*, a gathering of forces . . . matter itself was no longer a chaos to subjugate and organize but rather *the moving matter of a continuous variation*" (p. 340)? From this perspective, methodological labels have a temporal presence and virtual subjectivity. They move and shift, and they are only known through their variations and co-presence. Instead of creating networks of meaning word and labels without meaning, they create varying alliances and affiliations.

Massumi (2002) encouraged scholars to follow and create affirmative methods:

> techniques which embrace their own inventiveness and are not afraid to own up to the fact that they add (if so meagerly) to reality . . . *vague* concepts, and concepts of vagueness, have a crucial, and often enjoyable, role to play. (p. 13)

Furthermore, Massumi emphasized how paradox can be an effective logical operator for vague concepts. Furthermore, the question at hand is not about truth value but whether something works and can be useful for you. "What new thoughts does it make possible to think? What new emotions does it make possible to feel? What new sensations and perceptions does it open in the body" (Massumi, 1987, p. xv)?

Generally speaking, qualitative researchers do not lack communication, but maybe they have too much of it and they worry too much about it. Qualitative

Robert Ulmer

researchers may lack creation (see also Koro-Ljungberg, 2012). "*We lack resistance to the present.* The creation of concepts in itself calls for a future form, for a new earth and people that do not yet exist" (p. 108). "Concepts are really monsters that are reborn from their fragments" (Deleuze & Guattari, 1994, p. 140). These concepts in making and monsters haunting in the shadows of normative language can be seen as potential and a form of energy that has power to surprise and diversify. For Deleuze, the goal of philosophy "pragmatics" is to invent concepts that do not add up to a system that you enter but that will pack potential "in a way a crowbar in a willing hand envelops an energy of prying" (Massumi, 1987, p. xv). Similarly, Derrida's vocabulary is always on the move. "He does not relinquish a term altogether. He simply reduces it to the lower case of a common noun, where each context establishes its provisional definition yet once again" (Spivak, 1997, p. lxxi).

It is possible that language and labels fail to represent. Spivak (1997) explained that "in examining familiar things we come to such unfamiliar conclusions that our very language is twisted and bent even as it guides us" (p. xiv). For Derrida, a possibility of thought does not come through being or identity but in the thought's simultaneous separation and the sameness of the other. Half of the sign is "not there" (same as the other) and the other half is "not that." The structure of signs is determined by a trace that will always stay at least partially absent. If meanings and signifiers stay at least partially absent, why forcefully fit labels or why insist on language carrying particular meanings? Maybe qualitative researchers would do better to think about temporary, virtual, or quasi-conceptual links assigned to labels and words. From this perspective, scholars should always recheck and in some ways question normative language and labels, and they could adopt a position of linguistic openness and uncertainty. In that way, labels and language might become more of a game with constantly changing rules, a puzzle without an end, or a nagging thought that won't go away.

This ties nicely to a conversation we had about hegemony in Buffy's summer class. We arrived at the conclusion that we may not be able to imagine what is possible for race relations because we only had normative language to describe what might be possible bounding our ideas to what is not and what is possible.

—Darby

Even though normativity and socially accepted uses of the labels may prevail and dominate, especially in peer-review processes, we should not give up our desire to think the impossible. One cannot think the impossible only with the possible, since logic, language, and **labels must fail first**. Language and different uses of labels are always historical, political, incomplete, stuttering, and repetitive in their imperfection and inaccuracy, which, luckily, leaves room for impossible yet provocative methodological projects. How would qualitative researchers' normative practices and/or legitimizing uses of labels change if Lyotard's language games or Deleuzian endless language events informed our methodological processes and decision making? Think about these options as possibilities, events to come—not just any possibility but possibilities that will work for you (return of possibility).

READING LIST OF LIFE ——————————————————————

Coelho, P. (2006). *The alchemist*. HarperLuxe.

Frankl, V. (2006). *Man's search for meaning*. Beacon Press.

Hesse, H. (1951). *Siddhartha*. Bantam Books.

Michaels, A. (1996). *Fugitive pieces*. Vintage Books.

3

Data-Wants and Data Entanglements

Data Matter

Data is such a central concept in the world of researchers that oftentimes the role of data, its conceptualization, its theoretical connections, and its "doings" (i.e., the ways in which data works, provokes, generates, and moves) are taken for granted. It is as if data is already known and at least anticipated prior to its construction, emergence, and appearance. Qualitative researchers plan what to do with *it* (data), how to analyze *it*, how to present *it*, and how to increase the validity of *it* even before they have any encounters with data. Discussion in this section attempts to problematize these taken-for-granted notions of data and assumed ways in which data might function, happen, provoke, and relate (see also the special issue on data in *Cultural Studies ↔ Critical Methodologies*, Koro-Ljungberg & MacLure, 2013).

Robert Ulmer

I do not propose that researchers should surrender to data or that the agency of the data should solely drive future research. Neither do I propose that *I* know what data wants. More, I hope to show that when a researcher begins to shift his or her control of data, both data and analysis become infinite and ideally multiple. The final end of the analysis or the stability of the "conclusion" may become questioned. Not knowing what data really wants is both the dilemma and the possibility at the same time.

I wonder about data. Can data be pleasing in its appearance; can data be alive? How can data change and transform us as researchers? If data were not pleasing or alive, why would researchers act as if data had the power to influence behavior, demand attention, create change, shape attitudes, or illustrate injustice? As with Mitchell's (2005) argument about contradictions in the analysis of images, it is important to catch the power and powerlessness of data, data that are alive but also still/dead, both meaningful and irrelevant. **This paradox associated with "wanting" and interacting with data brings to the forefront differences and similarities between wanting, being, and being capable of wanting.** Data's wanting something does not reflect real, organism-like structures but provides a metaphor for thinking about data and data analysis differently.

In this section, in addition to wondering, I project and anticipate what data might want when data is seen as reactionary, when data is communicating with us in the form of insights, questions, feelings, and so on. How does data take or provoke action? If data wants X, researchers might respond by doing Y. Yet we cannot ever really know what data wants, especially if we see a degree of separation between data and us. Data will always stay somewhat mysterious, unknown, and tentative, leaving researchers uncertain about the *exactness* of data and its wants. This uncertainty, in turn, can translate to qualitative researchers' notions of findings, and this uncertainty might be productive, since our interactions with data are never finished, and our conclusions about data always stay reversible and open to other interpretations. Research is always unfinished and thus calls for ongoing attention and future work from the scholars.

Can scholars ever "really know" data or analysis?

So, one may ask, what is the point of this exercise? To answer briefly, it could be meaningful to play with the idea of thinking about our relationship with data differently, to imagine what could happen if a researcher's control of data were released, in a way (if that is possible). Alternatively, thinking about data's relationality, movement, entanglements, or multidirectional epistemological flows—that is, knowledge from data shaping researchers and research, knowledge from research shaping data, and/or knowledge within the data–researcher relationship shaping the data–researcher relationship, among others—might help us to change the direction of knowledge production in critical social science research and practice. I hope, this chapter will serve as a stimulus for those scholars who wish to reconsider the role of data in their own work, and to

Is data meaningful only when a person stops to reflect on its meaning? Or is the world full of the untapped potential of data, being limited only by the hegemony of human thought?
—Darby

open up alternative possibilities for data and data interactions. This line of thought could also have implications for overall research design, analysis, representation, and so on. Alternatively, researchers might simply read this section and ignore everything.

I will do both

I control   maybe interpret a little   and, for heaven's sake,

thematize

data, my interactions with data, data space

you and ways you should, I mean could, read

this data?   What data? Where data? How data?

Me and me/data/us

Knowing subject   What knowing subject? Who?

I feel controlled, created, seduced, led, pushed around

by data

I am not sure

I feel, think, sense, believe

Data matters   Data matter/s [data material]

Here, now

Also tomorrow

What can be gained when scholars consider data-wants and data's desires?

What happens if a researcher releases control of the data?

GLOSSARY

Data. Latin *datum.* Meaning is not ascribed to the object under study, but discovered (or given) to researcher who is able to empirically verify knowledge through the use of the scientific method (Crotty, 1998).

Data. "Created by chunking experiences into recordable units" (Bernard & Ryan, 2010, p. 5).

Data. Reductions of our experience (Bernard & Ryan, 2010, p. 5).

Data. A matter of seeing (Schostak & Schostak, 2008, p. 91).

Data. Data is fluid, a chameleon, able to take different "shades" of meaning based on the perspective of the researcher (see, e.g., Hammersley & Atkinson, 1995; Jackson & Mazzei, 2012).

Data. "Accounts gathered by qualitative researchers" (Polkinghorne, 2005, p. 138).

Data Directionality

Data, a word that itself might resist definition (see, e.g., Koro-Ljungberg & MacLure, 2013), is hard to conceptualize in independent and uncontextualized ways. Rather, it is possible that data is entangled with other labels, "collection and analysis," subjectivities, and positionalities, theories, letters and notes, memories, practices, and too many other things to list or maybe even know. It is often taken for granted that data and data analysis are essential and central structures of the main grand narratives of research. We have textbooks that tell us what data is and how to collect and analyze it; how to sort and shift it; how to tell the good data from the "bad" data, or a well-executed analysis from a badly executed one. Researchers aim to separate the data and processes that are trustworthy, relevant, valid, and meaningful from those that are not.

At the same time, qualitative research scholars and the field of critical social science acknowledge the dispersion of theories and theoretical frames. The slogan "My theories are not necessary your theories" is an acceptable and widely distributed position, at least within some qualitative research contexts and discourses. However, less often scholars conceptualize or use data in similar ways. We could think more often about when/if/how my data might (not) be your data or my understandings of analysis might (not) overlap or parallel with your understandings and preferences.

Data, like researchers, participants, and theories, are already particles and material within inquiry systems and an ecology of research (see also Barad, 2007). Data, I, this text, and you as readers—our physical bodies, cultural connections, and so on—are part of knowledge practices that make this knowing, these data readings, these data-wants, and these data analyses illuminate, valorize, and extend quite unpredictably. **Sometimes** qualitative researchers are or become the data, and as understandings are being crafted and explored, we might feel distance—material or epistemological barriers—between us and the data. I recognize the mutual constitution of entangled beings, particles, (e.g., data, analysis, this text, me, and analyst) and epistemological forces, yet the main focus in this section is on data-wants and how data-wants can constitute and create different interactions with researchers, participants, readers, and others. Furthermore, the notion of **"data-wants" is used as a reference to data's desire for, or wanting of, "control" in order to enable qualitative scholars to think differently about reversed knowledge flows.**

What we (researchers, scholars, students, teachers, etc.) do with "data" once we have "access" to it happens often unexpectedly, in unpredictable and entangled ways. I don't think I can model/illustrate/claim to know something that can take such a different form every time data is recognized as a happening. Instead of knowing or recognizing data or "the analysis" (at least enough to describe it and claim legitimacy that way), I suggest that we could begin by investigating/

rethinking/releasing data's positioning and relationships—the "role of data." Maybe we could pay attention to the ways in which data is playing games on us, interacting, or intra-acting. Rather than providing answers, I want to ask questions about data, the role of data, and how we come to know the relationship between data and researchers as one-directional but ultimately controlled by the researcher. How does this position of the researcher as knower bound and limit us, analysis, and data? Without finding some ways to move away from this assumed relationship between data and researchers, scholars keep proposing that they "know" or completely understand the data, analysis, themselves, and their worlds. I also wonder what would happen if scholars moved toward a temporal place of surrender (to data) that could prompt researchers to ask questions related to the data's potential energy to shift things and transform research, the point being that without ever really knowing what "data wants," researchers are bound to *consider data as multiple*, uncertain, and shifting instead of reductionist, fixed, and always already "knowable." Even though "data's desires" may not be known, something is still happening.

How can data displace itself and generate/create the subject and knower?

What might happen if scholars let go of their learned or socially constructed intentions and desires to control data? Maybe this move is impossible and might not lead anywhere, especially if scholars are not ready to trouble notions of linear logic, certainty, and correspondence theories of truth. For example, in my data work, I feel continuously trapped in a space where I make things and data connections happen or these connections happen to me, but I cannot describe them, since the connections keep escaping description, capture, and knowing. Simply put, I just don't know for certain who I am and how I am in relation to data or how to know what to do with data.

ALWAYS (not sometimes)! Data and the researcher are nested in a consistent reproduction through the process of research.
—Darby

Section key points:

- Shift researchers' focus toward what data (object) might want—how data might take initiative and create itself in connections with other data. Recognize how data (object) can make a discovery of the researcher (subject) during "data analysis."
- Suggest a possible return to "data object" that also **questions the subject's dominance over data and the one-directionality of knowledge.**
- Keep data and analysis open to revision and being responsive to differentiations from within, which can promote reactive scholarship, deeper engagement with data, and ongoing analytical creativity.

These ideals challenge researchers, particularly in the constructivist/interpretivist realms, to acknowledge that many often struggle with allowing space for "data-wants." Because, oftentimes, these researchers are either ignorant of the amount of control they wield or fearful to allow space for what data actually may want.
—Chandra

The Dilemma of Data-Wants

A profound thinker never really convinces us of anything; he or she can only awaken us to the choices we have made, and make us wonder about their meaning and their consequences.

—Levin, 1996, p. 7

In my final project for your class last semester, I tried to do this. Instead of finding a method, I looked at some interview data that I had which was screaming to be analyzed using Deleuze. I hadn't anticipated this, but it was so exciting that I couldn't think about anything else. I have never been this excited about research. I analyzed the data in a way I felt was good, which resulted in a kind of messy analysis, but something that was very meaningful. There were no prescribed steps, just thinking with Deleuze. What resulted was messy, but exciting and new; it hadn't been done before. At the same time, I kept hearing people talk about rhizoanalysis. I had no idea what rhizoanalysis was, but it was related to Deleuze. It was a very interesting experience for me to do something and realize that others had replicated that kind of method without progressive steps.

—Justin

Problematizing data, data entanglements, and data-wants is not necessarily a new approach to data, but the persistence of neopositivist discourses in the social sciences may still prevent the "problem" with stable notions of data from being accepted in mainstream research communities. Let me use a brief study to provide context to this phenomenon. In 2010, two mixed-methods faculty from agriculture and I sent a two-question open-ended survey to qualitative methodologists and members of the American Educational Research Association via the Qualitative Research Special Interest Group Listserv. We received 45 responses. We asked participants to characterize in their own words what "data" is and how it impacts research (see below). The following figure summarizes participants' responses. We presented participants' responses (data) in a way that illustrates researchers' control over data through over-summarizing and decontextualizing. Our systematic thematic analysis (see Bernard & Ryan, 2010) and the controlled interactions between data and us happened as a result of epistemological and methodological negotiations between my collaborators and me on this study. When I met with my collaborators, we talked about our data interactions, the ways in which we approached the analytical in data, and how other scholars viewed and interacted with data. Each of us wanted to experience data differently, and some of us worried about peer evaluations and "systematic analysis" of data. As a result, we engaged in "data reduction" (see the following example) but also expanded our interactions and understandings (see later in this chapter). We worked both with and against "normative" notions and functions of data.

Our interpretation was that these qualitative researchers were working from different epistemological and theoretical perspectives. Figure 3.1 illustrates that for some scholars, information had to be empirical or recorded to be considered to be data, and for others, information was fundamental to the goals and purposes of the research project or original so as to provide meaningful insights in order to contribute to the existing literature. For some scholars, data seemed to relate to a specific object, and there existed different kinds of objects, including various lists of materials, sources of information, shared materials, facts, narratives, language, linguistic objects, and so on. Data was also seen as an object that was created in response to a particular research question. In addition, data was a process that became visible and recognizable through acts of seeing, hearing, interacting, experiencing, and living (accounts and texts of living or data performances). Some researchers did not distinguish data from nondata, and they proposed that everything is data; for some, data was comparable to insights and inner thoughts. Overall, it could be argued that based on these interactions, data takes on different forms, and seemed considerably different for different scholars. Data was not just one thing, and data did not do just one thing.

In your own research, you could:

- Pay attention to the ways in which you generate and control data
- Consider your notions of data and how data is entangled with you, theories, the research context, politics, and writing
- Read different texts about the role and functions of data to expand your experiences and notions of data
- Talk to your peers and teachers about their notions of data
- Think about ways to avoid overconsumption/overgeneration/overcollection of data

I like this! How does this go beyond reflexivity? Does your questioning of data challenge reflexivity? I think the concept of reflexivity is limited in encouraging researchers to question the subject's dominance over data. Because in reflexivity, the researcher is still trying to understand how data is influencing them. Being able to articulate what data is doing and how they are responding to it. Oftentimes, we don't know what data is doing, or why it is doing what it does.

—Chandra

Data's Past

Despite the reductionist and controlled ways in which many qualitative researchers from our study seemed to approach data, different roles, functions, and responsibilities of data (broadly defined) have been discussed in the literature. For example, some researchers argue that data guides analysis and its own sampling (i.e., theoretical sampling in grounded theory; Strauss & Corbin, 1998); contributes to the changes in research questions (Marshall & Rossman, 2006); contradicts, traps, and captivates audiences; troubles language (St. Pierre, 1997); emerges unexpectedly; provokes and questions (Tuhiwai Smith, 2001); and even breaks your heart (Behar, 1996). Even though many of these perspectives are familiar to qualitative researchers, some qualitative researchers may still prefer to conduct "easy" or epistemologically comfortable research, to focus on procedures of collection and analysis, and worry about data and the roles of data may come only as an afterthought, when prompted

Figure 3.1 Some Potential Notions of Data

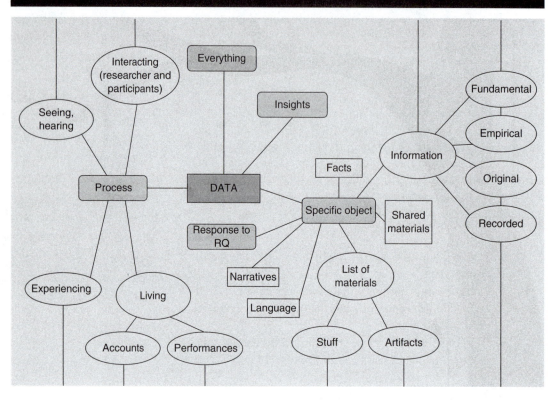

by reviewers, or perhaps not at all. Research time might be spent collecting data, documenting practice, capturing "lived experiences," or producing materials, evidence, and reflections instead of questioning, further developing, or reconstructing various well-known aspects of research.

Furthermore, being overwhelmed with the quantity of data and the volume of data materials in qualitative studies easily results in data interactions and findings that resemble lists of materials and examples of collected quotes. Sometimes data is collected, constructed, found, and lived without detailed plans for analysis, data integration, or considerations for why a particular type of data is needed. It can also be tempting to ask brief, uncritical questions about data and perhaps to let findings emerge and appear "magically" rather than pay attention to data's resistance or silence or the possible reversal of knowledge flow (from subject to object). Additionally, some scholars' overemphasis on large quantities of data may enable them to stay away from questions, tasks, and processes that are messy, uncertain, and uncomfortable. These uncritical and sometimes mechanical interactions with data are not only often prompted by personal preferences and

What are the pitfalls of not being receptive to data-wants?

time restrictions but are also sometimes guided by larger sociopolitical discourses and values. At the same time, big data and large quantities of data may be needed. For example, some scholars conducting qualitative research feel compelled to collect large samples to be able to "generalize" across contexts (Gobo, 2004), triangulate data to get to the "truth" (Perlesz & Lindsay, 2003; Silverman & Marvasti, 2008), and collect sufficient amounts of data to define the properties of emerging theory or "verify" the findings (Charmaz, 2010).

> *Eat data, bite it, blend data particles with drops of your saliva*
>
> *data for consumption   data for digestion*
>
> *data breakfast, data lunch, data dinner   or maybe just my secret data snack*
>
> *Wait data! Don't move!*
>
> *Stay still! Reproduce and multiply!*
>
> *So I can stick my fork in you   taste you again and again*
>
> *Data: tasteless but full of flavor*
>
> *Can I slice you up with my sharp analytical procedures?*
>
> *Swallow slowly as a piece of holistic Truth and true description?*
>
> *Wait a minute . . .*
>
> *. . . you taste bitter*
>
> *you taste odd   maybe too much salt or pepper perhaps*
>
> *What happened to my clean data?   Delicious data?*
>
> *What happened to my nerves that supply sensory innervation to the palate?*
>
> *Did I hurry data? Or perhaps overcook data?*
>
> *I just need to take a deep breath and digest   Approach data slowly*

Can data be consumed? Eaten bite by bite? It could be argued that when data is consumed all at once, data becomes still, quiet, possibly dead, and potentially a distant object to be possessed rather than an aspect of production and a part of co-creation and interchange. Researchers have no time to tailor their analysis, think critically about their data, or let data rest. So, why hurry with data? I wonder whether to do more with less data by letting "the same" data repeat itself and multiply (see, e.g., Jackson & Mazzei, 2012; Koro-Ljungberg & MacLure, 2013) might lead to interesting new insights.

For the project for the data analysis class, I released control and invited my data to take initiative. It wasn't a particularly successful maneuver; the poem below describes a failed dialogue. Instead, other data I wasn't even seeking kept asserting itself, jumping up and down, incessantly insisting to be analyzed. I told the images and phrases launching on new lines of flight in my mind to go away, but they refused to go unnoticed. Finally, I relented (see TQR 2014 paper proposal, "Deleuzian Lines: Intersections With Photography and Policy").

I tried talking to my data.
But it wasn't interested in
conversing.
I asked if it had any
methodological inclinations.
My data chose not to respond.
I tried to explain that I wanted
to be respectful—I would let it
choose.
Still nothing.
I told my data that maybe it just
sucked.
My data didn't care.
So I started a staring contest
with a visual version of my data,
repeatedly pressing "re-layout" on
the screen—
click, click, click, click, click
—as if pulling a slot machine
lever, holding out for the jackpot.
—Jasmine

Or whether, by opening up the concept of data (see, e.g., St. Pierre, 1997), researchers might get inspired to experiment with data. Or maybe paying more attention to different interactions with data and "data's wanting" rather than the stringent and uncritical execution of a method or distant and sterile interactions might remedy some researchers' urges to overgeneralize and decontextualize data. By "interactions," I do not refer to manipulation or documentation of data but rather processes and entanglements in which researchers and data act upon one another. Data interactions could entail reciprocal actions, effects, influences, and transformations. **What could happen if qualitative researchers were to shift their focus from acting on, manipulating, or analyzing data to data's working on the researchers themselves or data's taking the initiative?**

Data Object

The previously described analytical move that centers on *data object* (not still or stable in form but productive, alive, and interactive in form) rather than on the researcher might bring elements of uncertainty, humility, and movement into data interactions and analysis processes. It is also interesting to think about how data (object) can make a discovery of the subject (researcher). This approach to data and analysis also introduces a return to data object, questioning the subject's dominance over data and the one-directionality of knowledge. Additionally, this move can create space where data can produce uncertainty and possibly a mess, redirect researchers' attention, and ultimately maybe even produce "want." As a result, certainty associated with researchers' knowing will be questioned if they come to realize that they can *never really know* what data wants, and therefore analysis will stay tentative, uncertain, and always open to reinterpretations. Finally, this analytical move also implies that the researcher as a subject of power, knowledge, and history gives way to diffuse and insubstantial subjectivities (see Baudrillard, 2010).

Although I propose a move away from the researcher subject and *toward* data, this move does not imply romanticism or a humanistic project. Conceptualization of data and data analysis is likely impossible without relationships, including interactions with a subject (in this text, researchers and study participants). Yet it is important to strategically reconsider normative, romantic, or humanistic assumptions about data and researchers' relationship with data. To build my argument, I first discuss the ontological and epistemological context shaping this text. Then I introduce some examples from published journal articles to illustrate common analysis practices adopted by qualitative researchers. Last, I share examples from my data to show how different notions of data and various analytical interactions can produce differentiations of the "same data" and how some interactions enable redirection of knowledge and decentering of the subject (researcher) maybe more than others.

Interlude: Knowledge Context
· ·

In the following paragraphs, I draw from Baudrillard and his postmodern project, where reality is replaced by signs of reality. Signs of reality create a duplication, the hyperreal, which makes it impossible to separate true and false, real and imaginary. Baudrillard's antidialectical project reverses the subject's dominance over the object and reenvisions the direction of knowledge.

Baudrillard's ontological project was not only to reverse subject–object relations but also to give objects their escape, strategies, and resistance.

> The more an object is persecuted by experimental procedures, the more it invents strategies of counterfeit, evasion, disguise, and disappearance. It is like a virus; it escapes by endlessly inventing counter strategies. This behavior of the object is also ironic insofar as it breaks the foolish pretension of the subject, its desire to impose laws and dispose the world according to its own will, its own representations. (Baudrillad & Witwer, 2000, p. 79)

For Baudrillard, there are at least two options: One commits to certainty and a particular vision, or one takes the knowledge-seeking process less seriously, placing one's faith in the game and the rules of the game. In this context, I place my faith in the game, thus minimizing the value of any single point of view or piece of knowledge. I do not believe in one right notion or way of data or data analysis. Furthermore, hierarchies and rules are treated as ascriptive and provisional (see Levin, 1996). Therefore, I invite you to join the data game and create your own rules and notions of data and analysis.

I really like this part. . . . This is an interesting way to talk about data analysis. Why do we want to exert power on the data without considering the option of being under the power of the data? Manipulating the data gives the analyst control of what he/she will find. Submitting to the data opens up a world of possibilities that you never knew existed. The uncertainty also adds to the excitement of the find!

—Cheryl

In this game, I am aware that data objects want, speak, and strategize, but I can never be really sure how they will do it. Mitchell (2005) proposed that "the slogan of our times then, is not 'things fall apart,' but 'things come alive'" (p. 172). "The collapse of structure may be replaced by potentially uncontrolled growth of structures" (p. 172). Mitchell (2001) argued that physical objects have their concreteness but also abstract, metaphysical, and imaginary character—words, images, and signs circulating in different discourses. Baudrillard (1990) proposed that objects take revenge, and he would like the object to speak for itself. "Perhaps there is now the possibility that the object will say something to us, but above all the possibility that it will avenge itself!" (Baudrillard, 1990, p. 18).

In your own research, you could:

- Imagine how data can become alive or provoke and what might change methodologically as a result of that
- Reflect on and document how data might transform and approach you
- Redesign or reconceptualize your research from the position of the researcher as a lost subject

More specifically, for Baudrillard, objects can be material things, events, science, mummified royalty, or entire living people (see Weinbrot, 2012). Objects may transform subjects. They intervene between subjects, separating subjects from themselves, and connecting subjects with what they are not (Levin, 1996). Weinbrot (2012) wrote that Baudrillard's notion of "object" is not used to elicit questions about the existence of reality, but epistemological indeterminacy, uncertainty about knowledge, is built into the object itself. Furthermore, individuals may frequently find themselves within a Baudrillardean object or as component of it. In other words, researchers may find reassemblage and deep connections with objects. Objects are no longer stable, but they become interchangeable units, elements in a chain of signification, transmissible and recombinable (Levin, 1996). Objects belong to the order of destiny (Baudrillard, 1990). The meaning of difference highlights the unlimited differentiation within the same subject and object. Unlimited differentiations can be seen as a form of initiative, inviting the object to speak and push the subject to **lose its power and position as subject**.

WRONG! We hold the ultimate power as the ones who are giving it up! (It paints a more enticing picture this way to the reader).
—Jason

> They [advanced sciences] can only verify the way the object plays with its own objectivity. This is the object's perverse strategy; perhaps it is a form of revenge. Apparently, the object is a trickster; foiling all the protocols of the subject's experiment, so that the subject itself loses its position as subject. (Baudrillard & Witwer, 2000, p. 75)

Analytical Interactions
in the Existing Literature

To investigate researchers' interactions with data from another perspective, I conducted a brief analysis of published qualitative research articles. The following analysis is the second example in this section that illustrates the knowledge flow from subject to object and exemplifies my control over "data."

For the purpose of the study, I reviewed 25 articles from five highly ranked education journals (*Advances in Health Sciences Education*, *Early Childhood Research Quarterly*, *Exceptional Children*, *Journal of Research in Science Teaching*, and *Journal of Special Education*). In most published articles, data were collected from various sources without thoroughly considering how or why all data were needed to answer the research question(s). For example, in the *Journal of Research in Science Teaching*, one study utilized interviews, documents, participant observations, conversations, and field notes from 29 participants. These data were analyzed through domain analysis. In a study from *Exceptional Children*, there were 142 interviews, 400 hours of observation, and documents and artifacts from 71 participants. These data were coded.

Across all 25 sampled articles, the most common data analysis method was coding (36%), followed by thematic analysis (16%) and the constant comparative method (16%). Only three articles used more layered, in-depth analysis approaches (i.e., critical discourse analysis, narrative, hermeneutical analysis) that went beyond description, data summaries, or comparisons.

What did data want in these selected articles? Perhaps the researchers did not consider what data could want or what kind of analytical relationships scholars could establish with data. Consequently, the analysis approaches in the reviewed articles seemed expedited, objectified, and technical. Data did not speak, want, or interact with the researcher; rather, it was seen as a still object to be manipulated and "treated" based on researchers' preferences or predetermined moves with the data. The majority of authors (80%) proposed that data were to be manipulated, including being "counted," "coded," "sorted," "transformed into computer documents," or "bracketed and pulled apart." For example, an article that used the constant comparative method to analyze 25 interviews, 17 focus groups, 73 conference observations, and reflective notes stated that data were analyzed to form taxonomy. Coding, extraction, and sorting formed the analysis. In other words, data objects were ordered, and the created order was reported as a finding. Another article reported findings from five focus groups. The authors simplified their data by coding and breaking data into small meaning units so that conclusions were able to be drawn, findings examined and validated. Technical discourse and reductionist language were used to create distance between researchers and data, claim legitimacy, and increase the "validity" of the findings. Data analysis and conclusions were performed and depersonalized.

In contrast, it seemed that when researchers collected less data, they were more likely to analyze it with more layered and multifaceted approaches, which in turn led to different interactions, notions, and statements about data. For example, a hermeneutical analysis was conducted with four interviews, and a critical discourse analysis included teacher interviews with one teacher, some student interviews, and students' artifacts (the exact number of student interviews is unknown). These data were interpreted through repetitive iterative readings. Data analysis included movement between whole and parts of the text, producing a gradual *convergence* of insights coming from the research and text. In the critical discourse analysis, data's role and needs were taken into account in other ways. For instance, data had independence and they were viewed as "action-oriented medium" instead of transparent source of knowledge. Additionally, data participated in a dialogue, and contradictions within data were allowed to guide analysis, interpretation, and theory building even when competing themes and explanations were encountered or created.

Even though data in some of the articles were interpreted, participated in a dialogue, moved, and were "independent," none of the articles addressed how data created or changed the researchers. The direction of knowledge continued to move from the subject to the object. Similarly, none of the reviewed articles addressed how data could take initiative, shift expectations, or create the researcher. How did the authors invite data to speak? What does data want that it cannot have? What might absent or lacking data want?

> Are you sleeping? Are you sleeping?
>
> Brother John, Brother John?
>
> Morning bells are ringing. Morning bells are ringing.
>
> Ding, dang, dong. Ding, dang, dong.
>
> Are you sleeping? Are you sleeping?

In the next section, I share five differentiations of data prompted by my different (analytical) interactions with data. "Still data" (or sleeping data) has been created by a doctoral student, Sam, who attended the qualitative data analysis course I taught. I asked all my students to write reflections about their experiences and interactions when "creating a mess with data." The following "still data" is a part of Sam's reflective notes after the second class in that

Perhaps this is a matter of being respectful of/to data. Recently, as I was strolling through an art festival, a booth of mixed-media installations caught my attention. Though the compositions were aesthetically pleasing from a visual standpoint, the historical and literary figures portrayed were, in my view, misarranged with the surrounding images. In these pieces, for example, Herman Melville sailed through the Gulf of Mexico while William Faulkner was forcibly relocated from the American South. In examining the compositions, I thought of data making decisions. If these images had been given agency, I imagined that Melville and Faulkner might have made different choices. I hope not to dislocate my own data in a similar manner.

—Jasmine

> *I totally agree here. I believe that depth should supersede breadth in qualitative research. We want to gain a deeper understanding of a particular phenomenon. We are not trying to generalize to the population. Collecting 400 hours of text to code, categorize, and report themes does very little to provide the depth of understanding required for rigorous qualitative study.*
>
> —Cheryl

semester. My interactions with Sam's data are guided by the following pedagogical question: How do doctoral students describe their unstructured interactions with data and their learning to analyze data? By building from Sam's still data and other supplementary data, I illustrate different ways data can or cannot work with researchers and students and how data may take initiative, thereby creating unlimited and ongoing differentiations of themselves. Data, examples, reflections, and other supplements are not meant to show how to "do qualitative data analysis" as a "step-by-step" process, and I am not sure that the following would be considered to be "analysis" in any traditional sense. Rather, I hope that the following reflections, decision making, values, expectations, preferences, and dilemmas associated with learning about analysis and prompting students to interact with data create more interactions, additional questions, and different ways to think about how data might guide researchers in various processes, including data analysis and analytical interactions.

What Might Data Want?

Still data: *It honestly took me a few minutes to figure out why in the world we were spending an undisclosed amount of class time in blindfolds interacting with objects as they played the role of data. However, as the activity unfolded, I began to realize just how detrimental my eyes had been to me. Looking at coins had allowed me to undoubtedly identify them on quick glance; however, I remained very much unaware of many of the other characteristics and attributes. How could I be so unprepared to work with objects that I have been around and handled almost daily for years? This segued so well into the individual data analysis activity that followed. As I walked around Norman Hall trying to find a quiet place, it became clear that my walk was just as much about trying to mentally transfer the money activity into a plan of attack for my all-too-familiar data. Just like the money, my data is something that I have looked at, immersed myself in, and "knew." My plan quickly became to take away my "eyes" (which here meant the methodical analysis that I had been trained and encouraged to use) and force myself to look at this data from a different vantage point. Hoping that the newfound confidence and approach would prove transferable to this task, I sat down at a corner picnic table and pulled out my interview data. Reading through revealed the same information that I was used to seeing, the words almost losing meaning from the number of views. I stopped, reflected on the "no eyes" task at hand, and then reread the data. This time, I focused on really listening to what the participants were saying. No more interpreting, looking for good fits, or assuming what was being said. Surprisingly, the data really seemed to speak to me—and it sounded much different than before.*

The next 20 minutes were spent listening to the participants and identifying some preliminary themes that were emerging. I classified these themes as beliefs, issues, and tools surrounding the analysis of student work in the elementary mathematics classroom. These were much different ideas than what previous analyses had produced. This new approach was liberating and, more importantly, generative.

Feeling really good, I moved to my second location, unable to keep from smiling a little from my recent accomplishments. I sat down at location two and paused to reflect on what had happened so far, as well as where I might go from here. To clear my mind, I composed and sent an e-mail that was of reasonable importance. It quickly became evident that the events of the day had affected my writing. As I read through my e-mail, I couldn't help but notice that I had written it in a very clear and concise way—much like I had hoped my data would communicate to me. It was a good feeling to construct an e-mail about my thoughts just as they were. I had allowed my thoughts to express themselves just as I had allowed my participants the opportunity only minutes before. This e-mail, although arguably a marginal occurrence in comparison to data analysis, was important and thought provoking for me.

After putting my computer away, I refocused on the stack of data staring up at me from the bench. Still wary that I might be missing elements that my data were desperately trying to tell me, I asked myself why—really why—I had identified the themes listed above. Having nowhere else to turn, I reread the data and looked for support for my decisions, hoping all along that I had only translated what was said. The overwhelming support from the data reassured me that, for the first time, I had truly translated what my participants were saying. Things began to fall into place like pieces of a puzzle that I had not been able to see until now.

This activity really did give me a new perspective on analyzing data. Just because we have familiarized ourselves with data in no way guarantees that we have taken the time to explore and interact with it in ways that reveal its true meaning. It took being blindfolded to see a new perspective of analyzing.

In your own research, you could:

- Consider how your analysis might differentiate data or create another iteration of data
- Reflect on onto-epistemo-methodological assumptions, beliefs, and positions framing different interactions with data
- Talk to your peers about data-wants and what their data could want

Differentiation 1: Counting

If data are counted, they are likely to be minimalized, condensed, listed, or checked over. Counting Sam's data made me highlight particular signifiers that were used to "represent" the data. To minimalize Sam's text and "capture" different counts of Sam's data in thorough and systematic ways (as is expected from an accountant of sorts), I turned into a "calculator," producing lists of frequently mentioned words. I checked over the data and word frequencies, noting that the most common word in the text was "I." I was not surprised.

I	11
Data	8
Activity	3
Much	3
Eye	3
Around	2
Task	2
Objects	2
Trying	2
Different	2

Sam's story was written in first person (11 counts of "I"); he was the actor in this story, and his writing was personal. Counting also brought to my attention the main content of this narrative; Sam's text was about "data" (eight counts), more specifically about one type of data activity. The frequency of the word "data" indicated that Sam stayed focused on the task and engaged in reflections that were expected as a part of the course. Furthermore, other frequent words, such as "much," "around," and "different," might have been used as special qualifiers for the content words rather than any other types of signifiers or indicators of quality. Counting, checking, and listing prompted limited variations of data object. Counting data disguised elements of surprise, leaving the subject (me/researcher) and data mostly intact, the same as before, and counting did not seem to change the direction of knowledge. For example, I reviewed the condensed list of counted words and noted three counts of "eye," which seemed out of place in this particular context. I was trying to explain and rationalize what "eye" had to do with Sam's interactions with data beyond seeing the data. After counting I felt done and finished; in some ways I was not inspired to create alternative understandings, approach data differently, or extend data, Sam, or me. Counting did not create new openings or wonderings, at least at this time.

Differentiation 2: Coding

If data were to say they wanted "coding," what words would they use? Would they hail for "systematic analysis," scream "organize," whisper "categories or signifiers," or perhaps stutter "marks of representation of something"? Would coding change the direction of knowledge? Could coding prompt me, the researcher, to separate me and data from our familiar or secured stillness? Would I lose my position as a subject?

Before starting this interaction with data, I knew that codes generally commit to certainty, and they are sometimes used as a proxy for universal condensed meaning—a proxy that could possibly be read and interpreted similarly by different individuals. I wondered what kind of differentiation would be possible while coding. In the following interaction with data, I created "open" and "in vivo" codes to "signify the content" of the data and represent Sam's meanings and experiences in a systematic fashion, as might be expected from me as a coder.

Table 3.1   Codes and Data Examples

Codes	Data Examples
Wondering about the activity	It honestly took me a few minutes to figure out why in the world we were spending an undisclosed amount of class time in blindfolds
The importance of vision in analysis	I began to realize just how detrimental my eyes had been to me
Quick identification of data	Looking at coins had allowed me to undoubtedly identify them on quick glance
Unawareness of other characteristics of data	I remained very much unaware of many of the other characteristics and attributes
Feeling unprepared to analyze familiar objects	How could I be so unprepared to work with objects that I have been around and handled almost daily for years?
Finding a quiet place for analysis	I walked around Norman Hall trying to find a quiet place
Transfer of one activity to another dataset	My walk was just as much about trying to mentally transfer the money activity into a plan of attack for my all-too-familiar data
Worry about being too familiar with data	My all-too-familiar data
Plans to remove vision	My plan quickly became to take away my "eyes"

(Continued)

Table 3.1 (Continued)

Codes	Data Examples
Hope to take a fresh look into data	force myself to look at this data from a different vantage point
Hope for more confidence in analysis	Hoping that the newfound confidence and approach would prove transferable to this task
Reading data through assumptions	Reading through revealed the same information that I was used to seeing
Stopping and rereading data	I stopped, reflected on the "no eyes" task at hand, and then reread the data.
Focus on listening	This time, I focused on really listening to what the participants were saying.
No more interpreting	No more interpreting, looking for good fits, or assuming what was being said.
No more good fits	No more interpreting, looking for good fits, or assuming what was being said.
No more assumptions	No more interpreting, looking for good fits, or assuming what was being said.
Data seemed to speak surprisingly	Surprisingly, the data really seemed to speak to me—
Data sounding different	and it sounded much different than before

Sam's coded data produced categories of activities that he had engaged in. He questioned the class activity and wondered about the reasons for doing it. He felt unprepared to engage in "messy" analysis, and he worried how his interactions with data might be distorted by seeing familiar objects based on existing assumptions. To heighten his senses and be more open to unexpected dimensions of data, Sam searched for silent surroundings. Moreover, he worried about being unaware and too familiar with data and decided to try to move away from the comfort of the "scientific method." Sam was most concerned about his reliance on "seeing" and observing. To motivate himself to carry on the assigned activity, Sam created a framework for listening to data; he rationalized that this activity might be useful to gain more confidence. Sam promised himself no more interpreting, good fits, or assumptions. The final code, "data sounding different," concluded Sam's story with the "expected positive outcome" of this class exercise. Sam convinced himself that now the data sounded different and that the activity had been completed successfully.

When I finished this interaction with data (i.e., coding) I felt I had imposed an external order on data, organized data according to *my* frame of reference using *my* interpretive insights, still leaving data at least partially asleep or unused. At the same time, I (the subject) moved closer to Sam and data as a result of these interactions. I sensed a type of connectedness that was created through my readings and studying/constructing the "codes." The "codes" had some of Sam, me, and us in them.

Differentiation 3: Filling In and Extending

After experiencing the previous "systematic" and somewhat normative analytical interactions with data and configuring reductionist ways to respond to data, I was ready to let data object discover me. I wondered how data could invent, create, and re-create me as a researcher or how data might invent strategies of disguise and counterfeit. Maybe through additional materials, connections with other data, a sense of being filled by the Other, and supplied with different extensions, I could lose my position as a subject and data would grow and take over. Instead of worrying about "the problems" of truth, interference, subjectivity, or "bias" when filling in data, I wanted to open up me-in-data, provide additional connections, bring a situational context to data, and expand data through me. I was not sure that data wanted to be filled in or expanded, but I believed that this move would re-create both me and data. I worked though data by filling it with other texts, dreams, emotions, interpretations, and so on. Filling in and expanding data changed data, me, and my relationship with it, and opened up new connections and insights about Sam and me. In the following, I blend Sam's story with my notes and Sam's reflective extensions. My notes and Sam's extensions were added two months after the actual data activity took place. Still data is in quotation marks, Sam's extensions are marked in italicized font, and my notes are in brackets.

"It honestly took me a few minutes to figure out why in the world we were spending an undisclosed amount of class time in blindfolds interacting with objects as they played the role of data." [This activity took place at the end of class and involved an undisclosed amount of time. I told students that after they had completed the assignment, the class was over. Similar to this activity, I often use activities and assignments without a specified time frame to allow students to complete the tasks at their own pace. I also prefer not to model activities but encourage students to be puzzled and find their own ways. This lack of modeling is sometimes seen as problematic by the students, but I resist modeling since I believe it is likely to kill creativity.]

> *The cynic would say, "OK, so what is so wrong with that type of coding? Did you not generate rich hearty conclusions this way?" The response seems to be that maybe you did generate good conclusions this way, but are the conclusions TRULY ACCURATE based on the data? The answer is no. Because you forced them into your own system.*
>
> —Jason

"However, as the activity unfolded, I began to realize just how detrimental my eyes had been to me. Looking at coins had allowed me to undoubtedly identify them on quick glance; however, I remained very much unaware of many of the other characteristics and attributes. How could I be so unprepared to work with objects that I have been around and handled almost daily for years?" *It was a humbling experience to realize this and have it brought out in front of others, although everyone else seemed to be having the same difficulties.* [It is interesting that Sam introduces humility here as an afterthought. I would like students to feel more humble and tentative when interacting with data. However, can a qualitative researcher show uncertainty or fear when analyzing data? Do I fear rejection and "interpretive" misunderstandings, as if there were only one correct way to analyze data? Maybe.]

"This segued so well into the individual data analysis activity that followed. As I walked around Norman Hall trying to find a quiet place, it became clear that my walk was just as much about trying to mentally transfer the money activity into a plan of attack for my all-too-familiar data. Just like the money, my data is something that I have looked at, immersed myself in, and 'knew.' My plan quickly became to take away my 'eyes' (which here meant my methodical analysis that I had been trained and encouraged to use) and force myself to look at this data from a different vantage point." *I really struggled with even figuring out how I had always looked at my data.* **I settled on the "theme-searching" methodology that my department tends to use.** *So I wanted to try to put my "eyes" aside and look at what the data were actually saying.* [Even though Sam could experiment with data any way he liked, he relied on the authority. At first I thought I must have been one of the authorities he talked about. How depressing! Sam talked about the theme-searching tradition followed by the colleagues and professors in his department. Or maybe I was different. Maybe Sam did not use me as his "methodological authority or example," but he wanted to follow theme-searching methodology common in his own discipline. **Should I be worried or offended that he preferred to rely on his closest peers, knowledge, discourse, and traditions of his field? Why he was not willing to consider examples I offered?**]

"Hoping that the newfound confidence and approach would prove transferable to this task, I sat down at a corner picnic table and pulled out my interview data. Reading through revealed the same information that I was used to seeing, the words almost losing meaning from the number of views. I again struggled with actually putting my plan into action. I stopped, reflected on the 'no eyes' task at hand, and then reread the data. This time, I focused on really listening to what the participants were saying. No more interpreting, looking for good fits, or assuming what was being said." *Reflecting on what*

I had been taught to do, I realized that I was just trying to fit the data into nice categories and themes that work well for writing. Now, I wanted to actually see what was being said without thinking ahead to the writing process. [Instead of approaching writing as a method of inquiry that helped him to analyze and process data and his interactions with data, Sam saw writing as a separate and immediate step following the analysis. He also treated writing as a structured activity, a logical and coherent process of creating text, even though I have carried out various creative writing exercises in the class that question logical and overly structured writing. At the same time, I saw Sam struggling with artificial boundaries created around scientific writing.]

"Surprisingly, the data really seemed to speak to me—and it sounded much different than before." *One thing I saw in my data was messiness. There were still themes (albeit way more general), but it was not as clean as I had been wanting to see it in my previous work with the data.* [I found myself in the previous data object. I was transformed by Sam's struggles, conflicts, and fear of messiness. I began to question my pedagogy as it was reflected in Sam's data. I also became the uncertain "noise," background, and the Other in Sam's data. I was no longer in charge with the direction of knowledge. Knowledge began to flow in multiple directions; from Sam's still data to Sam's responsive data, Sam's text to my reactions, past to present, and from present to future. It was no longer my frame of reference that produced knowledge in Sam's data. Instead, data expanded, grew, and changed us—both Sam, me, and insights gained from this text.]

> *I think all graduate students grapple with methodological conformity, especially when it comes to making decisions about their dissertation projects.*
>
> —Cheryl

> *I am struck by how little power young scholars have or feel they have in the context of coursework or even in who they may become. I often wonder when I will have endured enough normative rites of passage found in the academy to return to my ideas and constantly worry if they will still exist.*
>
> —Darby

Differentiation 4: Dialoging With Themselves

The following example illustrates data changing through dialoging (see also Sullivan, 2012). As in the previous example, data in this dialogue evade the researcher's presentations of reality and escape normative notions of analysis and data themselves. Data's different assertions expressed in the dialogue can make researchers and readers different from what they have been in the past, thereby mobilizing analysis and moving interactions between subject and object somewhere else. Data become more alive and can thus be experienced in a different time and space. Data's dialoging with itself could be seen as a way of interacting at multiple levels, inquiring of oneself, and familiarizing or defamiliarizing oneself with nuances, complexities, and less dominant aspects and characteristics of data object.

February 29, 2012

Two different data iterations (1 and 2)
dialoging with themselves (data talking to data)

Data 1: *It honestly took me a few minutes to figure out why in the world we were spending an undisclosed amount of class time in blindfolds interacting with objects as they played the role of data.*

Data 2: There is something in this sentence that I cannot process. Call for honesty maybe? Expectations of course content, absurd blindfold activity? Perhaps objects playing the role of data rather than being the data? Data 1 produces a playful critique; I critique this data play. I critique myself. Data 1 contradicts, complements, diversifies, shares me, Data 2.

Data 1: *However, as the activity unfolded, I began to realize just how detrimental my eyes had been to me. Looking at coins had allowed me to undoubtedly identify them on quick glance; however, I remained very much unaware of many of the other characteristics and attributes. How could I be so unprepared to work with objects that I have been around and handled almost daily for years?*

Data 2: Why do I feel insecure and unprepared to interpret data with others? Where does this expectation of mastery and "easy" learning come from? Why is it not fine to stay unaware? Does Mirka exemplify desire for mastery in her own work? Does she expect mastery after all? Does she colonize?

Data 1: *This segued so well into the individual data analysis activity that followed. As I walked around Norman Hall trying to find a quiet place, it became clear that my walk was just as much about trying to mentally transfer the money activity into a plan of attack for my all-too-familiar data.*

Data 2: I heard that Mirka guided students to transfer processes from one activity to another and then modify the transfers. Maybe the transfer did not work. It was too rigid and structured a way to approach data. Even though transfer might have worked in the past, why was she asking students to do the same? I need my privacy and a quiet place to think this through.

Data 1: *Just like the money, my data is something that I have looked at, immersed myself in, and "knew." My plan quickly became to take away my "eyes" (which here meant my methodical analysis that I had been trained and encouraged to use) and force myself to look at this data from a different vantage point.*

Data 2: Looking at data still implies "seeing." I am not sure what I am thinking here. How could I build on or expand my comfortable use of the scientific method while interacting with other data? What would transformation from within look like? Why do I need to force myself to pay attention to another point of view?

Data 1: *Hoping that the newfound confidence and approach would prove transferable to this task, I sat down at a corner picnic table and pulled out my interview data. Reading through revealed the same information that I was used to seeing, the words almost losing meaning from the number of views. I stopped, reflected on the "no eyes" task at hand, and then reread the data. This time, I focused on really listening to what the participants were saying. No more interpreting, looking for good fits, or assuming what was being said.*

Data 2: Transformation seems too easy and too fast, without struggles and ongoing questioning. I sound too certain. I make promises, but to whom?

Data 1: *Surprisingly, the data really seemed to speak to me—and it sounded much different than before.*

Data 2: I am not sure that I can speak on my behalf. What did I say? What did I not say? Who spoke? Data, researcher, participants, context, ghosts, or all above? Why does this dialogue matter?

Differentiation 5: Multiplying

Why are you choosing these methods? Was there anything with the data that prompted you to choose these approaches?

—Jason

Can data multiply, or has it already multiplied unexpectedly in the previous examples? Could my interactions with data prompt, stimulate, and generate multiplication and doubleness within various contexts? What would contextually differentiated doubleness look like? When texts, images, behaviors, or notes are seen as still objects, they form static signifiers. However, once researchers begin interacting with data and analysis, data may begin to multiply also across contexts, and have diverse and contextually situated "vital signs" (see also Mitchell, 2005). Massumi (2002) proposed that

> every multiplicity is divisible by its reactions. The object "constancy" at the basis of cognition is not so much a persistence in existence of unitary things as it is a ratio between perpetual variations: the ratio between habit (pattern of reaction) and the sea of chaos in which it swims (doggedly holding onto itself, and its own lifeboat. (p. 150)

Additionally, vital signs (e.g., motivation, autonomy, and aura) in objects and data can create emotional reactions and conceptual/theoretical movement also in researchers, participants, and other data. By pulling together different forms and types of data in one image, data's multiplicity and doubleness could be singularly expressed (see Figure 3.2).

Different images of data multiplied bring diverse and potentially conflicting prompts and stimuli to readers at one time. Multiplication can include overlaps, emphasis, excess, and visible gaps, among things. For example, in Figure 3.2, the scientific process portrays the context and mental image that Sam uses as a reference when analyzing data. The linearity of the scientific model embedded in the image helped me see the conflict Sam experienced between the traditions of science education and the expectations I expressed in the class regarding this analysis activity. The way I, as a researcher, reacted to the figure of scientific process shaped how I read Julia's journal entry (see the following figure), the story of another student from the class, and interpreted the guidelines given to the team leaders (those students who led the activities in their assigned groups). Sam's subtle and gentle resistance, which prompted him to believe in the "goodness" and value of messy interactions with data, became multiplied as I read Julia's reactions. Subtle and gentle resistance grew into open dissatisfaction and questioning. Resistance appeared differently because my perspective on Julia's description was already shaped by past interactions with Sam's data. I felt connected with Sam's data and alienated from Julia's, even though it was clear to me that the data was not different, but just multiplied and presenting its different variation. When Julia described "messy" analysis, she felt uncomfortable and alienated; she did not pretend to agree with intentions associated with messy analysis as described by the instructor and resisted the reflections she was asked to do. In Julia's story, the resistance and absurdity of this activity became more tangible and visible, not only due to how she expressed her thoughts but also because her data created a pattern of repetition. The contrast presented in these two stories illustrated the variations of the experience and built on the repetition of frustration and not-knowing. Data patterned themselves in the chaos of other data. Reflection that was portrayed as at least partially beneficial to messy analysis in Sam's story was questioned as an insufficient ingredient of analysis in Julia's story. However, another repetition of reflection that was encountered in team leader notes connected the concept of reflections to meaningful analysis and productive interactions with data. The tentativeness of the reflection (students *can* consider) put forward in team leader notes and the hesitant yet suggestive tone of the activity made me reconsider Sam's and Julia's data in the light of resistance as a stance, not necessarily any longer as a part of analysis. In my thinking, I moved away from "data work" or data interactions toward "ethic work" and the ethical work of critical pedagogy. Data prompted me to reflect more deeply on my teaching and classroom activities as potentially dominating and controlling forces.

Furthermore, images of Sam doing the activity and the surroundings of Norman Hall generated other multiplications and connections. Seeing Sam collaborating with another student who was also blindfolded, Sam lying on the classroom floor in a relaxed position, and the sunny, tropical atmosphere of Norman Hall replaced me and my interpretive frames, inserting other objects into the image. Data from these images were linked to each other, but they also formed their own entities. Two blindfolded individuals working together, the architecture of Norman Hall, shadows produced by large palm trees, and empty seats behind Sam represented existing stories, stories not known, or stories not willing to be told. In this example, data desire to be multiplied and reconnected through intertextuality and the interplay between text and images.

In your own research, you could:

- Think about ways in which extensions beyond the text could assist you in your data interactions and "analysis";
- Consider different ways in which data might multiply and change when you interact with it;
- Reflect on how simultaneous and overlapping segments of data inform your notions of knowledge, truth, findings, representation, validity, and so on.

Figure 3.2 Sam's Data Multiplied

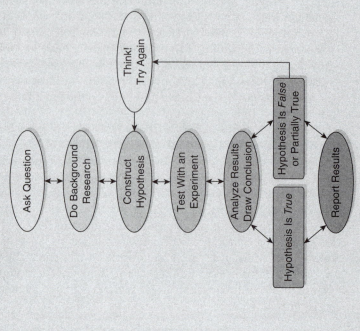

Julia: This whole process was strange to me, but not entirely bad.
I tried to keep in mind that there was no "right" or "wrong,"
but kept wondering if it was going to yield anything valuable,
or if this even counted as data analysis. Interaction as a form of analysis is,
in some ways, a given: We are always interacting with the data when we analyze it.
But in some respects, this was a whole new concept: Interaction has never been
so "spontaneous" or "ungoverned" as it was like this. And although I believe it is
always helpful to reflect, to me reflection is a necessary but insufficient ingredient for a successful analysis.
It would have been helpful to have other people involved in this process
to help and to challenge my reflections, because I think people can go in some strange ideas if left to themselves.

Sam: It honestly took me a few minutes to figure out why in the world
we were spending an
undisclosed amount of class time in blindfolds interacting with
objects as they played the role of data.
However, as the activity unfolded, I began to realize just how
detrimental my eyes had been to me.
Looking at coins had allowed me to undoubtedly identify them on
quick glance;
however, I remained very much unaware of many of the other
characteristics and attributes.
How could I be so unprepared to work with objects that I have been
around and handled almost daily for years?
This segued so well into the individual data analysis activity that
followed.
As I walked around Norman Hall trying to find a quiet place, it
became clear that
my walk was just as much about trying to mentally transfer the money
activity into a plan of attack for my all too familiar data.
Just like the money, my data is something that I have looked at,
immersed myself in, and "knew."
My plan quickly became to take away my "eyes" (which here meant
my methodological analysis [scientific method]

that I had been trained and encouraged to use) and force myself to look at this data from a different vantage point.

Hoping that the newfound confidence and approach would prove transferrable to this task,

I sat down at a corner picnic table and pulled out my interview data.

Reading through revealed the same information that I was used to seeing, the words almost losing meaning from the number of views.

I stopped, reflected on the "no eyes" task at hand, and then reread the data.

This time, I focused on really listening to what the participants were saying.

No more interpreting, looking for good fits, or assuming what was being said.

Surprisingly, the data really seemed to speak to me—and it sounded much different than before.

Team leader notes

Task 1: Students will interact with different objects on the floor (coins and potentially other small objects). Goal: Establish different kinds of relationships with data and experience data differently (video record)

    a. Blindfolded

    b. Talking out loud when interacting with objects

Task 2: Team leaders will provide extra stimuli by "doing unexpected things with the objects"

Task 3: Students will create something from the objects

Task 4: Students will organize the objects

Task 5: The blindfolds will be removed. Students will take some objects elsewhere to do something with the object (record if you can). When they return team leaders will ask students to report back (where did they go, what did they do).

Task 6: Students will reflect on their experiences. They can consider:

    What did you experience?

    What is your relationship with money?

    Describe a dream that included money (come up with one if necessary)

    What knowing do you bring to your interactions with these objects once you are able to visualize them?

©iStockphoto.com/DeirdreRusk

The Paradox of Wanting/Interacting

"The rose is beautiful" means only that the rose has a good appearance (Schein), it has a pleasingly luminous quality. There is no intention to say anything about its essence. It pleases, it arouses pleasure, as appearance, i.e., the Will is satisfied by the way it appears, pleasure in existence is promoted thereby. . . . The more it does so, the more beautiful it is; if its character corresponds to the purpose intended, the role is "good." (Nietzsche, 1999, p. 135)

Does this structure seek to control participants to change the direction of their data interactions and research? Had you only provided materials for exploration without regimented tasks, what might have happened? With ownership over the exploration, would Julia have been less resistant?

—Darby

There is no one way to analyze or interact with data, but "complexity always exceeds its reach," and data can, if so enabled, "proliferate through sustained entanglement and interference" (MacLure, 2010, p. 281). Maybe data are a complicated object, matter, and interaction, and the analysis has less to do with step-by-step approaches or direct application of documented procedures. Instead, instructors, researchers, students, participants, and data may want to distance themselves from normative discourses and search for spaces that enable unexpected and continuously changing interactions. Massumi (as cited in Rice, 2010) encouraged us to think about space that has the "ability to irrupt unexpectedly, to break out of or to break into the existing spatial grid, anywhere, at any moment" (p. 34). Even though I am inspired by alternative spaces, creativity, and nonnormativity in data and analysis, I am not advocating the dismissal of all existing structures and fixed analysis tools, techniques, approaches, or other conceptual devices altogether. Instead, I call for extensions beyond these approaches and technologies and look for different examples that might bend methodological normativity, thus enabling knowledge to flow in multiple directions. This section exemplifies my shifting knowledges (of data) and methodologies (such as analysis) as a moving theoretical and conceptual target. I want to problematize data from/within/by the data.

Different repertoires of tactics may be needed to keep data and analysis surprising and evolving. One might ask how to engage in (analytical) interactions with a pleasing quality, how to wake up data that are asleep, and how to invite data into a dialogue. How do we know when data are leading us? Baudrillard and Witwer (2000) reminded us:

The closer we come, through experimentation, to the object, the more it steals away from us and finally becomes undecidable. And do not ask where it has gone. Simply, the object is *what escapes the subject*—more we cannot say, since our position is still that of the subject and of rational discourse. (pp. 79–80)

By creating an opening for escape, room for uncertainty, and respect for humbleness, data could become more than an object of possession or a sleeping signifier for reality.

Can I, may I?   Dare I?

Leave space

for unplanned interactions with data

surprising interactions

interactions guided by intuition, creativity, emotions

and data

Data lead me!

Data take me to wanted and unwanted directions!

Silence me!

Please throw away the key.

What do you want, data?

Change, she replies.

READING LIST OF LIFE

Bender, J. (2012). *Dada data*. Lulu Author.

Boynton, S. (2012). *Fifteen animals*. Boynton Moo Media.

Bukowski, C. (2002). *What matters most is how well you walk through the fire*. HarperCollins.

Hemingway, E. (2006). *The sun also rises*. Scribner.

Kerouac, J. (1999). *On the road*. Penguin Books.

BPTU/Shutterstock

Irruption 1: Introducing Undirectionality and Uncertainty Through Images

Source: Benedict, J. (2011). Convenient Parking. Cedar Falls: University of Northern Iowa (Reprinted with the permission from the artist).

What do you see? What is happening?

Source: Benedict, J. (2011). Convenient Parking. Cedar Falls: University of Northern Iowa (Reprinted with the permission from the artist).

Source: Benedict, J. (2011). Convenient Parking. Cedar Falls: University of Northern Iowa (Reprinted with the permission from the artist).

What do you see now? What is happening?

These images remind me of data. Each is a representation of what "really" occurs. I note how the windows of the cars are also spray-painted gold, making it difficult to see out the windows (if in the car) and in the windows (if outside the car). We can do whatever we would like to do with data. We can rearrange it to tell different stories.

—Chandra

Source: Benedict, J. (2011). Convenient Parking. Cedar Falls: University of Northern Iowa (Reprinted with the permission from the artist).

Source: Benedict, J. (2011). Convenient Parking. Cedar Falls: University of Northern Iowa (Reprinted with the permission from the artist).

Which signs and objects prompt your uncertainty in this space?

What if there is not a right way, order, or correct direction in which to view these images?

What do you see now? What is happening?

What happens to directionality and order when a viewer enters this visual space?

What changes when a viewer encounters a parking lot and parking spaces on the roof?

How do your interactions within this space change throughout the series of these images?

How would a different ordering of these images change your interactions?

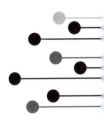

4 Fluid Methodological Spaces
Methodologies Matter

Methodologies are choices, often onto-epistemological and theoretical, and cannot be divorced from the values, beliefs, backgrounds, bodies, and affects of the researcher or the research context. Methodologies are political, and they have power to disempower, empower, and validate and invalidate experiences, data, lives, and material. Methodological choices not only generate and highlight data, but they also construct and contextualize studies, programs, scholars, and research aims. Methodologies can be informed choices, taken for granted, or just used uncritically without any alternatives. Alternatively, methodologies can be situational, complex structures or constellations that are in flux.

GLOSSARY

Methodology. Strategy or plan of action that provides a rationale for the choice of methods. Research design (Crotty, 1998, p. 7).

Methodology. Generalizable, rational form of activities that are embedded in historical practice (Novikov & Novikov, 2013, p. 8).

Methodology-against-interpretivism. A disruption of traditional qualitative research that seeks to think *with* data rather than force data analysis to speak only through mechanistic, discretely defined codes (Jackson & Mazzei, 2012, p. viii).

Methodology. Utilized to break down the false boundary between theory and practice (Coleman & Ringrose, 2013, p. 2).

Methodology. The assumption that researchers conceptualize research in a certain way (Creswell, 2007, p. 248).

In this section I work against given, stable, rigid, and predetermined methodological structures. Instead, I discuss fluid methodological spaces where multiple things and methods occur simultaneously and where frameworks and methodological foci are diverse and continuously changing. I provide examples of research designs and methodological flows with varied research objects, practices, enactments, and ways of representing realities. In these spaces that could also be called incorporeal (i.e., reality that is abstract) and fluid spaces, similar and different methodologies, tools, and approaches come together at different times. "Methods" and "tools" are not methods and tools in their stable meaning or rigid structures, but "methods and tools" begin and end in an unforeseen and unpredictable "order," forming incomplete methodologies without absolute identities or nonidentities. Methods and tools are conceptualized as temporary structures that are being regenerated again and again. Following this line of thought, methodological flows, tools, approaches, and techniques do not collapse, fail, or disappoint. Instead, they melt, transform, circumvent, infiltrate, appear, and disappear while opening up new directions for qualitative research. This section is about methodologies that always begin again by having "already begun."

Methods imply order,   they reflect traditions

My methods should be your methods   or

even better   our methods collectively; shared and identical methods

replicable methods

methods with more legitimacy, power, V-A-L-I-D-I-T-Y

They look good

They are recognized   preferably by funders

I have been trained in methods

I have acquired knowledge about methods

I do know methods   Wait a minute   I know what?

Methods, they demand

Methods, they teach

Methods they make me   (un)do

How could a method be wherever it is while not being everywhere?

More specifically, my argument here is more critical and ontological, with a focus on the ontologies of practice (see Mol, 2002). From this perspective, scholars acknowledge epistemological and methodological multiplicities and accept the uncertainly, fragmentation, and temporality associated with this multiplicity. They are concerned about knowledge, not as a singular but as a multiple event. I wonder how researchers can ontologically combine multiple and overlapping methodological events, forces, and practices (not multiple and distinct methods as often described, for example, in mixed-methods literature) that extend the objects of research, various roles, and social expectations. By *methodological extensions*, I refer to forces, events, and practices that might build from theoretical, cultural, and methodological traditions but at the same time move beyond documented tools of data collection and analysis, thus expanding the notions of normative research.

Robert Ulmer

Section key points:

- Methodological order, linearity, and containment can promote hierarchies and increase methodological surveillance and external quality control.

- **Fluid and multifaceted methodologies can offer new dimensions of research to better articulate, accommodate, and reflect anticipated conditions and preferred spatial dimensions for qualitative research.**

- In fluid and incorporeal methodological space, methodological moves might have temporary limits and porous boundaries before morphing into something else, whereas other research elements and moves may be completely unknowable and indescribable.

> *"Fifteen hundred years ago everybody knew the Earth was the center of the universe. Five hundred years ago, everybody knew the Earth was flat, and fifteen minutes ago, you knew that humans were alone on this planet. Imagine what you'll know tomorrow." Kay (Tommy Lee Jones),* Men in Black *[Movie].*
> —Jason

What Do Linear Methodologies Do?

The linearity and order in qualitative research processes as described in many introductory books (see, e.g., Bogdan & Biklen, 2006; Silverman & Marvasti, 2008) might help researchers conceptualize qualitative research practices without becoming overwhelmed with the plenitude of methodological and theoretical options. The research process begins with a literature review and research questions, then moves to the formulation of theoretical perspectives and overall design (see Figure 4.1). Introductory books and methods courses teach us that research design should be transparent and follow published guidelines and procedures and that methodological citations are needed. Furthermore, different tools of inquiry, including data collection and analysis methods, can be separable units and distinctive methodological containers. Novice researchers are often taught that the representation of findings and writing should follow thematic flow and descriptive structures so that readers can locate and verify validity and rigor. As a result, some qualitative researchers may be anxious to follow the "right" procedures.

Figure 4.1   Linearity and Order in Qualitative Research Process

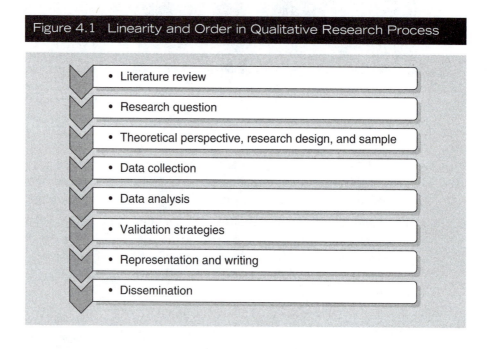

- Literature review
- Research question
- Theoretical perspective, research design, and sample
- Data collection
- Data analysis
- Validation strategies
- Representation and writing
- Dissemination

Cleanness, linearity, predictability, careful planning, and onto-episte-methodological consistency are sometimes considered hallmarks of quality qualitative research. Such order, linearity, and containment are likely to limit research, promote hierarchies, and increase methodological surveillance and external quality control, especially during peer reviews. **Sometimes order and linearity in designs fail, and scholars may encounter various unpredictable events, urgent decisions, and unexpected interactions.** These unanticipated hurdles can create possibilities for methodological adaptation and alternative representations of research processes beyond linearity and certainty.

The purpose of this section is to reconsider the linear logic and invariability in qualitative research designs. The circular, emergent, and messy nature of qualitative inquiry and research design has been acknowledged by many scholars (e.g., Crabtree & Miller, 1992; Lather, 2007a; Luttrell, 2010; Marshall & Rossman, 2006; Mason, 2002; Maxwell, 1996). For example, Luttrell (2010) characterized qualitative research design as a plan for researchers to make decisions that leaves room for individual judgment. Furthermore, she referred to various standards for study designs, including clear research questions, demonstration of study significance, definition of key concepts, data that match research questions, systematic and triangulated data collection, and reflexivity. Luttrell also noted that qualitative research design is interactive in that all design parts are interdependent, making a coherent whole and creating interaction between the researcher and the study participants/study context. Process is also iterative—going back and forth between different design elements.

In your own research, you could:

- Document what is gained and lost by methodological linearity and predictability, possibly embedded in your research activities

- Map your messy and multilayered interactions with different social and material study contexts and data

- Create your own labels for your processes, tools, and approaches

Even though some current notions of circularity in qualitative research designs take into account unexpected changes (e.g., Luttrell, 2010; Maxwell, 1996), this circularity may still build on historical origins, logic, standard labels, recognizable categories, and coherent identities. Massumi (2002) noted that as long as any event is ongoing, its outcomes stay uncertain, and its labels and identities are subject to change. In the context of qualitative research design, Massumi's ideas could indicate uncertainty and methodological open-endedness that ultimately also acknowledges risks and implies the need for creativity. Massumi also argued that science has its own "default design" that meets newness and innovations with predetermined procedures and available techniques. **In other words, Massumi cautioned scholars not to label and categorize newness and innovation by existing labels and structures.** At the same time, Massumi worried that science might result in indeterminability (not acting or creating

It's more than unpredictable events. Doctoral students who want to live on the periphery of their disciplines and recognize and seek to build bridges across gaps between disciplines will need a strong tradition in the basic tenets of methodologies in order to bend/blur them.
—Chandra

I think the clean representation makes young scholars feel as though they may be failing in their research endeavors because it is almost a secret that the research process NEVER works like this.
—Darby

What about newness to the discipline? Do labels have to be previously unused in order to be considered new to an audience that has never seen them before?
—Chandra

but maybe paralyzing), especially within the social worlds of predetermined order and discourses of methodological certainty. Often, methodological linearity and order are assumed and expected, and cyclical revisions and methodological reconstructions are merely seen as acceptable exceptions to the linearity (not as the option on its own or as an option outside the normative other). For example, within circular research design processes, linearity is always still present in the form of return. A return (e.g., to research questions, to data, to a theoretical perspective) serves as one expected point, a point of arrival and departure, thus contributing to linearity itself. From this circular perspective, fluidity is seen as a temporal change and exception rather than an anticipated condition or preferred spatial dimension.

What Might Happen in Fluid Methodological Spaces?

Instead of seeing continuing changes or methodological fluidity as a more or less accepted exception to linear logic, viewing methodology as always already fluid and multifaceted can offer new dimensions to research. Fluid methodologies might also stimulate deeper or more engaged ways to represent, accommodate, and reflect anticipated conditions and preferred spatial dimensions often present in qualitative research encounters. In this section, I discuss the methodological system or space where research designs are no longer based on stable structures—rather, research designs could be seen as forces and events that highlight or create different types of methodological extensions. These forces and events have temporal and spatial dimensions.

In your own research, you could:

- Propose, live, and document research designs as events and extensions
- Connect design events to a specific time and space
- Map overlapping research events and interactive spaces
- Solicit peer feedback on your maps

Surprise

Methodological flows and multiplicity in designs can promote conceptual and analytical surprise and contextual responsiveness that might be lacking from mechanical or uncritical methods and approaches (see Koro-Ljungberg &

Mazzei, 2012). Not only does analytical surprise or contextual responsiveness keep researchers more deeply engaged in their research but can also enable scholars to methodologically adjust to changing circumstances in which they practice scholarship and interact with participants, data, and the Other. However, analytical surprise or contextual responsiveness might become impossible and unimaginable in normative and tightly controlled methodological and political contexts. Thus, viewing and approaching methodologies as events or aporetic entities without methodologies could provide a framework from which critical social science and qualitative researchers could conduct research that leaves room for surprise, responsiveness, and creativity.

Methodologies without methodologies

rest in fluid spaces   occupy contested lands

challenge me, us, data, perspectives, theories, frames, positionings, knowledges, truths

to co-exist

to be present   in a single moment, in orderly chaos

Methodologies without methodologies

comfort my uncertainty

feed from my hunger for creativity and experimentation

provoke action   and change   turn me into a methodological rebel

against my better judgment   for my great joyment

Methodologies without methodologies

leave room for unplanned interactions   and analytical escapes

create a blind vision of absences and non-presence

Show me the impossible!   Impossible!

Work Against Methodological Norms and Grand Narratives

In fluid methodological spaces, similar and/or different methodologies, tools, and techniques come together without absolute identities or nonidentities. Fluid methodologies exist outside stable boundaries and cut-off points. In fluid spaces, "normality is a gradient rather than a cut-off point" (Mol & Law, 1994, p. 659). As a consequence, methodological flows and fluid methodological spaces do not collapse, fail (failure as inadequacy, lack, or not meeting the objectives), or disappoint. Methodologies and methods do not fail. The absence of failure also calls for different notions of validity and trustworthiness. Maybe "rigor" could be viewed as continually changing, situated, divergent (see, e.g., Lather, 1993, 2001, 2007b), and maybe even inaccurate and irrelevant.

In fluid methodological spaces, methods and research approaches melt, transform, circumvent, infiltrate, appear, and disappear. There is no "need for police action to safeguard the stability of [research] elements and their linkages—for there is no network structure to be protected" (Mol & Law, 1994, p. 662). In addition, fluid and incorporeal methodological spaces and extensions call for attention to change, divergence, and difference. *Incorporeal* refers to reality that is abstract—methodology that is "inseparable, coincident, but disjunct" (Massumi, 2002, p. 5). From this perspective, methodology will always stay indeterminate and ever changing. Following Massumi, one can access the incorporeal dimension of the methodology, not the methodology itself. Researchers can talk about different dimensions that might constitute a methodology, but knowing stays always uncertain. Incorporeal methodology travels alongside the methodology but does not become it. "With the body, the 'walls' are the sensory surfaces. The intensity is experience. The emptiness or in-betweenness filled by experience is the incorporeal dimension of the body" (Massumi, 2002, p. 14).

Complexity

Fluid methodologies are complex, but they do not necessarily complicate or confuse, especially when fluid methodologies are situated outside reductionist or essentialist frames. Complexity in this context refers to meeting and facing the limits of one's knowledge. I believe that complexity is not necessarily concerned with technically advanced processes but rather processes that exceed individuals' capacity to know them (see also Law, 2004). In fluid and incorporeal methodological space, methodological moves might have temporary limits and porous boundaries before morphing into something else. Sometimes research events and methodological moves may be completely unknowable, unrecognizable, and indescribable. I wonder how fluid methodological space would function without order or clear direction. How could a methodology be wherever it is **while not being everywhere**? How could a methodology leave room for whatever it left out? How might qualitative research methodologies respect and build from complexities? (See also Mol & Law, 2002.)

Conceptualizing Fluid and Incorporeal Methodological Spaces

In this section, I borrow from various philosophers and draw theoretical connections to Massumi's (1998, 2002) ideas on virtuality, movement, fluidity, and incorporeality; Deleuze's (1991) writings on virtuality; Baudrillard's (1983) concepts of reproduction; and Mol and Law's (2002) discussion on complexity.

Like ice in a glass. It fills the glass yet leaves room for other liquid to come inside, and the ice enhances the other liquid by making it a refreshing drink. But if no other liquid is added, the ice itself turns into the liquid and can serve as a refreshing drink in and of itself.

—Jason

Connecting With Massumi and Deleuze

For Massumi (2002), the virtual is real but abstract. The same problem, the same critical condition, is replayed in multiplying variations. Massumi (2002) discussed dimensions of the virtual as "multiple levels that have different logics and temporal organizations, but are locked in resonance with each other and recapitulate the same event in divergent ways, recall the fractal ontology and nonlinear causality underlying theories of complexity" (p. 33). Deleuze (1991) proposed that the virtual does not have to be realized but is actualized. Following Massumi and Deleuze, the fluidity is inaccessible but can be "figured out," worked through, and images of it may be constructed.

> How could fluid methodological space function without linear order or clear direction?

My call for methodological fluidity, representation of variations, and increased attention to methodological flows is not a call for unqualified relativism—relativism that absorbs and accepts anything unconditionally. Instead, an order might exist, but it is not linear, logical, or rational. According to Massumi (2002), variation is punctual; it is realized at structurally spaced intervals, often through predictable moves and positions. From the perspective of fluid methodologies, spontaneous connections are expected, and "accident zones" can create openings for different ways of engaging, knowing, moving, fracturing, and changing. Furthermore, the methodological, analytical, and interpretive potential of unique, multidimensional research situations may be better actualized if qualitative researchers focus on flows, cracks, and infoldings and outfoldings rather than linearity, order, and simplicity.

> How might qualitative research methodologies respect complexities?

> How can researchers ontologically combine multiple and overlapping methodological extensions (not multiple and distinct methods as often described, for example, in mixed-methods literature), objects of research, various roles, and social expectations?

It could be argued that one of the main purposes of fluid and incorporeal methodological space is not to represent but to resonate and add to reality. Massumi (2002) suggested moving toward affirmative methods that embrace their own inventiveness and add to (rather than confirm) reality. Methodology could be a spatial register of research intensities—intensities

How could a method leave room for whatever it left out?

of various research acts. These research acts and events form an immanent relation that continually changes. Methodologies and research events belong to this continually changing interaction as the dynamic corporeal or abstraction that is always unmediated. "When the event-dimension migrates to a new space, its elements modulate. There is no general model for the catalysis of an event. Every time an event migrates, it is re-conditioned" (Massumi, 2002, p. 81). Massumi (2002) also referred to the situations in which a system (in this case a methodological system) is momentarily inactive and in ferment. During this fermentation, methodological research events, acts, and objects come together and multiple methodological paths become possible.

True. It's important to remember that the net production of energy from fermentation is much less than energy produced from an aerobic process. Interestingly, multiple species can do both processes. Thus, I would argue that neither of these forms of methodologies can or should exist exclusively from one another. They each serve a purpose, depending on the environment/ context of the objects, subjects, etc.
—Chandra

Thinking about methodologies without methodologies through the process of fermentation serves as an interesting example of energy transfer in the absence of one main material (oxygen). In the enzyme-catalyzed fermentation process, sugars break down without oxygen, decomposition takes place in the absence of air, or microorganisms grow in bulk. In methodological fermentation, energy is being created in the absence of normative methodology, textbook tools, techniques, or simplified linguistic categories.

In your own research, you could:

- Map out different variations of the "same" problem, phenomenon, condition

- Create images of fluid methodological spaces in which you visit, inhabit, or experience

- Imagine how your research "objects," texts, observations, and you, among other things, blend into each other and interfere with each other in unanticipated ways; theorize and reflect on what you see!

- Allow your methodology to ferment and observe the "consequences," decomposition of knowledge, newly created substance, and future events following the fermentation

- Teach and educate others about the possibilities of fluid designs

- Work with local structures (IRB, committee members, funders, etc.) to allow more flexibility, revisions, and open-ended tasks during the research process

- Think about revisiting and revising ideas and projects from different perspectives
- Build different optional paths into your designs

Connecting With Baudrillard

Methodological events create interactions and movement between miniaturized method and theory particles. Baudrillard (1983) proposed that

> the real [of research and research design] is produced from miniaturized units, from matrices, memory banks and command models—and with these it can be reproduced an indefinite number of times. It no longer has to be rational, since it is no longer measured against some ideal or negative instance. It is nothing more than operational. (p. 3)

Similarly, methodologies can be reproduced in different variations an indefinite number of times. These variations combine elements from existing and maybe more widely accepted methodologies, but each new constellation is never the same as before. Baudrillard (1983) talked about this infusion of real and illusion that happens in simulacra and copies without the original: "Concrete trees with real leaves printed into them, a hog made out of reinforced concrete, but with a real hog's skull inside, concrete sheep covered with real wool" (p. 90). Following Baudrillard (1983), copies without originals could be seen as series of reproduced objects, and this reproduction absorbs the production processes and changes the production itself, as well as the producer and product. The methodological space referred to here is no longer linear or one-dimensional but cellular, including indefinite generation of the same signals or genetic code.

Connecting With Mol and Law

In fluid methodological space, social objects exist, draw upon, and recursively form the space. Methodological flows transform without sense or points of discontinuity.

> Sometimes fluid spaces perform sharp boundaries. But sometimes they do not—though one object gives way to another. So there are mixtures and gradients. And inside these mixtures everything informs everything else—the world doesn't collapse if some things suddenly fail to appear. (Mol & Law, 1994, p. 659)

Additionally, in the context of research, methodological flows can include multiplication of images created and re-created throughout the research process. Research processes can be actualized through movement from one sample to another, through infoldings and outfoldings, redoubling and reductions, the methodological past projecting ahead to the future. Fluid methodology is the reprocess—a methodology that is actualized by being differentiated and differentiating itself. Methodological originality as a concept or position is no longer helpful or appropriated, since originality is being replaced by virtual, endless reproduction, multiple tiny and fragmented methodologies. Fluid methodology dissolves binaries and hierarchies. Mol and Law (2002) proposed that "when investigators start to discover a variety of orders—modes of ordering, logics, frames, styles, repertoires, discourses—then the dichotomy between simple and complex starts to dissolve" (p. 7). Fluid methodology pays attention to the systemic relations and energies being transformed and transported from one event to another or one object to another.

Annemarie Mol's Fluid Methodology

Next, I discuss in more detail one example of methodological flow, namely, Mol's (2002) ethnographic work of day-to-day diagnosis and treatment of atherosclerosis. I do not use Mol's example as a generalizable model to be used with every study situated in fluid methodological spaces or frameworks, and I don't see her work as representative of all other cases. Additionally, there is nothing unique in her work per se (see Massumi, 2002), but it is exemplary in its detail and singularity. In this singular example (belonging to oneself and extendable to others at the same time), Mol illustrates how one object can actually have multiple variations. Massumi (2002) talked about an organization that has different logics and degrees of temporality that are resonating but also diversifying at the same time—following fractal ontology and nonlinear causality. This nonlinear causality is present in Mol's work. For example, Mol was interested in scrutinizing the ontological politics of medicine and how different medical "problems" and objects are framed and individual lives are shaped. Mol's work utilized different theories, including those of philosophy, anthropology, and technology—she referred to her approach as a study in empirical philosophy.

To provide more methodological details and demonstrate the fluid and incorporeal project, I crafted Figure 4.2 to represent Mol's methodological flow. This figure shows one example of multiplicity of a research object (in Mol's example, "body with atherosclerosis") and the various ways Mol studied, observed, and constructed the enactment of atherosclerosis. Mol moved from one moment, place, object, and treatment to the next as a different atherosclerosis was being discussed, treated, measured, and constructed. Mol did not want to tell a story of an object, body, or disease that was removed from the practices and contexts that sustained and created these particular objects and bodies. For her, reality was an act that can be done, intertwined, or undone.

In Mol's ethnography, various methodologies and techniques were used to study medical practices in one hospital, observe multiplicity of the research object, and document ontology in practice. To gather materials and document her interactions with the environment in a university hospital in the Netherlands, Mol visited clinics, operation rooms, debriefings, and staff lounges over four years. The coherence of atherosclerosis was made visible through various tactics, including transporting forms and files, scanning images, providing diagnosis, having conversations in different spaces, and so on. Mol explained that different enactments of the disease can be added up and patients can be distributed between practices. Furthermore, there was no one single passive research object to be discovered. "Instead, objects come into being—and disappear—with the practices in which they are manipulated. And since the object of manipulation tends to differ from one practice to another, reality multiplies" (Mol, 2002, p. 5). Mol argued that the body, patient, doctor, and technology were more than one and were always somehow related. Reality of "body" or "disease" was an act, something

Figure 4.2 Mol's Methodological Flow

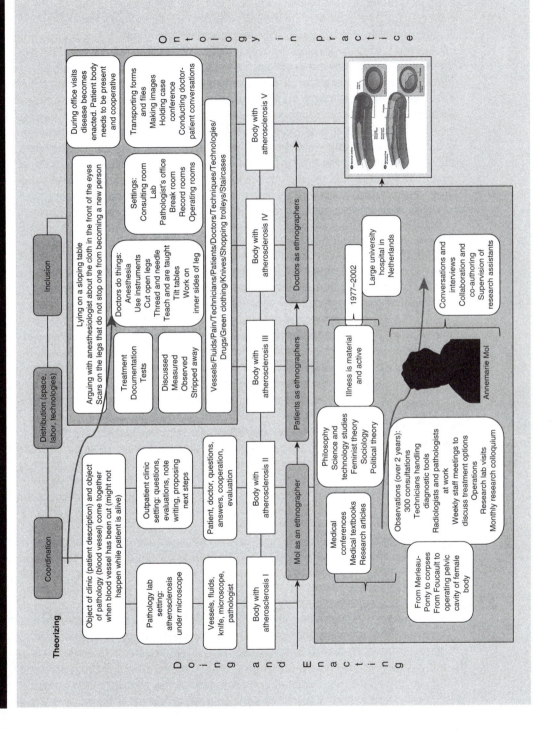

that may be done or left undone. Instead of focusing on getting the research or design "right," Mol illustrated methodological and conceptual movements in singular space and interconnectedness between objects and research activities, enactments, settings, actors, life at the hospital, and produced knowledge. For Mol, objects were interdependent and shaped by different modes of ordering. When different ways to enact an object meet other ways of enactment, practices interfere and objects transform. One goal of Mol's work was to describe a single/multiple object as a part of practices in which they were enacted and created. In this type of work, there was not one fixed point of comparison between objects, since realities and enactments are multiple. Objects do not magically glide or silently move from one reality to another, but materials interfere and interact with objects, creating emotional, material, and psychological effects. Objects become part of the real—objects encountered when living with the real. Focus shifts from the truth to the goodness and appropriateness of methods, tools, and research practices.

Ontologies of practice present an interesting dilemma by blending theory and practice within singular events and by bringing ontology to practice and practice to ontology. Ontologies of practice combine the questions of existence and truth with the questions of diverse, differentiated, and perceptual/affective practices. Ontologies of practice materialize theories of truth and truths themselves. Additionally, ontologies of practice could be seen as a question of power, legitimacy, and social structures that enable certain practices to exist and to be considered as true and others not. They also call for critical reflection and adaptation, different ontological politics, and various changing and complex connections between epistemologies, methodologies, and theories (for diverse connections, see, e.g., Carter & Little, 2007; Koro-Ljungberg, Yendol-Hoppey, Smith, & Hayes, 2009; Lather, 2007a). Mol and Law (2002) noted, "There is complexity if things relate but don't add up, if events occur but not within the processes of linear time, and if phenomena share a space but cannot be mapped in terms of a single set of three-dimensional coordinates" (p. 1). Similarly, in the context of educational research and sometimes also in qualitative research, things, data, experiences, and bodies don't always add up or follow linear logic. Complexity cannot be simplified into various digestible units and understandable or literal meanings.

> *There are two large arrows that go from left to right. Is this from doing to ontology or from enacting to practice?*
> —Chandra

> *Does the larger grouping next to ontology represent ontology? If not, what is that grouping? Why did you group these constructs? Does the large grouping near enacting represent enacting or something else?*
> —Darby

Another Conceptualization Beyond Mol's Methodological Singularity

In addition to mapping Mol's fluid ethnography and research design, I created a second map to use her work in a more general context of critical social science and qualitative research. Figure 4.3 is a conceptual illustration of fluid methodology where multiple methodological parts and objects come together in one space. More specifically, in this space, researchers no longer move from object to theory or from participants to text. Rather, qualitative researchers transfer from one way of acting, enacting, and experiencing the objects of research to another way. For example, a researcher could first observe objects being enacted in different contexts and then smoothly transition to writing about these enactments. These acts would not be separate research tasks but potentially overlapping interactions between the researcher and objects to illustrate the objects in multiple variations. The methodology or research process is not fragmented but involves fluid components connecting different acts of researching, living, and experiencing. When considering the value of this type of methodology, externally controlled or audible understandings of validity or rigor might not be sufficient or appropriate. For example, it is not enough to ask questions about the truth if multiple truths are visible or possible, and there are many ways to enact objects or methodology. Instead, it could be beneficial to turn the "validity" question into a question about the appropriateness of research acts and practices. From this perspective, knowledge is not a matter of reference but a result of manipulation and doing. "Instead of the observer's eyes, the practitioner's hands become the focus point of theorizing" (Mol, 2002, p. 152).

> If practice becomes our entrance into the world, ontology is no longer a monist whole. Ontology-in-practice is multiple. Objects that are enacted cannot be aligned from small to big, from simple to complex. Their relations are the intricate ones that we find between practices.
> (Mol, 2002, p. 157)

Following Mol's example, methodology occurs as different movements or sets of research moments joined together to create something that we can recognize as a methodological event. These methodological events and movements are unpredictable gatherings of analytical, theoretical, and interpretive momentums. These gatherings, in turn, can take place in different material spaces. In addition, methodology is created and enacted through different dense and intense spaces that methodology encounters or interacts with— these moments are created when research is complicated and messy. Fluid methodological moments can be found only in spaces where movements slow down, speed up, disappear, and appear again. When methodology is done, carried out, implemented, and created, it cannot be compared to others but only to its own variations—including variations of a methodology within a methodology. Methodology carried out this way is real and material yet incorporeal (see also Massumi, 2002). In this corporeal state also, one order becomes multiple.

Figure 4.3 Another Map of Fluid Methodological Space

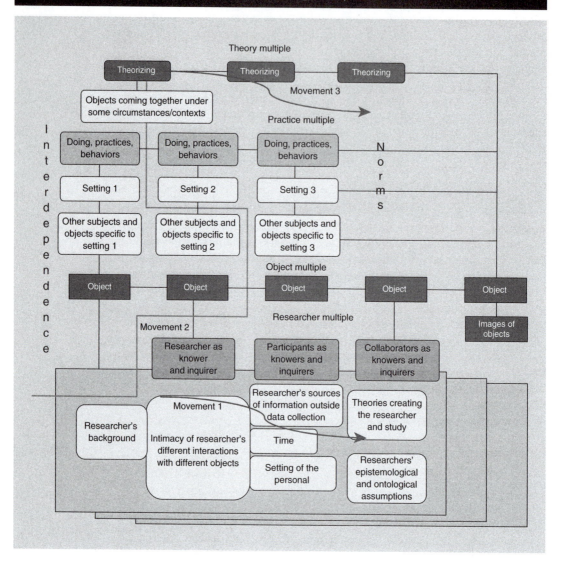

Researcher 1, researcher 2, researcher 3 . . . 15 . . . ∞   different variations of data, us

in relation to objects, practices, theories

Processes are messy and I want to leave them that way

No cleaning, no beautification

Can I, may I?   Even in research?   Or will I just do it anyway—without permission?

Secretly sliding in messy images

of research and life

silently working through complexities

just to illustrate that you also can do research and write differently

The Unexpected Lives of Methodologies Without Methodology

I hope that the above examples provoke and do the messy work of diversion and distraction. Maybe some **seeds** of productive complexity have been planted, and qualitative researchers could consider the methodological possibilities and new directions that variations embedded or exemplified through research objects and enactments could present. Multiplicity and simultaneity of processes, objects, intra-actions, and particles can create interesting and stimulating movement that may enable scholars to meet the unknown and movement that can resonate, maybe with otherness. This movement might be temporarily documented through **maps instead of linearity or fixed processes, as illustrated in this section.** Maps can also document methodological movement through particles in different cultural, geographical, and political spaces of knowing. As a result, documented methodologies are always partial and limiting because particles and objects do not stop moving or resonating.

Fluid methodologies serve as one alternative to linear and invariable research designs. Fluid methodology can create a space where scholars can reconsider their relationship with knowledge, data, traditions, and themselves. Notions of fluidity can also work against the stability of methods and the omnipotent power of "right" methodology that may portray methods as isolated, always (in)appropriate and (in)accurate, fixed, objective, and ultimately as controllable tools for research. Methodologies are not right or wrong, but when contexts and tools are continuously moving, the issue is applicability. Applicability, in turn, enables wonder and surprise. Incorporeal methodology adds to the "real" by complementing it rather than confirming it. "Generating a paradox and then using it as if it were a

A good metaphor, as we apply our order to a process where we cannot know its beginning or end, but rather only what we label as beginning or end.

—Darby

Exactly! Why does a research process have to follow a traditional text structure? Why can't it be a picture, or a map, or a chart, or a song, or a 3D tangible object! I think in a lot of cases these nontraditional depictions would better serve the research process and/or data!

—Jason

well-formed logical operator is a good way to put vagueness [of concepts such as methodology] in play" (Massumi, 2002, p. 13).

Fluid methodology can also work against notions of singularity of data, knower, theory, and method, thus becoming a move away from essentialism. Interconnectedness of various methodological processes, as well as researchers' and research's relatedness to data, participants, research contexts, and policy, can be framed within multiple and potentially simultaneous orders, repertoires, discourses, and styles. However, these multiplications may not be easily captured by words commonly used in methodology texts, such as *audit trails*, *thick description*, *categorization*, or *member checks*. Instead, fluid methodologies offer numerous variations, conceptual agreements, or traces of methodological paths, inviting scholars to travel and explore.

One might ask what it takes to implement and practice fluid methodologies. How to do it? (Un)fortunately I do not have an answer. I do not know how to do it or what to recommend, since this type of methodology is unanticipated and becoming. Readers can borrow ideas, read about different examples, experiment with existing methodological configurations, but in the end each scholar is responsible for creating her or his own flexible and continuously changing methodologies. Methodologies as such are experimentations and projects without an end. As a result, scholars might need to educate others about alternative ontologies and be prepared to negotiate with IRBs, committee members, collaborators, and tenure and promotion committees how, why, and where this type of scholarship is carried out. For those scholars who would like more scaffolding, "In your own research, you could" inserts put forward some ideas of how fluid methodologies could be introduced to your work. In addition, later (especially in the pedagogy section of the book) I will also discuss some potential pedagogical implications of this type of scholarship. Yet none of these ideas are strategies to be transferred blindly or uncritically.

Furthermore, fluid methodologies can open up or point to the concepts and practices associated with methodology that is already "already there" without proclaimed arrival. Representations, descriptions, and reflections on methodological relations, repulsions, and connectivity may create a flow that picks up speed, moves between researcher and data and back again, changes, encounters its momentary limits, and begins to evaporate. Methodological flow and multiplicity could transform one research project, research act, design, or methodological arrangement into another without disruption or discontinuity, thus incessantly, immediately, and continuously changing researchers, their processes, and expected or experienced outcomes. Critical social science or qualitative research does not necessarily need to be communicated or presented as a question/answer binary. Baudrillard (1983) explained that "*the referendum is always an ultimatum*: the unilateral nature of question that is no longer exactly an interrogation, but the immediate imposition of a sense whereby the cycle is suddenly completed. Every message is a verdict" (p. 117). What if qualitative researchers stopped translating complex events and conflicts into question/answer responses, codable categories, or verdicts? Qualitative scholars should be more concerned about the consequences of turning every message, finding, argument, or position into a verdict than confirming the norm and following grand narratives. Methodological fluidity cannot be premeditated, easily surveillanced, or protected. Maybe it can have a life of its own that we as scholars can only witness.

READING LIST OF LIFE

Camus, A. (2004). *The stranger*. Cambridge University Press.

Carroll, L., Random, H., & Torrey, M. (1955). *Alice in wonderland*. Random House.

Tolkien, J. R. R. (2004). *The lord of the rings*. HarperCollins.

BPTU/Shutterstock

5 Afterword

This Project (and Other Projects Alike) May Be "Failing" Productively

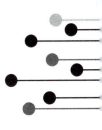

There is no ending to this project or the book. Conclusions and endings are likely to imply the final word, complete stops, and loss of beginnings. Rather than writing about concluding thoughts, I want to direct readers' attention to productive "failures" of unfinished research, since without a conclusion I am failing to "conclude" my text and thoughts. I also fail to provide you (my readers) a way out, a reason to stop reading, interacting, and thinking. Instead, I hope that this failure will be a productive new beginning and thus in itself quite desirable. By failure, I do not refer to a position or skill that does not meet specific criteria, external evaluation, or social expectation. Failures of that sort do not reflect my interest here. Instead, I use "productive failure" to work against finality, completion, and extreme methodological purification and predictability. Failure, as discussed here, indicates that more has to and can be done. Inquiry and research are not finished. Failure in this sense is a failure to conclude and deliver the perfected or anticipated, whether it is a question of a research project, text, example, interactions, policy, or thinking. Productive failure has to do with partiality and absence. Something about the research and researchers'/participants' interactions is still to come and to be continued and extended. Working through and with failure in qualitative research calls for creativity and critical reflection.

Robert Ulmer

Furthermore, productive failure does not imply that "everything goes" or that nothing needs to be done, since in order to "fail" one needs to put forward an "effort," set "goals," and have a certain degree of directionality. Qualitative researchers who approach scholarship and research through productive failure and who believe in the unfinished and raw elements of research are less likely to engage in research activities within contexts that call for specific research outcomes, predictable circumstances, and fixed variables based on rigid external expectations or evaluation criteria. Methodologies without methodology and methodological failure might be best nurtured in spaces that support risk taking and experimentation, since unfinished scholarship is never really done and as such continually revises and reworks itself, toward what everyone hopes will be more generative and generous interactions and methodologies.

O'Donnell (2014), referring to playwright Samuel Beckett's work, points out how failure is not about being but doing and making choices. "Failure is inevitable in practices that remain open to the world, through which the 'unknown' is allowed breathing space rather than resisted in an endless quest to master, confine and navigate the terrain of the known" (O'Donnell, 2014, p. 263). O'Donnell proposes that if individuals eliminate failure, they also close down life's openness and unpredictability. Experimentation and failure are immanent in any practices (including qualitative inquiry), explains O'Donnell. Thus, qualitative scholars also need to give up their desire to control methodologies and participants or justify their success or actions at any cost.

When one approaches methodologies without methodology from the perspective of productive failures, one commits to continuously reinventing, revising, and reenvisioning methodologies. The methodological work needs to stay moving and changing through diversified inquiry and careful and purposeful questioning. It is important to consider when methodological repetition is desirable and useful and when established methodological strategies needs to questioned, modified, or completely dismissed.

I also want to return to the notion of aporia (see Derrida, 1993, 2005) because aporetic spaces speak to the forces that may enable and stimulate "failing." Many qualitative inquiries, similar to many other methodological frameworks, are aporetic and undecidable, and as such continually and restlessly call for ethics, care of self, and "responsible" decision making. In addition, methodologies without methodology as aporetic strategies are likely to create a sense of failure, because methodological openness and theoretical/conceptual uncertainty embedded here prompt new questions and extensions. These questions might, in turn, problematize or bypass existing hierarchies and practices of nomination, creating new unknown or unexplored spaces and unexpected relatedness. Both aporetic research and qualitative inquiry can include momentary paralysis in the face of the unknown, and they call for a reflective pause when facing situations that seem impossible—situations that have no clear path to be taken (theoretically, methodologically, or in practice). In these aporetic situations that often lead to a sense of failure, duty is not the answer, but responsibility is the question.

Rather than expecting others (including literature and other scholars) to tell them where to go and what decisions to make, qualitative researchers ought to take more risks in their research and interactions with others. Without a risk, qualitative researchers cannot take a leap of faith, and they are unlikely to face the unknown responsibly (Derrida, 1995). In contrast, expecting and living with "failure" might become one possible means of responsible risk taking. Furthermore, approaching qualitative research as an unfinished and always already desirable failing project might assist scholars in being more open to the Other. For example, qualitative scholars could ask how to extend any methodological idea (similar to ideas presented in this book), how to perceive the Other who is still becoming, or how to welcome the Other who in its otherness is still to be met and encountered. Perhaps it is through brute and raw writing, methodological and theoretical flux and conceptual movement, that scholars may be able to stay inspired and continually growing (also methodologically). It may also be possible that uncertainty, rawness, and creative chaos prompted by doing, engaging, collaborating, and reflecting through failure and unfinishedness (without constant and continual purification and "cleaning" efforts) is conceptually stirring and theoretically life changing. Methodologies without methodology are not one but multiple, and thus there cannot be one method, practice, example, or preference but all methods, practices, examples, and preferences—methods on top of each other, methods continuing other methods, methods contradicting each other, and methods lacking and desiring something that cannot be described, understood, or achieved. The methodological future is not only coming but in some ways is already here in its absent, present, and absent-present methodological elements.

Scholars may also find it inspiring and productive to engage in epistemological and ontological experimentation across various porous and permutable "borders," for example, by creating passages between methodological, theoretical, experiential, performative, material, and spiritual (liminal) spaces. Experimentation, especially when departing from normative practices, is often seen as a form of failure by those who guard and control normative forms of scholarship. Experimentation can be seen as a failure to obey and follow approved and validated practice. However, failure to obey and resistance to normativity may be one of the forces that fuel qualitative researchers' experimentation. Failing and unfinished scholarship can also open up a space for more generative work. Generous and generative research includes types of practices that are committed to serving others (participants, collaborators, researchers, policymakers, others within it, students, theories, methods, and so on) in some way and to promoting scholarship that puts forward change and possibly unexpected actions in others. Generous and generative inquiry invites others and subalterns to work alongside the mainstream and alongside "the center," or practices that might be considered normative. It generously welcomes the Other and generates spaces for others to express, create, and speak—maybe spaces of displacement and shadow spaces (see Spivak, 1993). It aims to give until it has nothing else to give, and it shares until nothing else can be shared. However, since giving and sharing do not come to an end, this task (book, research, project, others, and writing) will not be finished, but they may fail while continuing to give at the same time. Actually, I hope that this book will fail in various ways. For example, I desire these texts to fail to provide satisfactory and agreed-upon answers, fail to please and confirm the norm, fail to meet expectations, fail to represent my scholarship and research interests, fail to resonate with all readers, and fail in many other unthought-of and unthinkable ways. And still be able to give . . .

Maybe the giving will happen through questions: provocative, challenging, nonsensical, liminal, wondering, caring, and loving questions. Rilke (1993) challenged readers to "live the question" rather than search for answers. Can one live to fail, fail to live, fail and live? Rilke also asks us to "try to love *the questions themselves* as if they were locked rooms or books written in a very foreign language" (p. 34, emphasis added). He reminds us about the distance and foreign elements embedded in a question. This distance and these foreign elements can introduce surprise and endorse exploration and discovery.

Inspired by Rainer Rilke, Harold Pinter, and Anne Reinertsen and Ann Merete Otterstad (2012), this section finishes with dialogical questions. I envision that these questions could serve as a (new) opening of sorts, acknowledging that my vision of this type of opening might be completely beside the point. For Derrida, even a question might be beside the point.

> No answer, then. Perhaps, in the long run, not even a question. The copulative correspondence, the opposition question/answer is already lodged in a structure, enveloped in the hollow of an ear, which we will go into to take a look. (Derrida, 1982, pp. xvi–xvii)

In his work, Derrida poses many questions and also wonders about the role of questions. For example, for Derrida (2007), questioning is one of the tasks of the philosophers and as such calls for theorizing and philosophical reflection. Philosophers want to give a question a chance. By questioning, one hopes to have an attentive audience. A question also functions as a welcome, a hailing, and an approach toward the approachable Other. It serves as an indication that I am talking to you even if I do not have anything to tell. Derrida argues that this welcoming and interactive "yes" before the question is actually embedded in the question itself. Posing a question also runs the risk of carrying its own answer, since a question may pre-impose an answer (Derrida, 2007). I will take the risk and see what happens.

You

my attentive audience

Y___E___S   you

read the questions

live the questions

ask the questions

and

try not to answer

    try not to impose or force answers

may your answer be another question

just another question

What is the future of methodologies without methodologies?

What is here to learn?

Does, can, and might somebody know?

Does anybody know? Does anybody know?

If there is one who knows, isn't there also a new grand narrative emerging and a new norm/normativity being created?

Who wants to take on the duties of a watchdog or the creator of new grand narratives?

Who? You?

Who wants to be the famous and governing methodological watchdog?

Who does not want to be a famous watchdog (i.e., to be published, known, funded, loved, tamed . . .)?

Is there a future of methodologies without methodology? Is there a knowable future? Or is future a reflection or residue of the knowable present?

Why does knowing matter?

How does knowing matter?

Does matter know?

How can one know without determinism and finality? How can one know without future? How can one know without the Other? How can one know without certainty? How can one know without language? How can one know without duty? How can one know without experiencing and living? How can one know without knowing? How can one know without a subject? Can one know?

Can "it" know?

Can know?

Know?

Is it possible to know uncertain, humble, unfinished, fragmented, stuttering ways?

What happens when knowing and unknowing come together and knowing becomes a matter of degrees? Is this viable in the context of research?

Does matter know?

Might knowing exemplify living? Or might living exemplify knowing? Maybe a living-knowing? Or knowing-living?

Might there be a knowing-living (monster) among us? Who is afraid?

What has a copy without the original to do with knowing?

What has singularity to do with knowing?

Is singular always already multiple?

* *

Are you afraid of monsters?

Does the loss of Real scare you?

Or is it the simulacra and copy without original that might create fear and maybe a sense of mourning?

What do you do when normative and simplified methodologies are replaced with failing and unfinished strategies and approaches? Where do you go?

Can you do it? Can you go there?

Are you ready to do it and go there?

Are you (never) ready?

Do you feel prepared and capable?

Is acknowledging one's unpreparedness a form of preparedness?

* *

Does the notion of capability include or imply a measure and external evaluation? Who structures and generates a (in)capability?

Who benefits from preparedness, discourses of capacity and resources, or docile learners and scholars?

Whom should we (not) listen to and believe?

What happens if we do not listen?

Where do these questions come from?

How can somebody bypass power-knowledge and normative discursive formations? Is it possible?

Is everything possible (also in research)?

Aren't all forms of life and thought entangled with power, various forces, and particles of life?

How can one work with power, acknowledging its energy to constitute and create oneself as its object?

What do students think? Where would the students like to go next?
(Note: In this section, students' comments are not posted in the sides, but they are presented in the following question diagrams.)

How do scholars live with the dilemma of doing and undoing, working for and against simultaneously?

How do scholars live with and react to unanswerable questions?

How can one erase one's thoughts, text, practices, or methods? How can one carry out conceptual and theoretical repairs or work through methodological malfunctions?

Where can one find the language lost and words erased?

> *Where can one find the language lost and words erased?*

> *Where?*

Figure 5.1   Student Advisory Board's Questions About Language and Data

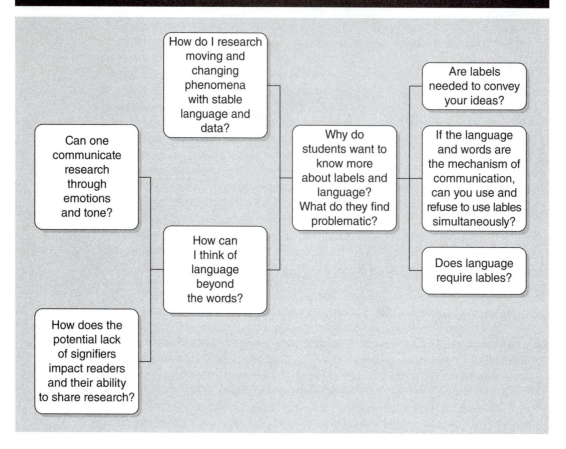

What about students; where will they go next?

Why it is so hard to learn without scaffolding, modeling, or examples? Why does one need an authority to point the direction and provide a confirmation?

How do teachers indoctrinate and build armies of dutiful and docile learners?

What happens to citizens who do not question?

What happens to noncitizens (aliens) who question?

What happens to responsibility beyond the duty?

Figure 5.2 Student Advisory Board's Questions About Methodology

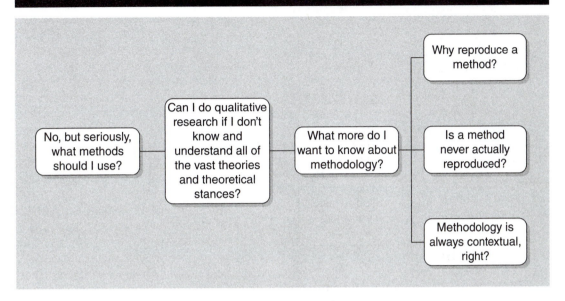

Where is fear of complexity and theory located? How is theory-scare being initiated and reinforced?

Who controls the gates?

Where do these questions come from?

Why does not-knowing appear so scary, inaccessible, distant, and potentially not respected?

What needs to happen to let theories loose and do their thing?

When might theory wash over us like a wave of warm turquoise water, creating an impact with a ripple effect? What might happen?

What needs to happen to let methods loose and do their thing?

Where will students go next?

All life is meeting—right? Where do you want to meet . . . life?

Are the methodological beginnings of participant-driven research (PDR) possible?

Figure 5.3 Student Advisory Board's Questions About PDR

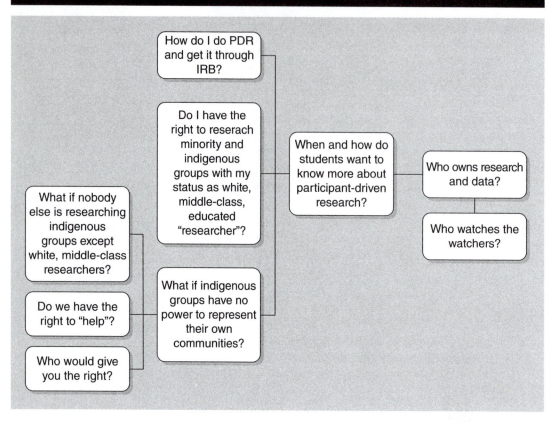

One might propose that many beginnings of PDR are always already there (in students' and scholars' work, mind-sets, practices, interactions, lives), and they have already shaped the present. Would that make a difference?

Is it plausible that many beginnings of PDR are ghosts or examples of historical linkages/extensions?

How does pedagogy infiltrate research?

How does one teach the unteachable?

To what extent does relationality influence my teaching today, tomorrow, always?

Where do these questions come from?

Figure 5.4 Student Advisory Board's Questions About Pedagogy

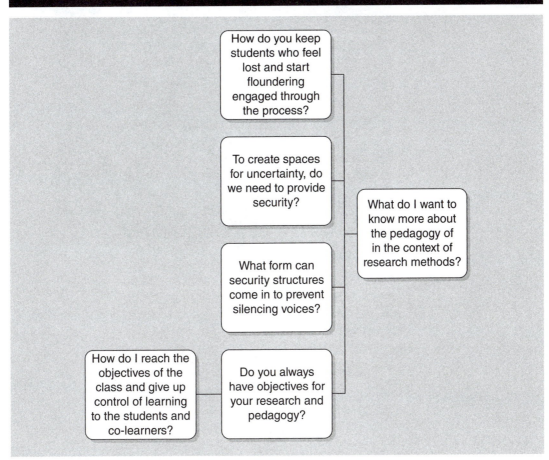

Is it about movement after all?

Is it about questioning and reflection after all?

Is it about power after all?

Is it about methodological work after all?

Is it about theories after all?

When is after-all?

Continuously and never.

Robert Ulmer

Irruption 2: Performance, Philosophy, and Not-Knowing

Learn more about performance philosophy at http://performancephilosophy .ning.com/.

Group Activity 1: Living Through Time

Meters **by Kaprow**[1]

Carrying a cube of ice in the mouth

Carrying a cube of ice in the hand

Walking on

Swallowing the melting ice till it's gone

Calling out: Now!

Walking on

Waiting for the hand to hold no ice

Calling out: Now!

Walking on

Waiting for the hand to dry

Calling out: Now!

Walking on

Mirka Koro-Ljungberg

What happened to your notions of time? How did you live time? Where and how was time? Did ice linger on your dry hand? Did time linger? Did you linger? How did your sense of time differ from the other group members' senses or experiences?

---

1. An edited version of unrealized activity by Allan Kaprow from 1972. Presented in the workshop by Laura Cull, Gainesville, 2012. Reprinted with the permission of The Getty Research Institute, Los Angeles (980063).

Group Activity 2: Taking Risks: Unthinkable Time Warp

Mirka Koro-Ljungberg

Please stand and close your eyes. You may choose to do this or just visualize it. Please keep your eyes closed. Jump to the left. Step to the right. Put your hands on your hips. Bring your knees in tight. Thrust your pelvis forward.

Hold your body or image of your body for a count of 15 seconds. Release the position or the image. Open your eyes. Sit down.

How did you experience holding and moving your body? What did you think when you held your mind and body in a potentially uncomfortable position? Can you hold yourself as a researcher and your data, analyses, and representations in an uncomfortable position? Can discomfort be useful and productive? How can one live through one's body and mind, simultaneously experiencing uncertainty and dealing with risk? How does normativity limit our holding of our bodies and minds?

6

Methodological Responsibility Outside Duty

Responsibility Matters

As a result of neoliberal movements in higher education, technocrats (individuals who have been charged to carry out teaching and scholarship in decontextualized, temporal, disengaged ways by focusing on fast delivery, easily attainable outcomes, and other cost-saving measures) have come to replace many teachers and scholars, qualitative methodologists not being an exception. I worry that creative and nonnormative qualitative methodology has suffered extensively from the past economic hardships in higher education, creating even narrower views as to what constitutes "academic work" or possible even a methodology scholar. For example, in some universities, qualitative research courses are now taught by "temporary" instructors from other content areas, as expertise in methodological matters has shifted to an overemphasis on "easy fixes" and rapid methodologies. In this sense, the current economic tension that permeates higher education reveals larger assumptions concerning what kind of expertise is needed, and how and in what ways methodological work is taught and valued. However, from this crisis extends opportunities for broader conversations, and I consider this contemporary moment an opportunity to rethink our responsibilities as research scholars interested in complex educational problems without easy and simplified answers. Further, the ambiguity inherent in responsible methodological work—that of not knowing what is to come, of dealing outside prescriptive methodological work—perhaps runs counter to institutionalized procedural norms and calls for general criteria for "good and rigorous" research and practices. I wonder how methodological responsibility differs from other forms of scholarly responsibility. Does methodological responsibility relate to tedious methodological compliance, or does methodological responsibility extend beyond duty?

Figure 6.1   Some Possible Responsibilities of a Researcher

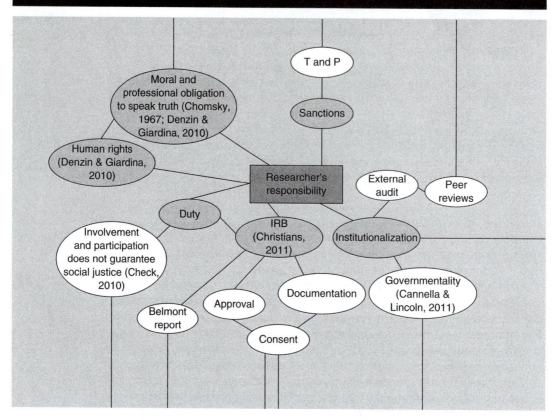

Similar to methodological knowledge (e.g., knowledge about how we know and have come to know, knowledge concerning various ways to design and implement one's research plan, knowledge about methodological traditions beyond one's personal interests, knowledge about methods and approaches to come), methodological responsibility can be viewed on a continuum. Methodological responsibility seen as a continuum includes the work of scholars who use qualitative methods only in their own research, scholars whose content area is methodology, and many others in between. I propose that increased methodological responsibility can promote complex understandings of inquiry and research approaches and their philosophical underpinnings. Scholars with such understanding can resist certainty, being informed by contemporary visions of coming to know in uncertain times. As a consequence, I argue that our era of uncertainty and complexity requires new methodological responsibility—a vision of methodological work that disrupts traditional institutional formations and fixed identifications of methodological identity.

Why Does Responsibility Matter?

In the context of qualitative research, researchers' responsibility is often treated as a question of ethics, morality, duty, or institutional review broad (IRB) compliance. It is scholars' responsibility to protect participants and avoid harm when engaging in inquiries or conducting research. Alternatively, some conversations have focused on plagiarism, faked or falsified results, and researchers' responsibility to be honest and professional. However, in this section, I discuss how researchers' responsibility can extend beyond participant protection and plagiarism toward ways in which scholars approach uncertainty and not-knowing. It is not my intention to completely divorce IRB compliance, ethical concerns, plagiarism, and falsification from researchers' responsibility toward uncertainty and the unknown, since all these issues influence each other and are parts of interrelated practices. Similarly, I do not propose separation of responsibility into philosophical stances or practical dilemmas, and I certainly see the need for protocols, guidelines, and systems of duty and responsibility. Yet I want to emphasize that the question of responsibility can include more than these aspects of philosophy or scholarly practice. It is my intention to stimulate conversations that move beyond reductionist and narrow views of responsibility. Derrida's notions of responsibility can serve as a helpful conceptual move away from normative duty and as one possible way to problematize how scholars view ethics and ethical dilemmas in qualitative research.

Robert Ulmer

GLOSSARY

Responsibility. The establishment of relationships of trust. The fulfillment of informed consent, completion of third-party review, maintenance of confidentiality and anonymity, and minimization of deception (Academy of Management, 2006).

Responsibility. The fulfillment of research that provides improved theories of human behavior (Wright & Wright, 1999, p. 1108).

Responsibility. The balance between career and scientific interests against the interests of prospective subjects (Baumrind, 1964, p. 421).

Responsibility. The expression of research that is more personal and compassionate in nature which leads to more robust and meaningful theory development (Frost, 1999).

Responsibility. The presentation of research that has both practical implications and relevance to nonacademic and academic readers alike (Wright & Wright, 2002, p. 175).

Responsibility as envisioned by Derrida draws from ethical practices and actions, and it concerns itself with onto-epistemological stances toward the unknown and the Other. For Derrida, responsibility is most challenging and always aporetic, especially during times of nondirectionality and when individuals encounter unexpected and unanticipated events and thoughts. Derrida's position on responsibility might be already present in the work and practices of many critical social science researchers. For example, the importance of staying open and welcoming the Other, making urgent decisions, deciding when the direction is not given, and taking risk can form a significant part of qualitative researchers' encounters with data, participants, and policymakers. Similarly, urgent decision making and risk may also characterize diverse research processes linked with data collection, analysis, and representation of findings. It is important to keep in mind that researchers' responsibilities should be not only procedural but also more deeply ethical and shaped by questions of goodness, knowledge, values, and the anticipated implications of one's actions for practice.

I draw from **Derrida's position on responsibility** because it complements the unexpected methodological moves and many unterritorialized aspects of research methodology, especially within qualitative inquiry. Derrida has written about responsibility in ways that extend beyond duty, and his conceptualization of responsibility is suitable for current times and uncertainties of multiple kinds (epistemological, social, cultural, etc.) that are present today. Derrida (1992) argued that responsibility begins with "the experience and experiment of the aporia. When the path is clear and given, when a certain knowledge opens up the way in advance, the decision is already made, it might as well be said that there is none to make; irresponsibly" (p. 41). Furthermore, saying that a responsible decision must be taken on the basis of knowledge seems to define the condition of possibility of responsibility (one can't make a responsible decision without science or conscience, without knowing what one is doing, for what reasons, in view of what and under what conditions), at the same time as it defines the condition of impossibility of this same responsibility. (Derrida, 1995, p. 24)

Great summary of Derrida's position!!!

—Chandra

Duties are everywhere, tasks are given, and protocols need to be followed

Rules are created to protect me from the other, unknown, unexpected

from myself

Duties and rules govern and are to be governed   easily institutionalized

intentionally institutionalized   simply institutionalized

simply lobotomized

Mechanical worker, dutiful worker, timely worker, responsible worker?

> *Not really*

only an idealized illusion, hope of the followers, hope of the ruling body

My body cannot decide   but there is no choice

Decision needs to be made, risks need to be taken

There is no choice

Derrida's work can be especially important and meaningful for qualitative researchers, who may continually adopt and create new research approaches to better meet the needs of participant communities. Responsibility matters for qualitative researchers, since their inquiries may provoke different and new ethical and practical questions about urgent decision making as they conduct participatory work in the communities. Since various qualitative research approaches are inductive and driven by emerging data and potentially new information sources, scholars need to stay open to other ways of knowing and engaging in research. **It is not enough that qualitative researchers view responsibility as a moral question or duty, since unexpected situations and circumstances might not be accessible, described, or covered under existing guidelines, policies, or accepted practices.**

In my opinion, this argument demonstrates that the perspective of critical social scientists should have some prevalence in all types of social science research.

—Chandra

Section key points:

- Responsibility can return to the researcher, not as a duty but as a response to, and openness to, other epistemologies, theories, methods, and conceptual ideas.

- Three ways researchers can imagine responsibility are (1) resisting closure, (2) responding to urgency, and (3) disrupting traditions when responsibility itself is always escaping and still to be achieved.

- Reconceptualizations of methodological responsibility can enable researchers to put other theories, methods, and conceptual ideas to work without hesitation, reservation, qualification, or judgment, and to set in motion new thinking regarding theoretical and methodological possibilities within educational research.

Who should worry about responsibility?

The Role of Research Responsibility in Forming Public Policy

Former American Educational Research Association presidents Robert Linn and William Tate have discussed the role of responsibility in educational research. Linn (2003) connected responsibility to accountability and called for shared responsibility in order to improve education, whereas Tate (2007) highlighted the role of civic responsibility and how multiple sectors of the community should work together toward high-quality educational opportunities, regardless of learners' geospatial locations. Additionally, Taylor, Anderson, Au, and Raphael (2000) argued that researchers have a responsibility to show how their work can be situated in the larger policy context, and Eisenhart (2001) asked, "How should we think about our ethical responsibilities to those we write about and on whose behalf we wish to take constructive action?" (p. 24). However, despite the documented overall importance of discussing researchers' responsibilities, it is troubling that some contemporary "scientific" educational discourse portrays responsibility as a form of duty or commitment that can be externally observed and evaluated. By authoritatively enabling and disabling particular types of inquiries and methodologies, many policy and science discourses imply a form of control and colonization of knowledge that sets in motion practices of methodological oversimplification, sacrificing complexity in the name of mechanicality and promoting evaluative externalism (see, e.g., MacLure, 2006; Tikly, 2004). Rather than being constrained by calls for duty, accountability, and methodological reductionism in educational research, I hope for the return of responsibility not as a duty but as a response to, and openness to, the Other: other epistemologies, theories, methods, and conceptual ideas.

Additionally, various forms of methodological colonization aim to improve the "quality" of educational research and standardize research processes. Burkhardt and Schoenfeld (2003) argued for the establishment of norms applied to research methods to create effective prototypes for researchers. Similar discourse is echoed in many international and national policies and through statements related to external funding priorities. For example, the British Educational Research Association (2010) described its funding priorities at a research project level by examining

Unknown? Known?

Irresponsible? Responsible?

Mirka Koro-Ljungberg

> what kind and scale of study conducted in what time frame is likely to provide the most clear and credible information about the initiative's impact on literacy for key target groups of children and adults. *So this is a world of compromises, best fits and limited resources, not of ideal scenarios with money no object.* (emphasis added)

Similarly, the U.S. Institute of Education Sciences (2010) invited applications for their grant program on statistical and research methodology in education to advance education research methodologies and statistical analyses. Their call for proposals clearly prioritized easy methodological practices and methodological simplicity by stating,

> The Institute is very interested in the development of practical statistical and methodological tools that can be used by mainstream education researchers (*rather than by statisticians or researchers with highly sophisticated statistical skills*) to improve the design of their studies, analysis of their data, and interpretation of their findings. *Easily accessible, stand alone* software with documentation written *for a general research audience* that is disseminated through well-established websites is *more likely to gain wide use by education researchers* than are programs designed for use by highly trained statisticians. . . . The Institute invites proposals to develop tools or methods for *making the analysis and interpretation of NAEP data easier for education leaders and decision makers* or to permit advanced analytic techniques to be *readily applied* to NAEP data. (emphasis added)

Inspired by these examples, I problematize the decontextualized, widely generalizable, and "readily applicable" uses of methodology and methods across all disciplines and research traditions. I do not want to view my duty as a researcher as being one of creating readily applicable and widely generalizable research to advance humankind or contribute to the scientific progress. I worry that current calls for methodological effectiveness might not promote "increased quality" of educational research from diverse epistemological and theoretical perspectives; rather, they reinforce easy methodological practices, decontextualized methodological decision making, and uncomplicated uses of methodologies. Furthermore, this strategic move toward improved educational sciences often silences and dismisses discourse of complexity and methodological uncertainty, methodological expertise, and knowledge. But most important, such discourses redirect attention away from (methodological) borderlands, researchers' responsibility, cultural values, troublesome questions, multiple viewpoints, and ideological and methodological impossibilities. Moreover, many of these strategic policy moves encourage researchers to view themselves outside methodological decision making, ethics, situated values, and epistemological beliefs promoting separation between the knower and the object of knowledge.

What are the disadvantages of viewing responsibility as a duty?

Exactly. Everything should be critiqued, scrutinized, and criticized. Constantly. That is when the real truth will emerge:

"Criticism may not be agreeable, but it is necessary. It fulfills the same function as pain in the human body. It calls attention to an unhealthy state of things."

—Winston Churchill

—Jason

On the surface, easy methodological practices can enhance and promote widely accessible methodological knowledge as well as fast knowledge transfers, but at the same time, they limit the possibilities of research and represent "easy fixes"— temporary solutions to the perceived crises in educational research. O'Byrne (2005), reconceptualizing such crises by reading Arendt and Derrida, stated that "crisis demands a critical response, but the practice of critique itself precipitates crisis, with the result that modernity, the age of critique, must also be the state of permanent crisis" (p. 392). She continued, "It is not the failure to supply answers that is the cause for concerns, but rather answers themselves as calcifications that have come to be regarded not as answers at all but as truths exempt from critique" (p. 393). Similar analytics could be applied to research methodology. **The problem is less about theoretical perspectives, research designs, and the types of collection or analysis methods used and more about how some scholars and politicians treat certain methods or research approaches as truths exempt from critique.**

It is possible that the emergence of discourse promoting easy and decontextualized methodological practices is a reaction to notions of contemporary educational research as methodologically complicated, advanced, and continually changing. Discussions about theoretical movements, intertextuality, and emergent research approaches in statistics and linguistically or performance oriented analysis have become popular, and research reporting

How do researchers mask or avoid their responsibilities?

has simultaneously become more detailed and sophisticated and thus more difficult to read and process by those outside the academy. It is no longer easy to understand educational research without methodological training and/or research experience. Additionally, educational "realities" have not become less complicated; rather the complexity of education and questions posed by researchers and practitioners is here to stay. By reclaiming researchers' responsibilities in the context of theory and methodology, scholars can generate intellectual and scientific hope that is currently often absent from educational research discourses and practices at the local and national levels. **This ethical move toward renewed responsibility and activism can also open up possibilities for working collaboratively toward sustainable social change and reinventing inquiries and methods in diverse interpretive spaces and cultural ecologies.**

Now I return to the concept of responsibility, both conceptually and methodologically. The ways I approach responsibility in general and responsibility in the context of qualitative research in particular can be traced to my readings of Derrida and other scholars who have interpreted Derrida's scholarship on responsibility. Later, I elaborate on three ways researchers can imagine responsibility: by resisting closure, by responding to urgency, and by disrupting traditions when responsibility itself is always escaping and still desirable.

> *The concept of Freirean praxis—reflection and action— clarifies who and what I seek as a researcher. The idea of generative themes provides hope in the face of what will always be partial truth.*
> —Darby

Return to Responsibility

Researchers' duty to follow protocols and guidelines and externally auditable selection of right, good, and economically effective methodological choices characterizes much of the current social science and qualitative research discourses. These signs of audit culture are problematic, since they position researchers as technicians rather than intellectuals and scholars who use different systems of logic to justify or ground their decisions. Thus, I believe that critical social science and qualitative research scholars could advocate a different kind of ethical approach to the request for duty: namely, different forms of responsibility. More specifically, we can return to responsibility from multiple angles and diverse perspectives. For example, Todd (2003) viewed responsibility as relational, arguing that "what counts as conditions of responsibility are therefore based in the quality of relations we have to others as opposed to adhering to predefined principles that we apply to the particular situations" (p. 141). Todd's relational view places emphasis on a mutual-relations-based construction of responsibility. Responsibility cannot be divorced from social interactions and cultural contexts. Alternatively, responsibility could be approached from a more individualistic perspective, similar to moral responsibility, which can encompass aspects of determinism, free will, and duty or moral integrity (Feinberg & Shafer-Landau, 2008). From the individualistic perspective, responsibility is about choice, vision, intentionality, or rational action. Cartwright (2006) conceptualized individual responsibility in two ways: responsibility as actions and consequences attributed to the reflective self and responsibility as rationality. In comparison, a definition that may be closest to Derrida's notions of responsibility is Davis's (2001) concept of reflexive responsibility. Davis differentiated simple responsibility, conventional and settled duties, from complex or reflexive responsibility that includes the ability to change plans in the face of unforeseen consequences and willingness to give truthful accounts of one's actions.

In your own research, you could:

- Reflect on your notions of responsibility and ask yourself where those notions come from

- Keep a journal documenting your reactions to unknown and uncertain research situations

- Think about ways in which different forms of duty create you as a subject

Derrida (1993) challenged us to think who would call a decision without a rule, law, or norm a decision. For Derrida, responsibility is linked to knowledge (the perceived presence or absence of it), and responsibility always carries seeds of its own deconstruction. It could be said that responsibility is a prerequisite to knowledge; it enables individuals (and researchers) to welcome the Other also within themselves and continually stay sensitized to themselves, data, and unexpected interactions with participants and communities. In the qualitative research context, there may be various decisions that have to be made without a rule or law—for example, how to interact with participants who all come from different backgrounds, how to conceptualize data within a particular research project, or how to involve participants in data interactions and analysis. All these tasks include decisions without clear rules or norms. One might even notice that rules or laws provide little help regarding when to begin or practice this type of responsibility. Students cannot find answers from the textbooks about when and how to face uncertainty or how to make urgent decisions without laws or norms. Derrida (1995) also explained that "the activating of responsibility (decision, act, praxis) will always take place before and beyond any theoretical or thematic determination" (p. 26). In the process of exceeding borderlines and impossible passages and operating outside thematic categorization, the aporia of suspension, nonways, indecision, and urgency both enable and disable researchers' responsibility (see, e.g., Edgoose, 2001; Wang, 2005). Acting responsibly calls researchers to view scholarship, data, interpretations, and presentations as questions rather than answers (Patrick, 1997).

Imaging Responsibility as Resisting
Closure and Holding a Space for the Other

According to Derrida (1995), responsibility will not be accomplished, and it is precisely this impossibility that can move researchers toward responsibility or keep scholars responsible. Responsibility is always escaping, and individuals are constantly responsible for other things to come. Similarly, qualitative researchers are responsible for the Other within their research, activities, and themselves—other interpretations of data and inclusion of other participants, methods, and implications to come. From this perspective, if responsibility is an infinite task and always becoming, scholars' responsibility and responsible decision making are never finished or accomplished. This becoming and open-endedness, in turn, call for different ways to "evaluate" or reflect on responsibility. Evaluation or reflection cannot be based on the outcomes or final impact, but responsibility can be experienced in its uncertain doing and unfinished process.

Evink (2009) referred to responsibility as contextual and infinite, a response to the call of the Other, which will withdraw from and transcend one's world. Responsibility is infinite because individuals are called to do more than they can, but Evink (2009) explained that this does not mean that individuals are called to everything—limits of responsibility exist, but they cannot be localized, and the borders of responsibility are beyond individuals' grasp. Wang (2005) proposed that "the responsibility of answering the call from the other opens the self to its own rupture with itself, a rupture attentive to the differences in the other and in the future" (p. 50). Ruptures within methodologies, research processes, and methods question assumptions and techniques accompanying these inquiries and scholarly processes. Furthermore, ruptures redirect researchers' attention toward changing subjectivities, disrupted knowledge projects, the unknown in methods, and the ineffectiveness or impartiality of research processes.

In your own research, you could:

- Engage in ongoing critical reflection of your responsibility as conceptualized by Derrida

- Consider differences between duty and responsibility in your research encounters

- Try to be consciously open to the Other (and to failure)

- Think about how to become a more responsible author, scholar, individual, citizen, and so forth

In the context of research, responding to the call from the Other can imply theoretically and methodologically unlimited and ongoing movement toward the unknown and beyond established knowledge, questioning and dislocating the knowledge one desires to produce. Engagement with the edge, or with the Other, and advance of the future, or the borderline, are preconditions for responsibility (Wang, 2005). Derrida (2005) explained that responsibility answers for itself and for the legacy before the Other, before that which is coming.

What does it take to stay open?

I wish I could teach you, show you, direct you, and help you

But I cannot tell!   Sorry to disappoint!

I may feel, sense, or do something that reassembles openness

but

I never accomplish or finish or recognize or know it, them,

its, theirs

This task is never done   since Otherness always escapes

escapes in its strangeness   new otherness   unexpected otherness

This is Derrida's point and my point and our point and pointless point

Openness to other is sunshine, moonlight, dark bottomless cave, open sky, sounds of joy, fireworks, gentle touch . . .

and and and

living   responsibly   always   if possible

More specifically, in the context of qualitative inquiry, responsibility as openness to the Other does not imply unpreparedness. Instead, "responsible" researchers prepare for decision making by gathering information, reading, writing, and interacting, but at the same time they leave room for methodological uncertainty and responsiveness by continually and without clear direction revising and reconceptualizing research purposes, processes, techniques, and approaches, as well as interactions with participants and data. "Responsible" researchers are faced with dilemmas without prescribed answers. This space of uncertainty and indecision asks scholars to be present and open to other ways of knowing, doing, and interpreting. Actions and interpretations are not closed in on themselves, but they transform the doer and texts in question. Research texts and interpretations do not saturate themselves—they leave something to be desired, something else to be interpreted, space for others to sign one's text (Derrida, 2001b).

Responsibility in this context does not mean that researchers need to choose between two options, right or wrong. Responsibility is not about binary choices; rather, it is an ongoing response, decision, act, or praxis. In other words, if other theories, approaches, and methods are possible and accessible, scholars and researchers are always responsible and engaged in doing, deciding, and responding. Even after reflections, research presentations, publications, and completed study reports, responsibility is not over; answering to the unknown within oneself is forthcoming, knowledge projects are continually changing, and more data and new knowledge are being constructed beyond our intentions and efforts as researchers, and beyond the desires of our participants.

> *What guidance will readers be provided to develop their ability to recognize this space? Who is responsible for providing this intentional scaffolding to move away from the norm? Or is the ability to engage in a third space innate?*
>
> —Darby

Some examples for this type of notions of responsibility exist in the literature. For example, MacLure (2006) interestingly introduced what she called "the baroque method": illustrating openness to the Other by resisting mastery and single points of view. She explained that "as the 'bone in the throat' of closure-seeking systems, the baroque method offers a hopeful figure for a productively irritating method" (p. 729). Methodologically, the traits of the baroque method could also promote research practices that activate responsibility. For example, MacLure wrote that the baroque method enables loss of mastery of self and the Other; attempts to represent the unrepresentable; practices confusion of opposites, such as reality and representation, surface and depth; and uses distorting textual devices, such as assemblage and parody. In her work, she also stayed away from "actual or procedural" analysis of data but encouraged researchers to add something to the data, such as artifacts, drawings, or anecdotes.

Working against closure could also be exemplified by researchers' evasion of infinite study conclusions or "right" answers to research questions. The multiplicity of possible conclusions, answers, or interpretations can activate responsibility among researchers but also among readers. **Readers are left with a space in which to interact with the text, draw their own conclusions, and create their own answers beyond what might be offered to them by the researcher.** This invitation to uncertainty does not diminish the value of research; rather, it sets up alternative ways to utilize research and interact with texts and interpretations.

Imaging Responsibility as Responding to Urgency

Responsibility can also be related to urgent decision making. Derrida (1995) encouraged us to make decisions here and now but at the same time question our decisions and desires to know and decide. Because Otherness in oneself and others

Robert Ulmer

is always immediate, the urgency of decisions is never ending. In the context of qualitative research, researchers are often faced with enduring and in situ decisions that cannot wait, and often they cannot be rationalized. These decisions can relate to different aspects of the research process, such as how to deal with participants who resist disclosure during interviews, how to handle conflicting viewpoints without being able to return to the participants for additional information, how to address unexpected changes in the field or a research team, or how to prioritize tasks and goals based on changing institutional circumstances or the immediate needs of participants or the researcher. Many of these decisions need to be made without certainty regarding the path to take or assurance about positive outcomes of the decision. However, less frequently, the urgency and uncertainty of these decisions are made public, and some scholars prefer to avoid such situations associated with urgency and uncertainty altogether by delaying their responses or by attempting to verify their responses ahead of time. In this case, researchers' decisions are already made, and thus no responsibility is taken.

In your own research, you could:

- Carefully document urgent research decisions and how your experiences of urgency shaped your actions

- Think about ways in which urgency manifests itself in your scholarship, and especially about why and how certain things become urgent

It could also be argued that the methodological nonlinearity or circularity often embedded in qualitative inquiries—the movement between different knowers, various aspects of data, and diverse audiences—fosters indefinite, contextual, and temporal decision making. Methodological decisions in adaptable research designs and practices are rarely definite, nor do they present a theoretical or practical ultimatum. Instead, being responsive to oneself and others calls for methodological adjustments, changes in research plans, and flexibility with data; such responsiveness can lead to various ruptures in knowledge. Often researchers cannot plan for conceptual or methodological changes or adjustments but find themselves within diverse "stuck places" and feeling unprepared. For example, when I think about my own research projects or teaching of research methods courses, I repeatedly find myself stuck, not knowing where to go next, what to expect, or what might be influencing my processes and practices. I could also argue that feelings of unpreparedness foster my ongoing learning and new forms of investigation and experimentation. Sometimes these personal and methodological stuck places and sense of unpreparedness might not be easy to explain or logically describe. It could also be argued that only when researchers experience uncertainty and limitations of theories, methodologies, and methods can they respond responsibly and begin their work from and within the limits of methodology.

Imaging Responsibility as Rupturing Tradition, Authority, and Order

Responsibility can also be manifested, experienced, or lived when one is working against tradition, authority, or order. Derrida (1995) suggested that

> the exercise of responsibility seems to leave no choice but this one, however uncomfortable it may be, of paradox, heresy, and secrecy. More serious still, it must always run the risk of conversion and apostasy: there is not responsibility without a dissident and inventive rupture with respect to tradition, authority, orthodoxy, rule, or doctrine. (p. 27)

Keeping open space for the Other can include different forms and degrees of theoretical, methodological, expressive, and pedagogical freedom, often followed by resistance, especially when one is not following a predetermined rule, procedure, or tradition. Along with methodological authority and order come rules and norms that do not often leave space for the type of responsibility envisioned here. However, I am not advocating complete dismissal of rules or traditions, but I envision qualitative researchers working from within the systems to push the limits, interrupting existing practices by changing their own actions, and simultaneously situating themselves inside and outside authority and order. Critical social science and qualitative research scholars need to take risks to interrupt existing methodological grand narratives. A part of the interruption can include taking what Derrida (2005) called "the absolute risk" that is specific to each situation, and one is required to rejustify oneself as if for the first time. He further explained that "in order to be a decision, it has to cut off this 'possible,' tear up my history, and thus be first of all, in a particular and strange way, the decision of the other in me" (Derrida, 2005, p. 129). It is not an easy task for anybody to take absolute risks, disturb one's comfort with history, or jeopardize expected positive outcomes in the future, because it requires deviating from the known past, rewarding social expectations, and documented methodological approaches. Aporia of responsibility can create what Derrida (2005) called "tragic pains" (p.129) related to feeling contradicted, insufficient, and unsatisfied. However, Derrida explained that these tragic pains can be productive by enabling action, decision, and resistance to fate.

How to carry on responsibilities at the time of uncertainty?

Researchers are always constituted within a tradition, and they continue to be a part of tradition at the same time that they might be capable of rupturing and changing traditions by not responding to its call for duty or not following its rules. Similarly, researchers' responsibility toward methodology is dual, including desires to sustain and revise simultaneously. The duality of responsibility acknowledges tradition and historical development of methods, but it also asks researchers to move beyond strict, theoretically, and methodologically bounded and controlled knowledge (see also Egéa-Kuehne (2003). Dual duty in the context of methodology does not imply that researchers ought to ignore legacy, tradition, existing knowledge, or previously established methods; rather, scholars could shift legacy and resituate or re-create tradition from within their discourses and disciplines.

In your own research, you could:

- Find ways in which ruptures to existing methodological traditions can be productive and stimulating
- Think about ways in which working both within and against methodological traditions might create a productive paradoxical space
- Consider how taking "absolute risks" could be done collectively with collaborators and research partners

Similarly, Derrida (1999, 2001b) argued that decisions are primed by knowledge and information, history and heritage. However, Derrida encouraged individuals, and in this context also researchers, to go beyond existing knowledge to the unknown. Derrida (1999) expressed, "We have to know as much as possible in order to ground our decision. But even if it is grounded in knowledge, the moment I make a decision it is a leap, I enter a heterogeneous space" (p. 73). There is always a context for decision making, but one cannot analyze the context to exhaustion; context remains open at the time of decision because there is something still to come and still to be identified. Derrida (2002) made multiple references to the leap of faith in his discussions on responsibility and decision making. This leap to the unknown, impossible passage, and aporia associated with responsibility are also described by Derrida (2002) as "profession[s] of faith." In the context of qualitative inquiry, the process of facing the methodologically impossible, struggling with inquiry, and getting messy with methodology becomes both the center and decenter of qualitative researchers' methodological work. Or alternatively, it may be one of the key considerations for the scholars who wish to work from the critical theoretical and philosophical frameworks. The acknowledgment of the impossibility of "getting methodologies right" exposes researchers to responsibility toward the Other—other ways of knowing, other methodologies, and other research approaches.

> Each time one must invent, not without a concept but by exceeding the concept each time, without any guarantee or certainty. This obligation can only be double, contradictory or conflictual, from the moment it calls for a responsibility and not for a moral or political technique. (Derrida, 2001a, p. 70)

BRILLIANT CHAPTER! I hope every researcher can read this!
—Jason

These uncertain and hesitant moves above and beyond normative discourses and possible reductionist approaches to research, data collection, and analysis are challenging but necessary shifts and conditions for methodological work at a time of overpoliticized and colonizing educational research.

Researchers' Responsibilities to Come

When reading Derrida, I began to imagine what could be gained by questioning clear, detached, objectified, purely technical or epistemologically smooth paths to inquiry and methodology. Britzman's (1997) question—"Can research be a mode of thought that refuses to secure itself with the consolations of foundationalism and the 'nostalgia of presence'?" (p. 36) —could be asked repeatedly across traditions and disciplines. Additionally, I would like to query what spaces of critique in the context of methodology could look like if they reformulate how methodologies are presented, used, and taught in academic contexts. Or how can one think innovatively and disruptively about how "users" of educational research can be informed and educated about complex methods and methodologies? Maybe it would be worthwhile to ask another question inspired by Derrida: What could be gained by thinking of methodology as methods without a project in which researchers are resisting "knowing the method" to complete and conclude their research? Derrida described pedagogy without a project as a struggle to hold open a space for noninstrumental thinking and action that might be filled with economical, scientific, or technological concerns.

> In Derrida's terms, it is a matter of constantly disrupting the model of product or project which, at its deepest, involves disrupting any tendency to think of ourselves as projects moving toward completion. Indeed, it undermines any thought of the self as a completed or complete-able being. (O'Byrne, 2005, p. 406)

What could be gained by not considering oneself as a researcher or one's research as completed or even completable? Or maybe we should engage more in what Derrida (1999) called "close readings" by reading events, analyzing situations, criticizing, and listening to various rhetoric, discourses, and individual and collective narratives. These close readings could possibly sensitize scholars to other ways of conducting research within those traditions that are unknown to them, and scholars might be able to create other points of reference regarding research standards and the legitimacy of scientific inquiry.

The moment I conclude that I am responsible for writing this section, I have created limits to my responsibility, simultaneously erasing my responsibilities. Thus, I would rather imagine methodological responsibility without knowing its constitutive limits. According to Evink (2009), there will not be a moment that responsibilities have come to an end.

I have written this book. I have finished my duty, completed my task, and followed the rules.

And? Or?

Have I been responsible? Have I taken on responsibility? Have I made urgent decisions without a clear path to be taken? Have I taken action now not later?

Many seemingly apparent decisions, only few urgent decisions, maybe no decisions at all but creativity processes, flow, undecidability

Does my responsibility begin when you open this book?

Does it end with the last words on these pages?

Does my responsibility extend beyond the limits of this book,

this writing project, and these texts?   Beyond your reading? Beyond you?

Far beyond me?

Where is responsibility?

Can it be located or recognized only

in the process itself?

still ongoing and becoming

No responsibility and all responsibility   all at once

Since a part of my responsibility is to stay open to otherness (critique, readers' responses, additional student comments, etc.), respond to the urgency, and rupture my "author/creator authority," this project cannot be concluded or my responsibility cannot be claimed. Instead, in my everyday actions and discussions about methodology and qualitative research, I continue to create new spaces for these texts, research, practice, and reflection that enable urgent responses and immediate actions, not only now but also, more importantly, in the future. Future research spaces, carried about responsibly, can also enable colleagues, students, and practitioners, among others, to speak for and act on complex and situated research "realities" that cannot be prepared for or calculated ahead of time.

Finally, the Other within a researcher and others is always coming and unanticipated in its coming. We ought to prepare for this coming of the unknown and the Other also in the context of methodology. The moment we are asked to only and exclusively complete our duties as researchers, or when we begin to feel certain about our research choices and conclusions, we lose the openness to the Other and avert theoretical and methodological responsibility. Lather (2008) asked qualitative researchers to put multiple othernesses to work and keep moving to circumvent dogmas and reductionism upon perceived arrival. Methodological responsibility can enable researchers to put othernesses to work without hesitation, reservation, qualification, or judgment and to set in motion new thinking about theoretical and methodological possibilities within educational research. Besides, some methodological possibilities could be created through conceptual and theoretical hazard, unpredictability, ambiguity, and the spontaneity of our relation to theories, epistemologies, and educational policies and practices. It might be unwise for educational researchers not to practice close readings, return to responsibility, and hold open spaces for incompleteness and complexity within methodologies and themselves. Where is your responsibility?

READING LIST OF LIFE

Faulkner, W. (1990). *As I lay dying*. Vintage Books.

Lowry, L. (1993). *The giver*. Houghton Mifflin.

Wheatley, M. (2009). *Turning to one another: Simple conversations to restore hope to the future*. Berrett-Koehler.

BPTU/Shutterstock

7 Teaching and Learning the Unteachable

Pedagogies Matter

With Chandra Bowden

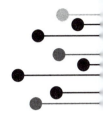

We work   within and against

structures such as   teaching,   learning, and   curriculum.

We stumble, stutter, reverse, return, and enter.

We have more than one

(method, student, teacher, content, goal . . .)

and

we are more than one!

To orient our readers, we begin by questioning how and what is (un)teachable in qualitative research. By *teachable*, we mean that part of qualitative research that can be learned though delivery-based, preconstructed forms of learning. We also consider how our past forms of being/knowing/teaching/learning influence what is (un)teachable, and where teaching takes place. In this section we utilize three main thinking devices (ghosts, events, and erasure) to process thoughts, materials, experiences, and memories associated with learning and teaching qualitative research in potentially less normative ways. These thinking devices come in the form of demonstrations—pedagogical experimentations if you will—experimentations as we have experienced them, as influenced by others, lived events and moments, and institutional structures and expectations. More specifically, we think with ghosts (borrowing from Marx and Derrida), through events (borrowing from Deleuze), and we resist institutional structures by placing writing and one potential curriculum for qualitative methodology "under erasure" (borrowing from Derrida).

I think you've raised questions that touch the heart of what it means to teach and to learn, because it suggests that to do either of these things well, one must know oneself and one's students rather intimately. A luxury often not available in a three-hour block once a week. How can you provide relevant or familiar stories and events that speak to people you barely know?

—Darby

I like the notion of "ghost" here. How often do we think about the fact that in using theories conceptualized by mostly dead people, we are actually collaborating with ghosts, or "duppies," as we call them in Jamaica.

I also like the word "haunting" here. Sometimes I wonder if we have become slaves to these "duppies/ghosts." We have subjected ourselves to their ways of thinking in the sense that we use their lenses to analyze data; we use their lenses to design research, sometimes with such precision that we find ourselves asking, "What would [name of ghost here] think?"

—Cheryl

Ghosts

We talk with the ghost and introduce our (pedagogical) ghosts. For us, teaching/learning is teaching/learning with **ghosts**: specters of past thinkers, texts, pedagogists, teachers, and forms of ourselves. We teach/learn *with* the past but not necessarily *in* the past. The past is with us in its **haunting** and pervasive forms but not in ways that necessarily close our options, release us from Derridian responsibility, or force us to follow established patterns and traditions. Rather, haunting and pervasive forces of past scholarship, research, theorizing, history, and dialogue shape our presence and absence. Our questions, negotiations, writings, and practices are shaped by the specters of other thoughts, writers, texts, and theories as well as the ghosts of anticipated readers. The presence and memories of other learnings, teachers, and students; imagined conversations with theorists; and conversations with ourselves about others who talk back to us linger and stay with us. "There are always there, specters, even if they do not exist, even if they are no longer, even if they are not yet" (Derrida, 2006, p. 221).

Events

We will think of pedagogy and learning through events: events of learning, teachers' delivery, and students' adaptation; feelings of satisfaction; senses of knowing, resistance, pleasure, desire, and refusal; and events of other kinds. In the second part of this section, we share some pedagogical events as processes, as a series of interconnected events. We intensify some events and speed up others, whereas many other events stay unapproached and also undocumented and unreported. Student events connect with teacher events, student–teacher events are becoming, and classroom events emerge unexpectedly, creating forces and vibrations. Williams (2011) drew from Deleuze's use of events when describing every event as an internal force and vibration between series of events. "The event is openness and chance in the present" (p. 90).

Curriculum Under Erasure

We work within and against institutional expectations and structures. In this case, we focus on three particular aspects of the structure, namely, curriculum, knowledge, and skill domains. To illustrate the indefinite deferral, the escape of origins, and stable signifiers, we use these terms, but we also want to note how these labels and ideas turn against themselves and illustrate the otherness within (i.e., within curriculum, knowledge, skills, and possibilities, and within questioning). We mark this turn by placing text and labels "under erasure." We hope this move helps us and our readers to be ontologically careful, avoiding the "totality" of these texts and the "essence" of these concepts.

GLOSSARY

Teaching. Messy (Waite, 2014).

Teaching. Always unfinished (Waite, 2014).

Teaching. Impossible (Biesta, 1998).

Teaching. Profession where we can "be sure beforehand of achieving unsatisfying results" (Sigmund Freud, as quoted in Biesta, 1998).

Teaching. Guiding change and transformation (Laroche & Roth, 2009).

Teaching. Being changed and transformed (Laroche & Roth, 2009).

Teaching. Balance between technique, attitude, and the art of applying method (Flick & Bauer, 2004).

Learning. Being changed and transformed (Laroche & Roth, 2009).

Learning. Doing (Flick & Bauer, 2004).

The Impossible. Cannot be conceived (Biesta, 1998).

The Impossible. Cannot be predicted (Biesta, 1998).

The Impossible. Releases the possible (Beardsworth, 1996).

Section key points:

- Learning and teaching (qualitative research methodology) often happen in a space of uncertainty and unknowing.

- Creative and continuously changing methodologies cannot be mastered (through a traditional sense of mastering, examination, and external evaluation).

- Teaching and learning always occur in the presence of others and ghosts (of the past).

- Qualitative research curricula may be necessary and at the same time inaccurate, misleading, and limiting in teaching students to view the world and carry out research in responsible and ethical ways.

Teaching Through the Teachable Past and Transferable Experiences

For better or worse, many texts have been published about what is teachable in qualitative research. The most prominent literature related to research methodologies focuses on "how to" effectively teach research methods to students (Early, 2014), using tools such as poetry (Raingruber, 2009) and technological learning objects (Raddon, Raby, & Sharpe, 2009) to "help teach" data coding. Teachers are also instructed "how to" use reflection to teach qualitative research and are challenged to respond to the call to create a pedagogical culture on teaching research methods (Wagner, Garner, & Kawulich, 2011). Qualitative research "training" has become overly focused on teaching the content of methodologies (McAllister, 2003). Methodologists are too often seen as technocrats and technicians who reproduce existing methods in sanitary ways. **This institutional and professional position may cause qualitative research courses to become even more technical, focusing on uncritical use of tools and execution of research approaches.**

> What does it mean to be "teachable"? How does "unteachableness" manifest itself?

It is no surprise, then, that students have also come to expect that qualitative research courses will teach them "how to" conduct qualitative research in a linear and quite simplistic manner. For example, Llamas and Boza (2011) analyzed syllabi from five doctoral programs and interviewed 11 students to understand how these courses prepared students for their dissertation work. Students noted that the main functions of their methodology courses were to teach them "how to" conduct research, expose them to diverse research methods, and to help them plan their research projects. Students also noted that these courses were useful in equipping them with the foreknowledge of "mental structuring" (p. 83) that is necessary to conduct research. Students most valued their methods courses that oriented them toward the subject matter they were studying and provided bibliographic material.

> *After being immersed in the somewhat uncomfortable tension between theory and application throughout my introduction to qualitative research, I had the distinct feeling of being robbed of a scholarly heirloom when my data analysis course instructor failed to mention even once that one ought to think about WHY they're doing what they're doing rather than focusing on the lockstep march of someone else's process and the prize of publication. Something in my mind had to fight to stay alive in that class, and as for my peers, perhaps they'll never know what they were denied.*
>
> —Darby

Many normative discourses in qualitative research methods rarely consider topics that have no definitive boundaries, such as (un)teachable, (un)learning, (un)knowing. Instead, these discourses amplify divisive issues centered on the "us" versus "them," "qualitative versus quantitative," and "inductive versus deductive" dilemmas and dichotomies. Next we will elaborate on some of these dilemmas to illustrate examples of potential resistance and argumentative structures that teachers of qualitative research might face when trying to teach qualitative research differently and outside simplistic and technical practices.

Dilemma 1: Qualitative Research Occurs "Here" or "There"

Can the teachable within qualitative research be delivered across disciplines, or is what is teachable discipline specific? According to Llamas and Boza (2011), doctoral studies are distinct from master's and professional studies due to their focus on research. There are educators who argue that research methodology courses need to be discipline specific because they reflect current disciplinary practices and norms (Welch & Panelli, 2003) and eliminate any attempt to present research methods as generic (Lorenz, 2003). From a pragmatic perspective, it may be beneficial to teach methodology courses with a specific discipline focus, as students may already have personal interests in the subject matter and professors are already invested in teaching the content (Bridges, Gillmore, Pershing, & Bates, 1998). But is this an acceptable solution to a logistical issue, or does it cause additional dilemmas and raise further questions?

Departments that do not want to expend resources replicating research methodology courses that are already taught in other departments at the institution end up outsourcing nearly all their research training (Benton, Androff, Barr, & Taylor, 2012). This may be advantageous for students, as they are exposed to epistemologies and theoretical frameworks that may be different from their own, but it is also risky, as there may be less epistemological compatibility (e.g., in terms of theoretical perspectives), logistical compatibility (e.g., students may be placed on a waiting list), or assurance that students will be exposed to how certain methodologies are utilized within their own disciplines (Benton et al., 2012). Is there a right way to approach course development and instructional resources?

> In my opinion, quantitative research is a science . . . technical application of steps/methods. Qualitative research is an art . . . possibly unteachable but definitely learnable.
>
> —Cheryl

Dilemma 2: Qualitative Research Methods as Luxury or Necessity

In many academic departments, quantitative research methods are privileged as "essential," while qualitative research methods are marginalized as **"luxury"** (Morse, 2005). Consequently, if qualitative research courses are seen as "luxury," fewer resources will be allocated to these courses, which, in turn, is likely to create a need to cover the complex field and diverse practices in more simplified ways and potentially in a shorter time. As a result, some qualitative research methods courses, particularly introductory courses, are packed with a lot of information without giving time to study methodologies more deeply. For example, Hein (2004) stated that the topics of his introductory course include qualitative and quantitative paradigms commonly used with qualitative methodologies, ethical issues in qualitative inquiry, designing qualitative research, formulating research questions, participant selection, interviewing and other forms of data, analyzing data, writing up qualitative findings, and evaluating qualitative research. We wonder whether there are necessary topics or required qualitative research skills, and if so, for whom?

Dilemma 3: Qualitative Research Methods May Be Personally Favored but Socially Marginalized

When students express interest in qualitative research, some of them may risk marginalization. For example, four recently graduated PhD students applied an autoethnographic approach to analyze their experiences as qualitative researchers at four different departments of social work (Benton et al., 2012). First, students reported that marginalization occurred because of the structure of the doctoral program. There were no research methodology courses offered in their home departments, which limited their access to knowledgeable and supportive faculty within their discipline (Benton et al., 2012). Second, marginalization occurred because of the opinions of influential people (namely professors) within the department. Statements asserting that students completing qualitative dissertations were not marketable, as well as public praise of the departmental "Quant Jock," perpetuated feelings of loneliness and isolation. The Quant Jock is the "cool" graduate student in right standing with faculty and a representation of the type of student that departments often want to produce. This student moves quickly through the graduate program, learns complex statistics, develops a dissertation based on a large quantitative dataset, and secures a tenure-track position at another elite university once he or she graduates (Benton et al., 2012). Often students with qualitative research interests find that they are indeed pursuing dual research paths, where the quantitative portion satisfies departmental expectations and the qualitative portion satisfies *them* (Benton et al., 2012). Are these practices needed as a sort of survival strategy?

Learning With(out) Teachable Teaching

To highlight situated methodologies and creativity in research, some scholars have argued that qualitative research can be seen as a **craft** (Wolcott, 1994) and a bricolage (Kincheloe, 2001; Lévi-Strauss, 1966). When research is viewed as a craft or a kind of trade, it calls for facilitation that is practice oriented and can provide a variety of skills, tools, perceptives, and theories that can be applied differently in different situations. Often these skills are something that has been passed to others (i.e., future professionals) through more or less normative social processes of acceptance and craftsmanship, often outside artificial classroom settings (Hurworth, 2008). In other words, some skills may be learned through example, whereas others one may need to be invented by the learners themselves. Where does this leave teaching and learning?

For example, to learn without being "officially" or systematically taught calls for openness and exposure but also attentiveness. Teachers and students are likely to share their knowledge by "doing" and "being," and by teaching and learning creatively in order to teach the unteachable (McAllister, 2003). Sharing and exposure to otherness within oneself and others is likely to promote attentiveness and critical reflection as well.

Alternatively, authentic learning opportunities may stimulate engagement and deep involvement with the content matter. According to Preissle and Roulston (2009), engagement in "authentic" research provides students the opportunity to learn about multiple facets of the qualitative research experience. Preissle and Roulston use three different types of authentic research experiences for their students: (1) supervised classroom projects, where a student's individual project is granted approval by the instructor (see also Hein, 2004); (2) individual projects, where students conduct research on projects that have gained IRB approval; and (3) authentic team projects, where an instructor gains IRB

Interesting terminology. Like "witchcraft," which, in the spirit of us-versus-them, qualitative-versus-quantitative discourses, is what many "purely" quantitative researchers seem to think I am doing when I talk to them about qualitative research. I am not rigorous, not scientific, not academic, but rather using magic to come up with what they would put in ironic quotes: "research."
—Becky

Robert Ulmer

approval of a class project and students present data findings to an end-user group. Authentic team projects are also likely to address and promote the role of ethics and responsibility in conducting qualitative research.

There is also a call for "being" as a researcher. "Being" allows the instruction of qualitative research to be more than directly transferred knowledge and how-to guides. It calls for research methods that are iterative, creative, and reflective, as this may best prepare an environment for effective qualitative research (O'Connor & O'Neill, 2004). From this perspective, "qualitative researchers" come in various types, forms, and temporary configurations, which, in turn, has an impact on the curriculum. Qualitative research methods curriculum could, for example, be more flexible, provide options for students' learning experiences, and emphasize analysis, writing, ethics, and rigor instead of mainly focusing on data collection (Hurworth, 2008).

Questioning *in lieu of* telling can also be an effective method of challenging both teachers' and students' fixed belief systems about methodology and the pedagogy of the methods. By not attempting to correct students or counter students' arguments, teachers could practice and promote aesthetic dissonance, feelings of indifference, and potential disagreement (Cooper & McNab, 2009). "A critical curriculum does not supply answers. It supplies questions" (Edelsky, 1999, p. 31). By questioning, both the teacher and student are stretched to expand beyond their current realm of knowledge and explore what was previously unknown. Obviously, not all students will be comfortable with this form of questioning, as it forces them to challenge what was deemed unchallengeable, unfixable, unlearnable. For example, in their context, Cooper and McNab (2009) took note of the students' discomfort, offered alternative suggestions to address these questions, and *waited*. The students came around and were able to question/challenge the very things that seemed unquestionable/unchallengeable. Questioning could allow students to begin with a local focus (i.e., thinking of their own story) and transition to a universal focus through sharing and experiencing the stories of others. This type of education may enable students to become citizens of the world (Freire, 1998).

Cook and Gordon (2004) discussed the difficulties in teaching qualitative research due to the complexity embedded within qualitative paradigms. They proposed that if students can make associations and connections with their own previous meanings and experiences, they might be better equipped to approach knowledge creative and imaginative ways. Hunt (2010), in turn, proposed that "active waiting," the balance between moving forward and fully developing one's ideas, is essential for qualitative researchers. Active waiting assists scholars in creating a space of critical reflection that can point to the possible deficits and unproductive presupposition arising from habits and **taken-for-granted practices**.

Harry Wolcott (1994), in turn, in his widely read text on teaching qualitative inquiry, referred to the "postholing" problem in qualitative research: a problem originating from the diversity of the field and practices, a problem that has to do with dealing with too much coverage and fast comprehension in too little time. Wolcott also preferred not to "teach" per se, since learning is out of teaching's reach, as it is more unpredictable and opportunistic. Instead, he explored conceptual and practical possibilities and approached a broad range of problems with his students to enable future qualitative researchers to cope with research situations that cannot be fully anticipated.

> *Seems like there is a happy medium in here somewhere. My background as a music teacher is always evident in some way when I teach. It is based on my experiences, and I use those experiences in contexts new and old. When I feel "lost" doing qualitative research, I still call upon my musical nature to help me navigate critical reflection.*
>
> —Becky

As illustrated previously, many wise teachers and pedagogists have envisioned, theorized, and documented teaching of qualitative research in the past. For example, previous suggestions to improve student experiences in methodology courses include extending the duration of the course (Bernauer, Semich, Klentzin, & Holden, 2013), teaching by example, adding more theory and hands-on activities, using play (Waite, 2011), increasing opportunities for student participation, using resources available through virtual classrooms, and increasing the coordination and communication between professors of differing methodology courses (Llamas & Boza, 2011).

We are not against these suggestions; however, we do recognize that these suggestions may not adequately address the deeper issues that haunt the teaching of qualitative research and learners interested in qualitative inquiry. We are not sure how to encourage students to be more patient with unknowing and move beyond their comfort zone, exercise creativity, and question taken-for-granted notions of scholarship and culture, or how to be comfortable with uncertainty. It seems to us that these notions associated with some forms of qualitative research are more attitudinal and motivational rather than directly driven by a discipline. Mechanical qualitative research and linear execution of research processes might be easy to teach, but complexity introduces uncertainty, and uncertainty often creates resistance both within learning and teaching.

How do you learn qualitative research?

How does your qualitative research practice provoke, stimulate, and impact your learning and teaching?

Banner and Cannon (1997) proposed that the basic elements of teaching are qualities that can rarely be taught. Instead they are "ingredients of our own humanity, to which contents and methods are adjunct. We must draw them from ourselves, identify, develop, and then apply" (Banner & Cannon, 1997, p. 2).

> *Teaching is a creative act,   a spontaneous process,*
>
> *and a set of improvised efforts and practices.*
>
> *Teaching and learning are   momentary,   situated, and*

full of infinite surprises.

Sometimes independent and

interactive uses of knowledge,

imaginative implementation,   and

the transference across contexts

could be

associated with   inspiring and   powerful   teaching/learning.

Furthermore, some pedagogists might favor scaffolding and modeling to teach the unteachable. Modeling the processes and practices can be helpful but also limiting. It seems that some students may be consumers of models rather than critical users of examples. We certainly have encountered students who do not know how to use examples in productive and inspiring ways, but they see examples as a way to reproduce the identical and the same. For example, when teaching, Mirka is careful when sharing examples, and she keeps reminding students that they should not copy the "original." Instead, students could focus on letting the examples show differences, particulars, and normative deviations. Similar to Shor (1992), Mirka encourages students to go deep and move beyond the visible and surface levels of their scholarship and research practice. When moving beyond the surface, students often notice that no knowledge is value free, and all-knowing is ultimately connected with power. Teachers become students and students become teachers, all in the shared temporary context and variable space. Sanchez and Barbour (2012) characterized teachers who approach teaching as a form of art as critical facilitators who are aware of hidden curriculum and complexities. When thinking about teaching as art, some teachers use their skills consciously, and they build from creative imagination. Sanchez and Barbour also highlighted the importance of enabling students to become critical thinkers and individuals who can identify and act upon various links between knowledge, power, and democracy.

What if we know all along that we cannot teach qualitative research?
Does this knowledge make qualitative research more teachable? Might acknowledgment of past influences on teaching and the complexities associated with teaching (qualitative research) release us from the pressure of the "correctness" and accuracy of teaching and thus make the unteachable teachable? We are not sure. Maybe this is a question of ethics and care of self (Foucault, 1986). More specifically, who am I to teach, and who am I to teach this way? Maybe teaching qualitative research is possible because we need to do it and impossible since we are not sure how to do it. From this position, every class,

session, and interaction with texts (content) and students is new. Decisions need to be made, and risks need to be taken. Sometimes lessons fail and interactions are less productive, but even the failed attempt moves learners and teachers somewhere.

Maybe learning and teaching is about movement—movement that sometimes appears smooth and fast and sometimes slow and stuttering.

Teaching With the Past: Some Ghost Stories

....

My work takes place between unfinished abutments and anticipatory strings of dots. I like to open out a space of research, try it out, then if it doesn't work try again somewhere else. On many points . . . I am still working and don't yet know whether I am going to get anywhere.

—Foucault, Burchell, Gordon, & Miller, 1991, pp. 73–74

Teaching (qualitative research) might be more about trying and connectivity. Waite (2014) and Mirka have argued that qualitative research is somewhat unteachable because it has many complexities and **uncertainties** and quite a bit of "unfinished episte-methodological business." At the same time, this space of "unteachable learning" is exactly where the productive contradictions and inspiring challenges lie. Unfinished structures, messy processes, complex relations, questionable hierarchies and assumptions, micro and macro politics, personal qualities and flaws, material environments, and so on influence teaching and learning in various ways (see also Waite, 2014). As stated earlier, learning and teaching qualitative research present unique challenges, since the field is very diverse and epistemologically dispersed, and qualitative research practices are often tailored and culturally situated. The use of any particular or singular teaching method or approach can easily prioritize or privilege some epistemologies and methods over the others in unproductive and constraining ways, thus shaping the ways in which students experience qualitative research activities and processes and ultimately how they view research. In addition, learning and teaching that are rigid and overly systematic tend to "produce" and create learners who are also rigid and overly systematic, and often operate within normative systems that are reproducing themselves.

Perhaps the idea is not to teach qualitative research but rather accommodate or facilitate the "mental structuring" or posturing necessary to carry out qualitative analysis. This becomes an unending process, because each project brings new experiences that bring about new learning. No one knows everything about qualitative research!

—Cheryl

Yes . . . but we have been socialized to be uncomfortable with uncertainty. This is problematic and perhaps one of the reasons the qualitative paradigm is frowned upon by the establishment!!!!

—Cheryl

Where does learning take place within methodological discourses and practices?

How can one avoid reproducing oneself within existing normative and hierarchical systems? Let's consider some potential strategies for critical reflection and pedagogical movement. Derrida viewed ghosts and haunting as a necessary element in every hierarchical system. Sometimes ghosts are associated with unspoken rules, or undocumented traditions, that influence particular people and haunt others. "Haunting belongs to the structure of every hegemony" (Derrida, 2006, p. 46). However, it is impossible to know what the mode of presence of a ghost or specter is, what the being of the specter is, or what questions the ghost will pose at any given time. Haunting and ghosts appear unexpectedly, and their impact and influence are impossible to predict.

Living with ghosts . . .

Do you?   Will you? Can you?

We do. We can. We will.

Again and again.

We live with our ghosts

who shape our teaching and pedagogy.

We have spectral conversations about many things

including learning qualitative research.

We also talk to our own ghosts . . . have long spectral conversations between ourselves and ghosts

about pedagogy.

As we enter

into simultaneous space of absence and presence in pedagogy

We are called to rethink   "where"   and   "what"

is being excluded in these texts and examples.

The ghosts

of our teachers in us

and spirits of us in our teachers

are all here.   And simultaneously nowhere.

We envision that a ghost has a virtual, absent body and thus is also **absently present**. Ghosts are with us, but they are not in their physicality. They are with us as personified thoughts and visions. Similarly, teaching and learning are not things or objects per se, but they can be seen as productions by the ghosts, illusions, and appearances. Sometimes we merely appear to learn and teach. Maybe teaching and learning are not about living or death, present or absent per se, but they become evident and project our hovering between past and becoming. Teaching and learning may not have ontology, essence, or a stable form of being, but they could be encountered through performative interpretations (interpretations that transform what is being interpreted). What becomes possible then?

> I call it "power in absentia."
> —Cheryl

Ghosts and various other forms of the past are often present during learning. It is possible that ghosts direct our learning and teaching in a manner similar to the ways in which those with flesh and material presence interact with us. Past learning (memories, senses, images, texts, etc.) shapes the present, and absences (things unlearned and lives not lived) are always present. Derrida (2006) argued that it may always be necessary to learn with spirits and ghosts. He encourages us to involve ghosts in our learning, to live with ghosts and in their companionship. This learning through living with ghosts would also involve working through cultural and pedagogical inheritance and engaging with the politics of memory. Next, I share some ghost conversations with ghosts that have played a significant role in the ways in which I approach pedagogy and teaching qualitative research.

A Conversation About Teaching the Unteachable (With the Ghost of a Critical Friend [GOCF])

GOCF: *I don't think you can ever teach thinking, theorizing, or values (e.g., epistemological diversity and equity), since these are experiences of different forms of living. Can you teach living?*

Mirka: *I am not sure, but through my living I am also teaching. Teaching in living, living in teaching. Learning in living, living in learning. I live my life through qualitative research, and qualitative research lives me. Does that make sense?*

GOCF: *No—I don't follow. Can you explain?*

Mirka: *Teaching and learning can be seen as forms of living, and when I live I also teach and learn in various ways. When I refer to teaching as living, I do not mean to diminish the role of teacher training or teacher education. Quite the contrary. To become "educated to teach," and to become a skilled, informed, aware, and present teacher, one needs to be attentive to life and cultural complexities, nuances, problems, relationships, dilemmas, and uncertainties of living, since learning is a part of living and vice versa. Yet I am not sure how to teach living or different approaches to life. How do I teach one to live life in meaningful and humble ways? How do I teach teaching or teach the unteachable in meaningful and open-ended ways? How do I make informed choices if there are no clear paths to be taken (I see the ghost of Derrida again)? How do I teach others to live qualitative research, philosophies, or theories? How do I help students see how qualitative research lives through them? Through examples and discussions, maybe. I am not sure.*

GOCF: *This still does not make sense. Do you mean that teaching or learning about qualitative research is about learning to live socially?*

Mirka: *In some ways, yes. It is about learning to live with multiplicity (of theories, methods, approaches, cultures, individuals, roles, etc.), uncertainty (associated with unknowing and methodological adaptation), and complexity (complexity of social phenomena, experiences, understandings, etc.). And during this process of learning to live, one has to think about ways to inquire (methodology) and live with or through methodology and research. Living in methodology, methodology in living. Still confused?*

GOCF: *Yes.*

In your own research, you could:

- Release the expectation to become an "expert" (of qualitative research or pedagogy)

- Explore connections between your lived experiences and your practice of research and pedagogy; deliberately draw connections between the (dis)similar and (un)familiar

- Engage in regular research methods "coffee chats" where you share your experiences, feelings, and reactions and the connections between your research methods and your life

- Keep a reflection journal chronicling when and how you experience the convergence of "life" and "research"

A Conversation About Learning the Unteachable (With the Ghost of a Former Instructor [GOFI])

GOFI: *You know, I was disappointed, Chandra, when you first told me you were leaving the natural sciences to study qualitative methods in social science.*

Chandra: *I know. I remember you telling me to stick with "real science" and that I was too gifted to waste my time on a fluffy pseudoscience discipline. I was surprised at your unfiltered honesty. I considered you a mentor.*

GOFI: *But you didn't listen.*

Chandra: *No. My dissertation chair resigned, and I needed to find a new home. I didn't know what I was getting into when I transferred departments, but the leap was worth it— though I am not certain I landed on my feet, or if that was the ultimate purpose of the decision.*

GOFI: *What are you saying?*

Chandra: *Well, much like this dissertation experience, I consider/ plan the route of my journey not knowing that I will reach the destination I originally planned. I prepare, but along the way I learn, unlearn, understand, misunderstand, expand, retreat in my knowledge, and need to make changes accordingly.*

GOFI: *It sounds like backtracking.*

Chandra: *Perhaps. But is that necessarily bad? Backtracking is not about going backward; it's about reaching newer/deeper levels of understanding/knowing/unknowing while (un) learning along the way.*

In your own research, you could:

- Make comparisons and note differences in your sense-making/ understanding from before and after each research detour
- Find critical friends who will listen and support your nonnormative methodological choices

A Conversation About Theory and
Writing (With the Ghost of Bettie St. Pierre [GOBSP])

Mirka: *Dear Bettie, you talk directly and indirectly to me during every paper I write and every class I teach, especially when I talk about the role of theory in qualitative research, my scholarship, and my life. You and images of your bookshelves overburdened and extended with theory and philosophy books haunt me. You make me read again, return to the text, not claiming to understand, but to reinteract again and again. You call me out. You inspire me to read with theorists, live through theorists, live with theorists. Bettie, who is smart, and when are they smart?*

GOBSP: *Read, read, read. Read without "understanding," or clarify. Read hard texts, read difficult texts; let impossible, uncomprehendable and sometimes unreadable texts wash over you. Stay with the text.*

Mirka: *I try and I also ask my students to try. I try (did I say it already?). We fail to understand and thus we may feel frustrated with our desire to know, but we move, change, and transform ourselves into something unknown, something that is still becoming. Bettie, who is smart, and when are they smart?*

GOBSP: *Think, think, think. Think hard questions and ask questions without seeking answers. Avoid oversimplifications or use simplifications tactically and purposefully. Use examples and think in examples.*

Mirka: *Easier said than done. Examples diversify and deviate. Examples bring forward new connections. Through examples, a thought shifts and alters simultaneously.*

GOBSP: *One more thing. Write. Write yourself into the text. Write every day. Think through writing. Think about writing as a method of inquiry. I think you know this already.*

> *Maybe Mirka's ghost visits me when I have to write and keep a research (or personal) journal. I find it a difficult task. I have 17 volume series of thoughts in my head that hide when it is time to put them to paper. They came to haunt me in your class when we had to keep a methodological journal. It was torturous until I took a leaf from my own book (remember when you discussed earlier in this chapter about previous experiences and active waiting?) and wrote my journal as a narration of photos (set to music, of course). Then— writing became accessible.*
>
> *—Becky*

Mirka: *Maybe. I write every day and ask my students to write every day. I write until writing is no longer a burden but a horrible pleasure. I write hoping that writing will come to a happy joint, curious stop—until the next time. I write with many ghosts, through the ghosts, and through the voices of my ghosts. I write myself into our texts, shared past, and into our ghosts. Where my qualitative research ends and your theoretical voice begins is impossible to tell. Your words, my words, and words of others blend. My texts have always already been written elsewhere.*

In your own research, you could:

- View writing as inquiry; something that will always stay unfinished and moving
- **Commit to uninterrupted writing every day**
- Maintain all previous versions of text and periodically reread and edit what you've previously written
- View peer reviews as an opening and an opportunity to make your text "stronger" and more accessible

A Conversation About Theoretical Perspectives (With the Ghost of Michael Crotty [GOMC])

Mirka: *I have used your book* Foundations of Social Research *for over 10 years now as one of the main texts in my Introduction to Qualitative Research class. Most often I find students overwhelmed, and they resist being introduced to philosophy. Some of them report that they can't understand a word you say and that they can't wait until we have finished your book and can move on to more "practical aspects" of the course.*

GOMC: *It is interesting how "hard" my quite simple introduction to different theoretical perspectives can seem. I assume that you are encouraging students to co-read my text along with dictionaries and other supplementary texts? Do you paraphrase, scaffold, or let students figure it out on their own?*

Mirka:	*All of the above. I not only encourage co-readings, but I also emphasize the usefulness of reading and writing groups, annotated bibliographies, all kinds of glossaries, and different forms of note taking. Understanding what one is reading and being able to apply theories and theoretical perspectives is one of the most challenging tasks—maybe even sometimes an impossible one—when learning qualitative research.*
GOMC:	*True. Additionally, learning about different theoretical perspectives may challenge students' (neopositivist) notions about research, science, and life. This stuff (philosophy and theory) can be very transforming if students open up a space for it and they allow theory do its (unanticipated) job.*
Mirka:	*I have also heard from the students that your book is one book they keep returning to, especially after they have gained some distance from it. Students return to your text throughout their dissertation work, but also later in their work as researchers and professionals. Your text takes time to process. I love it. No piecemeal or readily digested packages. Reading (without understanding everything) is hard work.*
GOMC:	*I know. It is also hard from the teaching perspective to choose which texts, theorists, and philosophies to introduce and include in my book. Many theoretical perspectives and influential authors are left out, especially since all perspectives are always incomplete in their diversity and complexity. Theories also evolve fast, and theoretical ideas need continual revising and updating.*

A Monologue About Passion for Qualitative Research (With the Ghost of Jude Preissle [GOJP])

This conversation is a monologue (in the presence of Jude's ghost, who at this time is only listening, not talking back) about passion to live one's life as a qualitative researcher. It is not about the meaning of passion or how to conceptualize living and loving qualitative research, but this monologue is about doing—more specifically, what happened or what I think happened when I engaged in doing qualitative research with Jude Preissle, and how "I's" (various versions of me within and across qualitative research tradition) were created.

I knew a little bit about qualitative research prior to my travels to Athens, Georgia, but in retrospect I was very novice in so many different ways. I was not attached to qualitative inquiry even though I had practiced it. I did not know about the multiplicities, rigor, creativity, and excitement associated with qualitative research practices. Jude, you showed me how to engage and love qualitative work! I was ready to be contaminated and infected by scholarship that spoke different language, scholarship that cared and lit fires. When studying in Athens, I audited your classes (often the same ones) numerous times, to learn the content but also to grow as a teacher. During those classes, not only did my knowledge of theories and qualitative inquiry expand, but also my awareness of different aspects of scholarship in general grew. No two of your classes were identical. Every lesson was new, and I learned something different about qualitative research each time. I looked forward to your classes, Jude, since they moved me personally and they deeply impacted the ways I viewed inquiry! I heard about novels as dissertations and learned tips about how to get your paper accepted at AERA—wow. You taught qualitative research with your mind and body moving between experiences, content, emotions, advice, and critique. You deeply cared about qualitative research and helped us to care on our own. You care, Jude!

I remember struggling with language, and not only with English language. I also had to study and learn the language and terminology associated with qualitative research and philosophy. Jude, you are a patient teacher! Tediously and carefully you corrected my use of terminology as well as English grammar at the same time that you encouraged me to speak and share my experiences. Sometimes you used red ink to indicate your voice within my text, and you always wrote lengthy and detailed comments about the strengths and weaknesses of my work. You encouraged your students to form writing and reading groups, which again pushed my thinking and learning and my knowledge about myself. There were groups, panels, conferences, writing retreats to provide an introduction to the life of scholars. You live qualitative research, Jude!

Not only did you listen, but you also shared. You talked about your life as a scholar, qualitative researcher, and writer. You shared examples from your ongoing projects and talked about your book collections when we visited your home. Jude, you exemplified how to live one's life as a qualitative researcher and how to love every day of doing this work. I listened, and I remember being fascinated by your experiences and vast knowledge. For you, and later for me, research became inseparable from living and life. Personal life blended with professional ambitions, sometimes creating harmony and sometimes resistance. Through your presentations, lectures, class assignments, images, texts, and persona, you colored qualitative research in positive and inspiring colors. Inquiry became inviting. Inquiry became personal and approachable. Inquiry became you, and you became inquiry. These epistemological moves became fatal. There was no return or escape. Thank you, Jude!

Curriculum Events and the Erasure of a Ghost Curriculum[1]

In our everyday work within and outside the classroom, we work for and against teaching and learning, for and against structures like language, labels, curricula, core competencies, and basic skills. **As illustrated in this subsection, we sometimes use language that is necessary yet inaccurate, language and labels that represent and resist, appear and disappear, and create assumed conceptual linearity while twisting and breaking up the linearity.** To illustrate this ongoing paradox associated with working, writing, and reading with and against pedagogy and curriculum, we have put most of this subsection under erasure. For Spivak (1997), drawing from Derrida, to put something under erasure is to write it and then cross it out, still printing and showing both the insertion and deletion. Spivak wrote, "In examining familiar things we come to such unfamiliar conclusions that our very language is twisted and bent even as it guides us. Writing 'under erasure' is the mark of this contortion" (p. xiv). In this context, our use of labels such as core curriculum, common experiences, skill domains, and so forth are put under erasure to indicate their departure from stable signifier–signified connection and to illustrate labels' inevitable traces and the presence of other labels. We also use these partial deletions, deletions that do not delete, to mark "betweenness" and "undecidedness." We let concepts such as curriculum and core competencies go as soon as they are introduced because we want to bring them to readers' attention, but simultaneously also desire to delete these signifiers that we find inaccurate and often unnecessary and overly controlling. Derrida (1997) talked about signs being under erasure, since they are always ill named. In the following passages, we use different labels to express our ill-named conceptualizations of curriculum, content, skills, disciplines, and so on.

Many qualitative researchers have experienced and continue living within systems guided by the discourses of scientific rigor, accountability, exclusiveness, and conservatism—discourses that portray qualitative research as a discipline belonging to everybody and nobody. These discourses often portray qualitative research as overly simplistic and nonscientific. We may have heard from our colleagues or administrators that everybody is qualified and capable of teaching, learning, and practicing qualitative research, since the skills required are intuitive and maybe unsophisticated and qualitative research is mostly about interviewing, coding, and categorizing. At the same time, nobody

> *I used to see inaccurate language as an obstacle, because it made me question what I knew or could even learn; however, I've come to see it as a necessary scaffold to hold me close enough to the process that I no longer get caught up in it. How can we be honest with our students about the purpose of teaching inaccurately to open a door to the unteachable?*
> —Darby

---

1. All texts with a strikethrough indicate erasure as a representation of the necessity and limitation of (1) labels and (2) the structure of curriculum.

(i.e., no qualitative methodologist) should or would need to teach qualitative research, and universities may not include qualitative research courses as part their curriculum or required research course sequence. In other words, everybody can teach qualitative research, but nobody (who has specialized in qualitative research) needs to. Naturally, both options will save universities financial resources.

Inspired by somewhat limited public conversations about what qualitative researchers and methodologists actually do (e.g., tasks, projects, techniques, responsibilities, relationship building) and what skills might be needed to carry out these tasks and projects, we developed some knowledge and skill domains that might be included or applied to learning modules and curriculum decisions if one was to think about teaching qualitative research in those terms.

A Conversation About the Curriculum (With the Ghost of a Colleague [GOC])

GOC: *Hey Mirka . . . do you have a minute?*

Mirka: *Sure.*

GOC: *I have wondered why our school does not have any core content or standardized curriculum shaping the learning experiences of those interested in qualitative research and interpretive/critical methodologies.*

Mirka: *I am not sure . . . maybe different scholars see the discipline of (qualitative) research and methodology very differently. Sometimes I wonder what would happen if our faculty and students agreed on some important or common experiences that all students taking qualitative courses should have. This might provide a sense of continuation regardless of instructors' preferences and staff changes. However, at the same time, I believe in teaching that is in flux and continuously adjusted based on learners' needs. Thus, I am afraid that ANY form or shape of curriculum that might be utilized in a standardized form and normative ways might be actually working against the work qualitative researchers do and desire to engage in. I am not quite sure what to do. A core curriculum that may include options or tracks, a core curriculum with differentiations and individual choice, or an individualized core curriculum? Or, simply, no curriculum at all? Just individual goals and objectives?*

GOC: *I have also wondered about the qualifications of the instructors. Who should or could teach qualitative research courses? Are qualitative research course instructors randomly assigned, or should one express interest or maybe have more intensive experiences in qualitative research than others?*

Mirka: *Of course, there is no right or single answer to this question. From my perspective, I would like to consider instructors' disciplinary emphasis and their relationship to the diversity embedded in qualitative research traditions and practices (i.e., if they use mostly qualitative methods themselves and if they have interest or experience in developing and advancing methodologies more broadly), past experience with methodological and epistemological diversity, and methodological curiosity. By methodological curiosity, I am referring to an attitude that values innovation and creativity when working with research and the importance of ongoing methodological learning and change. At the same time, there is not just one prototype of an instructor for a qualitative research class. I would like all instructors of qualitative researcher courses to push the limits of existing methodologies.*

GOC: *What about differences in the curriculum for those students planning to utilize qualitative methods (students focusing on required research courses) and those planning to develop and study methods (students having methodology as a major)?*

Mirka: *This is another point of tension, since some colleagues believe that all serious researchers are naturally methodologists. However, I see a difference in the responsibilities between a methodologist (mostly or solely focusing on methodology and methodological developments) and a researcher who is using qualitative research. Does this need to impact or change pedagogy and curriculum choices? Maybe or maybe not.*

GOC: *Furthermore, the idea that you put forward in the following tables seems quite structured and rigid.*

Mirka: *I agree, and since I am not sure I believe in highly structured curricula, I want to address both the* possibilities and impossibilities associated with these common domains. By the possibilities, I refer to some prospective benefits and different opportunities for personal and collective growth and professional development. And by the impossibilities, I point to potential ideological and practical dilemmas and questions associated with the domains. Therefore, the decision of whether these pedagogical structures presented are useful for the users of this book and their particular contexts needs to be determined by each reader.

Table 7.1 Knowledge and Skills Domains for Students Interested in Methodological Questions: A Proposition, Possibility, and Impossibility

Domain	Content proposition	Possibilities	Impossibilities
Theoretical foundations: Knowledge	Understands the epistemological history of qualitative research	Recognition of power, binaries, paradigm wars, epistemological preferences	Whose history?
	Understands the philosophies and current epistemological underpinnings and trends in qualitative research	Variety of philosophical and epistemological options	Breadth or depth?
	Understands how theories shape design and research activities	Thoughtful and purposeful design choices with awareness of theories' practical implications	What is theory?
Theoretical foundations: Skills and practice	Makes informed theoretical choices and knows how to use theories in purposeful ways	Increased theoretical awareness, utilization of theories	How to read unreadable and difficult texts? How to deal with "theory emotions" (e.g., theory fear)?
	Is capable of discussing the role of theory and philosophy in qualitative research in sophisticated ways	Sharing and communication	How does familiar or strange language work?
	Applies different theories in different contexts	Stronger links between theory and practice, impact of theories	How to teach and learn creativity and adaptation?

Domain	Content proposition	Possibilities	Impossibilities
Methods: Knowledge	Understands the methodological history of qualitative research	Methods cannot be separated from discourses, power, and practices of domination	Whose history? Trendy methods?
	Gains knowledge about different methodological traditions and practices	Respect toward different ways of knowing, tailored methodological applications	Where to start and when to end?
	Understands methodological alignment (connections between theory, research questions, design)	Informed and consistent methodological choices	What about blurred genres? Undesirable alignment?
	Understands the situatedness of methods and research approaches	Cultural appropriateness and personal preferences	What is culture? Who am I to study this?
	Understands how to adapt methods and modify practices	Avoidance of uncritical methodological uses, increased methodological responsiveness	How to teach and learn creativity and adaptation?
	Understands how data can be constructed/viewed differently depending upon traditions and epistemologies	Critical reconceptualization of what constitutes/ functions as data	Working against prevailing grand narratives and neoliberal discourses
	Understands different and situational evaluation criteria for qualitative research articles, proposals, and projects	Diversity of legitimized and culturally acceptable evaluation and rigor	How to move beyond normativity and episte-methodological preference?
Methods: Skills and practice	Uses methodologies and methods creatively and critically	Methodological adaptation and multiplication	How to teach and learn creativity and constructive criticality?
	Practices different "validation" strategies and evaluation approaches	Movement away from solely external validation; gaining experience in doing validation and evaluation across different epistemological traditions	Whose validity or validation? Or no validity at all?

(Continued)

Table 7.1 (Continued)

Domain	Content proposition	Possibilities	Impossibilities
	Gains practice in most common data collection and analysis processes, including narrative, discursive, visual, and performative forms	Experiential learning, learning through senses	What are common methods and methodologies?
	Designs studies from different theoretical perspectives	Theoretical diversity	Is theoretical diversity desirable?
	Demonstrates and carries out in-depth analytical practices within one method/approach and within multiple methods	Deeper insights, experience with layered analysis processes	How deep is deep? What will depth bring?
	Involves participants and community members in methodological decision making	Works against separation between academia and public	Whose time? Whose resources? The role of social capital?
	Practices writing and presenting methodologically focused texts and articles	Adds to the methodological developments of the field	What audience?
Ethics: Knowledge	Is familiar with institutional review boards and professional ethical guidelines	Ethical responsibilities	How can ethics extend beyond duty? How to handle IRBs with limited knowledge about qualitative research?
	Understands different ethical traditions and perspectives	Situational ethics and complex ethical decision making	What to do when "my ethics are not your ethics"?
	Understands limits of one's knowledge	Care of self	How to care for oneself at the same time as caring for others? (care of self is a social process)
Ethics: Skills and practice	Demonstrates the ability to apply and adhere to ethical and legal standards in research	Collaboration with IRB and information sharing	Who oversees and why?
	Serves as an advocate for participants and their rights	Sustainable change and ongoing relationships with the communities the research serves	Who needs advocacy? What about false consciousness?

Domain	Content proposition	Possibilities	Impossibilities
	Practices reflectivity related to ethical decision making	Ethical impossibilities open new ways to interact with others	How to become the Other?
Advocacy: Knowledge	Understands how to conduct research for the public	Research moves from labs to public spaces	What about resistance? Whose interests? Whose public science?
	Understands different forms of advocacy	Critical and community-led advocacy	How to react to changes and immediate needs?
Advocacy: Skills and practice	Engages in a participant-driven research project, including design and implementation	Research becomes public science, networking, collaboration	Where to find time, resources, and collaborators?
	Disseminates research findings outside journals and academic conferences	Wider usability, wider audience for research	What to do with tenure and promotion criteria, faculty assignments?
	Engages in community education to increase methodological awareness	Methodological capacity building	What about resistance? Need?
Grant development and management: Knowledge	Understands the elements of a successful qualitative research grant proposal	Possibilities for external funding	Can one use quantitative criteria to evaluate qualitative proposals?
	Is able to locate funding mechanisms for qualitative research projects	Targeted and tailored effort	Where to find appropriate funding opportunities?
	Understands how to manage grants fiscally and work collaboratively	Informed decision making, distribution of labor	How to balance individual effort and investment and research goals?
Grant development and management: Skills and practice	Gains expertise and practice in grant proposal development and writing	Experiential learning	How to practice with a "real" target and purpose? How to become an independent collaborator?
Consultation: Knowledge	Understands the context of collaboration and is sensitive to collaborators' methodological needs	Situated and tailored consultation practice	How to handle pressure to be effective and minimize costs?
Consultation: Skills and practice	Offers different methodological alternatives for collaborators	Promotes methodological alternatives and multiple ways to know	What if a client/collaborator does not want alternatives?
	Offers educational and learning opportunities when needed	Needs assessment and timing of services	What about time? Resources?

A Series of Unthinkable and Unknowable Classroom Events

For us, the boundaries between research and pedagogy blur and shift. Research bleeds into pedagogy, and pedagogy often shapes the ways in which we design and carry out research activities. For example, when Mirka experiments with literature, activities, and different class teaching structures, she also studies this process, analyzes her reflections, and publishes her experiences (see, e.g., Hayes & Koro-Ljungberg, 2011; Koro-Ljungberg, 2007; Koro-Ljungberg, Cavalleri, Covert, & Bustam, 2012; Koro-Ljungberg & Hayes, 2006, 2010). In Mirka's work, classroom experiences and everyday dilemmas such as mentoring, individually based evaluation, individualized or coconstructed curricula, and course content itself (i.e., how students create research questions, validate their studies, and analyze or try to line up methods with epistemologies and theories) have become areas of further analysis and reflection.

Massumi (as cited in Rice, 2010) encouraged us to think about space that has the "ability to irrupt unexpectedly, to break out of or to break into the existing spatial grid, anywhere, at any moment" (p. 34). We hope to reach that space by illustrating, discussing, and theorizing movements and example moments in unthinkable qualitative research, and teaching these possible unthinkable processes. During these unthinkable events, researchers' lives, practices, emotions, and material experiences fold into each other in unexpected ways. Researchers take risks. Unthinkable events may include "unreasonable" interactions with data, participants, texts, or others that are generally systematically excluded from researchers' consciousness and acceptable academic discussions about research. Unthinkable events may attempt to counter normativity and cultural dominance (see also Lemert, 2007). Furthermore, movements and moments in unthinkable research events are situational, but they hang together in some ways. Different worlds, people, data, analytical tools, interpretations, practices, and settings come together in new, unpredictable, and constantly changing ways in senses, experiences, discourses, images, and texts. How do students respond when we encourage them to try out something new, unexpected, crazy, absurd, and wild? Sometimes they get frustrated, disengaged, engaged, or curious, and sometimes they get inspired.

According to Deleuze (1990), events are impassive, and thus allowing the interchange between the active and passive, cause and effect, too much and not enough, already and not yet, can take place more easily. Events are not about binaries but reversal and commonly are a result of being simultaneously both too much and not enough. "Events are like crystals, they become and grow only out of the edges, or on the edge" (Deleuze, 1990, p. 9). Events are sought at the surface, in a misty space away from objects and bodies, in a reflection. Events travel.

"We can speak of events only in the context of the problem whose conditions they determine. We can speak of events only as singularities deployed in a problematic field, in the vicinity of which the solutions are organized" (p. 56). "The event is not what occurs (an accident), it is rather inside what occurs, the purely expressed. It signals and awaits us" (p. 149). In Deleuzian becoming, presence is always absent in a way, since in the absence of presence, past and future are jointed and interacting. Becoming is intertwined with language; "everything happens at the boundary between things and propositions" (p. 8). Every event has a double structure (past–future), and events are not collective or private, but they are singular, including both the private and the collective, the particular and the general, the individual and the universal. Events make language possible, but events do not belong to language; expression differs from the expressed. In the following passages, we share some of the events that blend and twist both research and pedagogy connected with qualitative inquiry.

Event 1: Messiness on YouTube

<u>Mirka:</u> During my qualitative data analysis class, my students and I experimented with different kinds of interactions with data. Before any "textbook" methods, tools, or approaches were introduced, I asked students to document their "messy," intuitive, impulsive, passionate, and unexpected interactions with data. Honestly, I had no idea what I was asking students to do, and I had no expectations what would happen as a response to this pedagogical and methodological prompt. I was curious how doctoral students would describe/enact/live through their unstructured interactions with data.

I introduced Law, Mol, Deleuze, and Lather (movements, messiness, fluidity, etc.) **to those blank faces.** Students did not react or respond. I was speaking in an unfamiliar language. I waited and then rephrased and introduced some examples, hoping for some positive reactions. Maybe some students looked at me, nodded, and expressed interest. I am not sure; I cannot remember. Most students continued to respond with silence and disconnect.

Maybe I was sensing fear. I also began to fear that I sounded strange, nuts, or maybe even anarchistic. I wondered how I could put this "mess" forward and ask students to join the messiness, since methodologists and methodological work should be all about precise methods, ontological order, and systematic analysis. Students shifted in their seats, looking at each other instead of me. Some students opened their computers. Others left to visit the bathroom.

If their faces were blank, does it represent a lack of expression or an inability to see?

—Darby

I think many students were uncomfortable with the flexibility/latitude Mirka gave us as learning researchers. I remember how one student commented during a rhizoanalysis-(dis)ordered presentation that she didn't believe that we should create disorder from order. She did not participate in the experience. I remember thinking to myself, why did she believe that we created "disorder from order" rather than the other way around? Could it be that our discomfort with (dis)order led to this (un)natural order that is fabricated and hence fake?

—Cheryl

Think about a time when you felt uncertain about your teaching. What prompted the uncertainty? How did you regain confidence or how did you move on?

Feeling very uncertain, pedagogically unprepared, and unorganized, I sent students out of the classroom to complete this unfinished and unclear task. No boundaries, expectations, or guidelines, just a request to videotape or otherwise document processes and interactions students had with their data. And I asked them to post this "experiential evidence" on YouTube or elsewhere where it would be accessible for me and possibly others to review. To follow up with students later and collect some of their reflections, I asked them to write me a one-page or one-paragraph story or narrative that related to the (un)teachable moment/event they had experienced in my class. In the following passages, we will share some of these events.

Event 2: Release

<u>Jasmine:</u> "From" your class . . . I've been debating how to read that aspect of the prompt. I'll interpret that not as a bounded "in" or "during" class, but as an unrestricted "from" that can emanate beyond the specifics of meeting location or time.

What prompted Jasmine to choose the data experiment option—the most risky alternative?

How does Jasmine deal with uncertainty when working through data and data examples?

I had intended to *collect* data alongside Deleuze in this experiment. Instead, I *released* data in an (un)teachable moment. A reversal, and most certainly a transgression within a course based on data collection. Yet because (un)teachable moments exhibit the potential to be simultaneously transgressive and acceptable, rather than abandoning the beginnings of an unconventional idea, I continued to release data to explore what might happen—a nomadic self in the middle of data and tweeted methodological memos, working within virtual and cinematic realms. (Un)teachable data *release* culminated in more writing/reading/theorizing/unwriting/experimenting/producing/rewriting/learning than otherwise would have occurred.

What conditions were in place to support her decision? Does a choice of uncertainty require some degree of comfort or an understood environment of acceptance?
—Darby

Classes serve as a catalytic agent for the open-ended methodological productions that ensue. Maybe creativity, innovation, and epistemological awareness are encouraged. Though it is easy to conform, perform, and comply within clearly delineated assignments and rigid requirements, flexibility is significantly more challenging. Like the data project, for example, this "can take many forms." It can be a report/movie/installation of (a) a research project (data collection and preliminary analysis), (b) a conceptual paper manuscript about the concept of data, (c) a data experiment, (d) or something else you negotiate with the instructor" (Qualitative Data Collection Syllabus). I chose **(c) data experiment** even though—and precisely because—I was uncertain about what a data experiment was.

Classes address theory, method, and process. Then we are released: "Researchers of the world, create!" (Koro-Ljungberg, 2012).

(Un)teachable moments can stem from release.

Mirka: I love the way Jasmine flew with this assignment and made it her own. I was also pleased to notice how the open-endedness (of the assignments) stimulated her thinking and pushed her to try something new. Interestingly, she decided to collect and create data alongside Deleuze—not for him, inspired by him, or to promote his ideas—but alongside Deleuze. Jasmine released herself, me (Mirka) as an instructor, and she and Deleuze released each other.

(Un)teachable moments may need epistemological freedom, be created and expanded, and occur within open space.

Flexible assignments can be quite challenging since they require responsibility, a potentially deeper level of activation, inspiration, and creativity. When Jasmine learned through/within/alongside the "release," she exceeded the expectations of methodological repetition, modeling, and imitation. Yet her powerful experience is hard to "evaluate externally." Jasmine was able to transfer and transform normative notions of data and data collection into something more meaningful that escapes normative scales and percentiles. She processed the materials and different notions of data by engaging in messy yet productive and reflective writing/reading/theorizing/unwriting/experimenting/producing/rewriting/learning.

Robert Ulmer

Event 3: The Dead End

<u>Melanie:</u> I wanted to be a *relevant* educational researcher so bad it hurt. And when I say *relevant*, I mean Black. I wanted to do research that had positive and meaningful implications for Black communities, and I wanted to do it in ways that did not further pathologize Black folks as damaged goods. I was learning about different methodological approaches, but I wasn't grasping the ways that epistemology, theory, and methodology coalesced into ways of researching that either harmed or honored community. I think I was looking for someone or some book or some program to tell me step by step how to do culture-focused research and how to be a culture-focused researcher. I was waiting for someone to give me an identity I could easily assume and then just keep it movin'. This proved impossible because no such person, book, or program existed. I was frustrated, confused, and unsure if I would ever come to appreciate research or my role as an educational researcher without a way of researching that reflected my desires.

In hindsight, this dead end proved to be a transformative moment for me because it forced me to rethink my dependence on the external in terms of claiming a researcher identity. I was moved to learn more about myself as a knower. As I engaged in independent study on "alternative" epistemologies, I reconnected with parts of me that had been buried, or lay dormant due to hermeneutical injustice and a serious case of miseducation. I was also moved to learn about traditions of intellectual activity embedded in Black communities and used for centuries to help Black people maintain their sensibilities, assert their existence, and mobilize for change. I think I was moved to begin charting my own course and making my own mark in educational research. At times this was risky because my ways of knowing and making sense of the world did not align perfectly with the dominating methodological paradigms. How do you do the kind of research that makes sense to you and achieve academic legitimacy at the same time? It was challenging. I began to do the dance of negotiation with my thoughts and actions as a researcher in a process of remaking methodology. This was certainly not what I expected I'd be doing as a doctoral student and emerging researcher, but it is one of the most personally and professionally empowering and engaging activities I am doing as a scholar.

> *(Un)teachable moments can be birthed when the student recognizes there is a disconnect between what they know and their momentary sense of self.*

<u>Chandra:</u> Melanie's sense of knowing and sense of self were at odds. It wasn't until she found it impossible to validate her sense of self through external means that she began the process of reuniting them. Melanie, like other students in similar situations (e.g., Benton et al., 2012), chose to embark upon the "Underground Railroad," where students do the work that is required to appease

the defenders of the norm (e.g., the graduate committee), while continuing to passionately explore and uncover the epistemological and methodological truths that describe who they are beyond being PhD students, but are the essence of what makes them scholars.

Event 4: Walking the Dog

Kathryn: Doing data analysis outside the box in Mirka's class sparked a shift in my worldview that led to a new way of thinking. Our class activities broadened my paradigmatic thinking from positivist to post-positivist concepts of research, data, method, and Truth. Once you experience that paradigm shift, it's hard to go back. A number of interactive class activities that encouraged engaging with data in novel ways helped spark the shift in my thinking—such as cutting pictures from magazines and building representations of data with them, and acting out the process of data collection and coding.

Perhaps for me the most memorable experience was walking my dog and recording my data analysis out loud. After I had been thinking and analyzing for a few hours, the walk was a chance to refresh and process more. I was never really sure if I was doing my data analysis "right" because it was intuitive, and creative, not following a prescribed method but seeking out meaning and tracking how I did it. At any rate, when I shared my video with the class, I felt like people got it. Seeing that happen confirmed for me that there is a sense, a something in the creative act of data analysis that is organized in its chaos. Doing data analysis can be an embodied process that follows its own (il)logic, yet leads to careful arguments that consider and collapse multiple ideas into sensible frameworks for examining phenomena.

> (Un)teachable moments can begin in confusion but culminate in greater "understanding."

Mirka: It was interesting to read about Kathryn's epistemological awareness and her paradigm shift. Many students, like her, come from epistemologically singular frameworks. Sometimes students who are trained in post-positivism, empiricism, and current forms of neopositivism may have a harder time with qualitative research courses and the open-ended assignments often embedded in those courses. To help these students learn qualitative research, we may begin with learning and experiencing "other" ways to know and carry out research beyond normativity. However, this broadening of epistemological and methodological horizons is ideally accompanied by a sense of hope (of an epistemologically diverse future) and the trust that one will be accepted in the research community. Additionally, doing something quite mundane and yet out of the ordinary in the context of data analysis (like walking your dog) can create productive spaces to rethink and relive data analysis. Kathryn's walking

How can teachers help students to think about data analysis in their everyday lives without losing interactions with data?

her dog brought mind and body, mental world and external/experiential world, life inside and outside academia, together in a particular time and space. This time–space connection, the dog-walking event, set into motion other events: the creative analysis event, the talking-to-the-dog-about-the-data event, the dog, the summary of data stories, the trees and asphalt, pull and the movement of the dog, and so on. Data, Kathryn, dog, street, clouds, and trees became a part of her analysis. Data analysis organized itself in its own chaos.

Event 5: "Becoming" Paper

Justin: I was in way over my head the first time I took a course with Mirka. My classmates were throwing out names and talking about books I had never heard of, and we were reading philosophers who seemed to be speaking gibberish. I was motivated, however, and had always wanted to read Heidegger, Foucault, and Butler. As the weeks progressed, I began to slowly understand the language that theory was using. I focused my final paper on the work of Gilles Deleuze and Felix Guattari. I spent 10 hours on a plane going to and coming back from Phoenix, Arizona, reading just the first chapter of *A Thousand Plateaus*. It was intriguing and exciting, but my brain was clouded and fatigued from reading. I just couldn't quite grasp what they were trying to say.

I really like how this section comes together here. First Bettie tells you to write, and now Justin and Chandra are doing the same things with you.
—Jasmine

After this experience I began writing. **I was told to think of reading and writing together as a process of understanding.** This was when I began to grasp a little bit of what I was reading. I started to *experience* Deleuze, to see him in everything around me. I took pictures of what I thought comprised rhizomes and I tried to think in Deleuzian ways. I was given enough latitude on the final paper to create something that too many would have seen as a messy assortment of garbled notes, but to me it was Deleuze or at least it was my "becoming" paper. A molecular "line of flight" that made me feel alive. I can't remember ever writing a paper that made me feel as liberated as that one did. I burst out of striated space into the realm of the nomad, and it was beautiful. This was a difficult, and at times impossible, task for me. But I had the motivation and was given the freedom to create, and the support necessary to **succeed**.

What forms of support can serve the dual role of nurturing and pushing? Safety in chaotic moments?
—Darby

> *Some (un)teachable moments can be "self-led," yet they may*
> *require support to develop and the freedom to breathe and move.*

Chandra: Justin felt overwhelmed at his task of understanding theorists. (Un)teachable moments may not always be instructor or classroom led. Sometimes (un)teachable moments are spurred from within the individual.

No matter the source, (un)teachable moments call for a supportive environment in order to thrive and generate movement.

Event 6: Liberation

Darby: As a fledgling doctoral student, I resisted allegiance to the fortified dichotomy of qualitative versus quantitative methods presented in my introductory seminar, recognizing its rigidity to be an oversimplification of the field of education, the authentic practice of children and teachers, and the potential of the individual. Fighting a tension I could not articulate, I responded with what I determined to be epistemological agnosticism. Satisfied at having outwitted the compulsory question forced upon me as a rite of passage into the academy, I entered my first qualitative research class. My refusal to reduce the limitless potential of my inquiring mind was, and is, I discovered, an action that spoke louder than words. In refusing to be boxed in, I had chosen my *side*. By refining my knowledge of the epistemological complexity beyond artificial binaries, I came to love the possibility of theory, which is too often masked by these sparring camps—theory, not as it reduces researchers to things or prizes a single way of knowing over others, but in its ability to facilitate understanding and new insight about the way scholars engage with their world. Early on in my qualitative class, there was a discussion about the impact of subject position on one's research or the way we live our lives, see our world, and construct meaning. The idea that my epistemology was more than what I produced through certifiable research resonated with me. It was liberating. In the vast yet familiar nature of my own ontology, I found the will to embrace the process of participating in the evolving discourse of qualitative research. I am comforted in my heightened awareness that the reduction of one's life and work to an artificial label is a choice; for me, accepting the choice was easy. Static *Truth* is a facade. **The meaning I seek can only be found in the dynamic process of evolving understanding, grounded in an interdisciplinary, qualitative perspective.**

> *It's interesting to look back at how my thinking has evolved over the course of the past year. I am far less certain now of where I stand than I was when I initially wrote this; however, my comfort in my uncertainty is much easier to accept.*
>
> —Darby

(Un)teachable moments can be provoked by the mundane.

Chandra: Darby's (un)teachable moment transpired when learning the basics of qualitative research. (Un)teachable moments do not always occur when there is great conflict/misunderstanding between the instructor and students, or when the students fear that they do not understand the expectations of them in completing an assignment. (Un)teachable moments can often go unnoticed as each student and instructor brings with them their pre-understanding. Conversations that are not necessarily meant to inspire (un)teachable moments can be the very catalyst that teaches what is (un)teachable.

Beginning Again and Again:
New Projects, New Methodologies

Think about a time when you felt that you "got it" while taking a qualitative methodology course. What was the concept in question? (How) did you come to a place of understanding/ confidence/learning or to a place of misunderstanding/ unconfidence/ unlearning?

According to some authors, one purpose of teaching qualitative research methodologies is to socialize students into a "culture of research" (Eisenhart & DeHann, 2005, p. 7) and to create a space where students can develop creative and innovative scholarship (Preissle & Roulston, 2009). This may occur when qualitative research is not taught in a linear-like process, and when theories are introduced in open-ended ways that allow students to make appropriate choices in research (Preissle & Roultson, 2009). We believe that one way to avoid "pinning creativity down" or turning open-endedness to another grand narrative, social expectations, or normative practice might be accomplished by continuous revision, reformulation, and reconceptualization of how cultures of research affect us and shape our practices. Through critical reflection and examination of our desires to close down and prioritize certain theories and methods, teachers and students may be able to avoid methodological nepotism at the same time as they create a sense of knowing and conceptual awareness. Creativity could also be met with other forms of creativity—maybe with a creative multiplication and theoretical cross-fertilization or experimental overexposure. These moves may help scholars and students to stay uncertain and humble and always in a process of creating new methodologies for new projects and new projects for new methodologies.

Scholars have also postulated that students learning qualitative research often traverse between clarity and confusion (Hein, 2004; Preissle & Roulston, 2009). According to Dewey (1939), action and knowledge, theory and practice are inseparable human activities. Students might benefit from hands-on experiences to practice qualitative methodologies within the field (Hein, 2004; Preissle & Roulston, 2009). However, without reflection and theorizing, experiences and practices may stay uncontextualized, remote, mechanical, and overly technical. Reading alone may generate theoretical knowing and stimulate pragmatic ways "to know"; however, doing is impossible without applications and action (Roulston, deMarrais, & Lewis, 2003). Doing theory and methodology and putting theory to work call for movement and decisions. Decisions are hard, and movement implies change. How can instructors help learners face uncertainty and make hard decisions? Working through discomfort (e.g., discomfort associated with theories and other hard concepts) may help novice researchers resist their desire for simplicity, and conceptual/practical struggles and "empty spaces" might enable learners to navigate complex processes of analysis and **interpretation**.

Accepting confusion is a deeply personal and vulnerable state. At times, uncertainty feels like a threat to everything I claim to be or think I am, but clinging to the known prevents becoming.

"A perfection of means, and a confusion of aims, seems to be our main problem."
—Albert Einstein
—Darby

Maybe qualitative research might be unteachable, since there is no right answer but many answers—answers that could be somewhat right or possibly right within particular contexts. Additionally, qualitative research might also be unteachable since it is an epistemological curiosity, an in-depth and engaging inquiry, an individual and collective desire to use research to serve others and to investigate research problems critically in culturally specific ways. Therefore, it may seem and feel hard to teach students how to be unsatisfied with the most obvious and how to be persistent, encouraging them to continue studying data, people, contexts, and materials beyond the normative and visible. It may also be challenging to guide students to use theories and philosophies in their work, since each use is ultimately different and no reading of a theory is identical.

In the context of the unthinkable, qualitative research researchers take risks that extend social norms and move beyond authoritative expectations. Ideally, scholars and learners move toward the unexpected, enabling researchers to meet the Other and experience other ways of knowing. For example, students might experiment with research processes that they have no prior knowledge about, or students could engage in research with communities that they have never worked with before. Alternatively, students might be asked to "do unexpected things" with their data and step out of their comfort zones through various exercises and activities. These uncertain moves "above and beyond" documented practices are challenging but necessary "conditions" for methodological work that is unthinkable and always becoming. Unthinkable methodologies utilize the energies gained from conceptual hazard, unpredictability, ambiguity, and openness to spontaneity as qualitative researchers relate their work to theories, epistemologies, and educational policies and practices.

Maybe teachers of qualitative research courses should worry less about "getting their teaching right," having the right content to teach, or making students competitive in the job market. We argue that we teach for life; our lives are those of critical qualitative scholars who can advocate conditions and values they see as important. We should promote scholarship that can create and generate innovative tools and research designs, potentially as a response to constructive cultural critique. We might teach for the creative and responsible life of a scholar, a life where qualitative researchers and methodologist can take "calculated" risks to improve and change the lives of others. Laroche and Roth (2009) described ideal learning environments as those with bounded randomness and an edging of chaos. These spaces might be filled with hidden and unspoken structures that temporarily slow down and enhance learning and teaching. But rather than unproductively feeling stuck or lost within these structures, teachers and researchers could approach these challenges as transformational spaces where things gain speed and temporal directionality. Let's focus on teaching that produces rather than protects.

READING LIST OF LIFE ————————————————

Cullum, A. (1971). *The geranium on the window sill just died, but teacher you went right on.* Harlin Quist.

Everett, P. (2001). *Erasure: A novel.* University Press of New England.

Fusco, M. (2013). *Teaching for what?* CreateSpace.

Gaines, E. (1993). *A lesson before dying.* Alfred A. Knopf.

Galloway, S. (2012). *The ghost that saw too much: What happens when a ghost is suddenly haunted?* CreateSpace.

Plath, S. (2006). *The bell jar.* HarperCollins.

Sarcone, G., & Warber, M. (2014). *Impossible coloring book: Can you color these amazing visual illusions?* Arcturus.

8 Productive Paradoxes in Participant-Driven Research

Communities and Audiences Matter

With Kristi Cheyney and Chandra Bowden

Whom do we conduct research for? What would happen if social science researchers were to reconceptualize the reasons and ways in which they engage in research? What if there were an expectation and a norm for carrying out only the kind of social science research that is collaborative and participant driven? We are obviously drawn into participant-driven research, but we also acknowledge many challenges and dilemmas associated with it. What if research were always (through some kind of relationality and extensions) to be linked to practice, not only as a form of practice that scholars claim to know or address but practice as experienced or described by the public, laymen, participants, our friends, neighbors, fellow residents, and so on? **What would happen if the form of research that students in the social sciences knew best were participant-driven?** This section provides insights into potential paradoxes associated with such research and previously mentioned propositions. We draw our examples from research studies, students' body maps, and a dialogue across our colleagues and collaborators.

> *I wonder who would teach these classes. Would participants/ scholars in residence teach or co-teach these courses?*
>
> —Darby

Many forms of qualitative inquiry call for collaboration within and outside academia. **No research project should serve only the scholars' egocentric purposes of recognition, vita building, or studying topics that have little relevance to the public.** We call for more public science—science that provokes and creates change outside academia. Qualitative inquiry serves individuals, especially those underrepresented, unheard, and ignored. Ideally, qualitative inquiry should be responsive to the needs of different communities, cultures, and ways of life. Furthermore, without collaboration, it may be hard to study complex problems, generate meaningful inquiry questions, and mobilize allies. Within research collaboratives and communities, it is easier to face the complexity of the social world and phenomena, since collaboratives are often composed of different voices, sociopolitical perspectives, and resources (in terms of both social capital and financial resources).

I agree! We need to bridge the gap between research and practice by creating "third spaces" in which practitioners are able to work with researchers to translate research and engender transformation.

—Cheryl

We believe that this move toward more participant-driven research (PDR) would encourage deeper and more meaningful relationships between universities and "the public." This move could also shift existing hierarchies between existing discourses inside and outside academia and those practices separating "academia" and "the public." However, participant-driven work is full of paradoxes, unanswered questions, exploration, and negotiations. Rather than simply creating a methodological framework for participant-driven work, we will share examples of complexities and productive paradoxes associated with this type of qualitative research.

Can the words *public* and *research* both be used to describe my personal program of study?

Massumi (2002) described lived paradox as space "where what are normally opposites coexist, coalesce, and connect; where what cannot be experienced cannot but be felt" (p. 30). For Baudrillard (2000), we live in paradoxical situations that call for paradoxical ways of thinking. For Baudrillard, paradox is "beyond the end, beyond all finality . . . too much reality, too much positivity, too much information . . . faced with extreme phenomena, we do not know exactly what is taking place" (p. 67). Paradoxical ways of thinking assume no principles of truth, causality, or discursive norms; instead, "we must grant both the poetic singularity of events and the radical uncertainty of events" (p. 68) and stay enigmatic and ambivalent. According to Deleuze and Guattari (1994), philosophy is paradoxical not when it is contradictory but when "it uses sentences of a standard language to express something that does not belong to the order of opinion or even of the proposition" (p. 80). In this section, we use "methodological paradox" to mark the unanticipated and uncertain within PDR practices, PDR processes, and the ways in which PDR is felt and experienced among us and our colleagues.

Robert Ulmer

Many potential problems arise from narrow purposes and understandings of research, particularly when participants are members of a marginalized community. Even if the intention of a researcher is to create new knowledge and discourses or to bring to light phenomena, ideologies, or policies that have served to create or sustain marginalization of people, unless we include participants in the research process in a purposeful way, there remains a meaningful risk that their experiences and perspective will be lost under the more voluble influence of the researcher. For example, participatory action research (PAR) methodologies provide explicit pathways for minimizing researcher privilege. However, attempts to incorporate both etic (researcher) and emic (participant) perspectives, not to mention participant/researcher goals, also creates tensions that are not always easily resolved. The effective PAR researcher not only expects these tensions but also incorporates into the research design purposeful procedures to guide the process of negotiating these tensions.

In this section, we differentiate participant-driven research (PDR) from participatory action research (PAR), action research (AR), critical participatory action research (CPAR), and community-based research (CBR), among others. Even though all previous labels are similar and often serve related purposes, our use of the participant-driven research label highlights our emphasis on the role of participant and participatory involvement without a specific commitment to action research (to study one's own practices), a particular type of critical framework, or only community-based research. Our point is to use PDR as a proxy (but not a direct or stable signifier) for scholarship that addresses the needs and desires of those who are impacted by research and policies but often do not have much impact on the focus or outcomes of research. We also advocate scholarship that does not assume or make predictions about participants' interests and needs but rather involves participants in decision making. Yet we acknowledge that this kind of research is complicated and in many ways problematic and challenging, and thus there are no shortcuts or simplified methodological solutions.

The main content of this section might not be new for those who have engaged in participant-driven research before. Our intention is not to redefine PDR or provide introductions to this kind of scholarship. Instead, we will highlight the importance of conducting complex and challenging research that serves others and builds from research activities that move beyond scholarly or solely scientific interest. We also want to show that PDR can be done in the classroom. Students can be exposed to this type of research early on in their programs and careers. Finally, we argue that participant-driven research processes are methodologies without *methodologies par excellence*, full of paradoxes and imperfection. **In PDR, normative and simplified methodologies break down, hard questions (almost always without answers) need to be asked, and researchers are often faced with impossible processes and tasks.**

I always struggle to honor the participants' voice while identifying a manageable question. I worry that in following one path over another, I may fail to respect their experience in the world.

—Darby

What are some of those productive methodological paradoxes that qualitative researchers might face when engaging in PDR, and how do they appear? We are not quite sure, since PDR is situational and context specific, but we wonder if some of these paradoxes are born within each interaction between subjects and between subject and material. Or maybe these productive paradoxes are generated through dissonance and difference. However, paradoxes are not binaries but possible situations on a continuum that can create opportunities for change and transformation. Paradoxes force scholars and participants to act and take a stance, since paradoxes often generate questions and break down normative notions of participation and processes of research. Paradoxes may also create breaking points when researchers' and sometimes participants' sense of control is being lost and existing knowledges are being disrupted. To replace the sensed loss of control or perceived lack of directionality and knowledge, paradoxes might call for deeper and renewed engagement among individuals or some other types of action. Furthermore, paradoxes could be epistemological, practical, pedagogical, theoretical, ethical, relational, and so on, and they can include different events and manifestations. In this section, we focus mostly on the following paradoxes:

Relational paradoxes:

> *Uncertainty and impossibilities related to oneself and the other* (e.g., belonging, commitment, investment). How does one construct or not construct a sense of belonging in a context of research? What are some potentially distancing boundaries of belonging and collaboration? How can one stay both committed and independent while engaging in PDR? How does one establish relationships with the Other that might not be known? How will relationships change overtime?

Theoretical paradoxes:

> *Uncertainty and impossibilities related to theory and practice* (e.g., movement between theory and practice, knowledge [practical, theoretical, tactical, etc.]). How is theory translated to practice and practice translated to theory? Where and how are theory and practice (not *what* are they)? How do different and potentially conflicting situated knowledges and knowledge interests shape PDR process? How does the absence of theory generate theory? How can situated knowledges be shared? When will "my theory/my practice" become "your theory/ your practice" (i.e., theoretical colonialism)?

Ethical paradoxes:

> *Uncertainty and impossibilities related to the goals of research and advocacy/activism* (e.g., definitions, roles, responsibilities, audience). Whose goals will be driving research and collaboration processes? How and when will collective goals shift? Who can and will advocate for whom? Where is the audience? Who will listen? When does research become research activism? **When community needs meet policy needs, what happens?**

> *What if the co-researchers have a political or activist agenda that will benefit their group but will/may oppress or harm another group? What if the researcher disagrees with the ethics of the agenda of the co-researchers? What if the co-researchers wish to show their group in a particular light (bias)?*
>
> —Becky

Practical paradoxes:

> *Uncertainty and impossibilities related to the resources/ financial support and volunteering* (e.g., funding, cost sharing, researchers' assignments, community service). Where does funding begin and end? Where and when does financial support turn into social capital? What are the researcher's responsibilities, duties, and desires, and how do these responsibilities interact with participants' responsibilities, duties, and desires? If a researcher is a part of the community, what happens to volunteering or serving the community? How do you navigate IRB? Publishing? Intellectual property?

Pedagogical paradoxes:

> *Uncertainty and impossibilities related to pedagogical* processes (e.g., assignments, grading, knowledge exchange, professional preparation). How can democracy and activism work together in a classroom context (activism versus simulation)? When does pedagogical power shift and participants become teachers? How can one teach the unteachable?

Considering these paradoxes, one may need to rethink the relationship between the researcher and participants and/or co-researchers (some scholars prefer to call participants co-researchers). Who knows within a research project? How does the flow of knowledge move (from researchers to participants, from participants to researchers, or in multiple directions at once; see Figure 8.1)? Where does knowledge begin and maybe temporarily pause? When, where, and why is knowledge? Who controls the practice?

Ideally, within participant-driven projects, knowledge is not dominated, solely created, or controlled by the researchers. Knowledge in PDR should

I love the apparent simplicity of this image, yet I realize that as a teacher/learner/researcher this process requires me to be fully alert and always questioning my role in the relationship. Studying my actions is fundamental.

—Darby

I like this figure, except (for example) when working with groups in the developing world, such as groups with low literacy or who are just organizing themselves, a certain facilitation aspect has to happen where the research almost has to in some ways teach the co-researchers how to do research. So in that context, there is still at least some flow of information from the researcher to the participant.

—Becky

What does the word _research_ do to you, and how does it operate in your particular context?

Who is "qualified" or encouraged to conduct PDR?

not be continuously guided by the researcher's interests, his or her agenda, and creation or domination of knowledge. Figure 8.1 illustrates the potential flow and directionality of knowledge in PDR projects. We are not proposing that researchers do not have impact or influence on knowledge or that they cannot share knowledge. However, we crossed out the one-directional flow of knowledge and power initiating from the researchers, especially when one-directionality is being seen as the only and dominant way to engage and interact within research. Rather than relying on researchers' information, knowledge, and influence, we see more generative potential, value, and importance in knowledge that flows from the community to academia and researchers. For example, participants in collaboration with researchers redirect knowledge, create the need for knowledge, manage knowledge, distribute knowledge, and validate knowledge. Knowledge can be initiated by the participants, shaping the ways in which researchers interact with it or create knowledge in the future. **Alternatively, knowledge is negotiated through reciprocal and mutual processes, within back-and-forth movement between researchers and participants.**

A part of the movement could be related to negotiating methodologies and ways to interact with "data" across contexts and disciplines. One way to promote fluid interactions, methodological movement, and sustainable change is to consider divergent ways of gathering data. O'Neill (2012) introduced ethnomimesis as a way to combine the arts and PAR. According to O'Neill, ethnomimesis can lead to democratization of images and texts that can move readers and bring them in touch with their subjectivity and reflexivity within projects that represent public scholarship. Community arts such as exhibits and public displays can transgress barriers and interfere with fixed and limiting boundaries between "academic science" and "public science."

Effective and meaningful communication can possibly transgress barriers. For example, Denzin and Giardina (2014) suggested that scholars should not be innocent actors in academia but should communicate directly with the public, reaching beyond journals and traditional academic outlets as the primary means of dissemination. Instead of considering themselves private intellectuals, qualitative researchers should engage in disruptive public intellectualism (Denzin & Giardina, 2014). Mayan and Daum (2014) argued further that research that generates knowledge to solve everyday problems serves the dual purposes of knowledge generation and action. Community

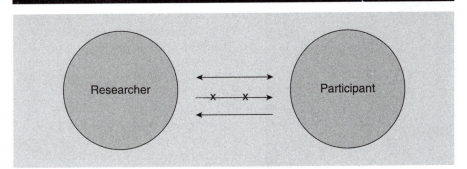

Figure 8.1 Directionality of Knowledge in Participant-Driven Work

Researcher

Participant

partners serve as guides to embedded experiences and studies evolving those experiences, informing knowledge, practices, and expressions.

One might ask why we need to think about the role of knowing the subjects, audience, or purpose of our research. First, we see research as one form of public service to improve the lives of us all citizens. From this perspective, researchers should be accountable not only to the university as a system with social responsibilities but more importantly to the public. Research could be viewed as a response to public inquiries. Those who currently view or constitute themselves outside academia or academic communities could continue asking questions about academia's purposes and about ways in which scholars' privileged positions might serve others and public initiatives. Second, social science research often investigates complex issues, issues that cannot be decontextualized or approached too narrowly. Multiple theoretical and practical perspectives might be needed to highlight the diversity and layered appearance or existence of social phenomena. This complexity also calls for continuous collaboration and different types of engagement and interchange. Theories blend with practice, and boundaries between researchers and practitioners/individuals not associated with universities blur. We could pay attention to how scholar-activists, from W. E. B. Du Bois to Cornell West, Michelle Fine, Mary Margaret Fonow, Jacqui Alexander, Linda Tuhiwai Smith, and many others, carry out their scholarship and community engagement. At the same time, not all scholars can or will become tiny Wests, Fines, or Smiths. Instead, community engagement and participatory goals are likely to operate on a continuum—more or less activism, engagement, and participation. However, the continuum, as envisioned here,

One example of international support of PDR initiatives: The UK–based Antipode Foundation funds social science research in the field of radical geography. Its Scholar-Activist Project Awards support research collaborations among academics, nonacademics, and activists in action research and publicly focused forms of geographical research and investigation. The organization is driven by the vision to build connections between academia and the public in order to develop a more just and equitable society. More information can be found on its website (http://antipodefoundation.org/scholar-activist-project-awards/).

Robert Ulmer

does not have clearly defined beginnings or ends, and therefore it is not a question of activism or no activism but activism and collaboration by degrees and on a continuum.

One of the goals of PDR is to bring new, contemporary, and potentially critical knowledge to society and existing practices. One could argue that the purpose of many PDR initiatives, like the ones sponsored by the Antipode Foundation, is to contribute new knowledge in the context of depth, diverse meanings, questions, nuances, imagery, and stories in many cases; through humanization, decolonization, emancipation, and policy; and through recursive, cyclical, political, and/or rhizomatic processes. Additionally, some scholars aim to defamiliarize the familiar and familiarize the unfamiliar in the context of both theory and practice; to show unexpected interconnectedness at the individual and collective levels; and to make research everybody's right rather than an exclusive privilege. Participant-driven research methodologies simultaneously belong to everyone and no one in particular. PDR is not bounded to specific individuals, schools, and community groups. For example, PDR has been used across various fields such as education, sociology, feminist studies, and more; among and by critical theorists, interpretivists, and, to a lesser organic extent, scholars working with populations in developed, developing, and undeveloped nations. PDR scholars and communities are everywhere and not specifically anywhere, both politically and geographically. Table 8.1 displays examples of PDR across multiple contexts.

Many practitioners and advocates of PDR receive support and disseminate their work to a larger audience through agencies dedicated to promoting participatory projects. Table 8.2 outlines a selection of prominent agencies or foundations that fund, support, celebrate, and disseminate findings of PDR projects across a variety of disciplines.

Table 8.1 Examples of Participant-Driven Research Projects

Project Title	Location	Issue	Collaborators	Methods	Community Action	Website
Science for Indigenous Activism: Mapping the Impacts of Oil Companies	Northern Peruvian Amazon	Ancestral territory has been affected by oil industry activities since the end of the 1960s	Martí Orta (Autonomous University of Barcelona), Jordi Noè (AlterNativa Intercanvi amb Pobles Indigenes), and Yanet Cavallero (Programa de Defensa Indigena – Solsticio-Perú)	Created cloud-based tools for collaborative management and publishing of information about oil spills collected by an indigenous monitoring team	Linked indigenous people to government policymakers; prompted the state government and oil companies to take the necessary steps to mitigate the environmental and health impacts related to oil extraction activities	http://antipodefoundation .org/scholar-activist-project-awards/201213-recipients/sapa-1213-orta/
Challenging the "New Urban Renewal": Gathering the Tools Necessary to Halt the Social Cleansing of Council Estates and Developing Community-Led Alternatives for Sustaining Existing Communities	London, England	Urban residents were being forced out of their homes and neighborhoods due to gentrification	Loretta Lees (University of Leicester), Just Space (http:// justspace.org .uk/), Southwark Notes Archive Group (http:// southwarknotes .wordpress.com/), and the London Tenants Federation (http://www .londontenants .org/)	Collected stories from tenants, leaseholders, and local communities about what gentrification is, how communities can resist it, and the alternatives to demolition and displacement.	Created the handbook *Staying Put: An Anti-gentrification Handbook for Council Estates in London*	http://antipodefoundation .org/scholar-activist-project-awards/201213-recipients/sapa-1213-lees/

(Continued)

Table 8.1 (Continued)

Project Title	Location	Issue	Collaborators	Methods	Community Action	Website
Balancing Work and Family project	Windsor-Essex County, Ontario, Canada	Due to cultural obligations, South Asian women had greater demands in balancing work and family responsibilities than other groups, which affected their job placement and economic ability	D. Rosemary Cassano, MSW, PhD Associate Professor, School of Social Work, University of Windsor; Women in Action Committee (WIAC) of the South Asian Centre (SAC); and other immigrant-serving agencies in Windsor, Essex	Originally, focus groups were to be led by WIAC members who were actively involved in developing the research study, including the literature review, design, data collection, dissemination, and follow-up. However, the executive director of SAC desired to hire a community member to facilitate the focus groups. Neither the executive director nor the paid facilitator assisted with the report write-up. Only the researcher and WAIC members contributed to the report write-up.	Created "The Women Balancing Work and Family: Needs Assessment Report," where the WAIC provided information about the issues and problems experienced by South Asian women balancing work and home responsibilities	http://www1.uwindsor.ca/criticalsocialwork/participatory-action-research-with-south-asian-immigrant-women-a-canadian-example

Project Title	Location	Issue	Collaborators	Methods	Community actions	Website
Participatory Risk Mapping for Targeting Research and Assistance With East African Pastoralists	Rangelands of Southern Ethiopia and Northern Kenya	People living in arid and semi-arid regions generally receive ill-matched research and development assistance based on outsiders' anecdotal assessment or superimposing issues experienced in subtropical and temperate zones	Kevin Smith (International Rescue Committee); Christopher Barrett (Cornel University); Paul Box (Utah State University); the Boran, Gabra, Rendille, and Samburu peoples of Kenya; the Boran, Gabra, and Guji peoples of Ethiopia	Utilized a risk-mapping technique where participants first identified risks in an open-ended survey and then ranked the risks they had identified	Presented findings to participants for member checking	http://dyson .cornell.edu/ special_ programs/ AFSNRM/ Parima/ Papers/SBB_ participatoryrisk .pdf
The Changing Role of Practice Nurses in Australia	Queensland, Australia	Unaccounted-for barriers prevent nurses from fully implementing the new model of service for patients at a well women's clinic	Jane Mills (Monash University), Mary Firtgerald (James Cook University), and three registered nurses employed by the general practice	Observations, critical reflection group sessions led by university researchers, and a modified course action occurred in cyclic fashion as improvements were made to the model of service	Identified the barriers that impeded full integration of the new model of service, and assisted the practice in acknowledging and capitalizing upon the role of employees in implementing new models of primary care	http://www .ajan.com.au/ Vol26-1v2_ Mills.pdf

Name	Activities	Website
Antipode Foundation	• Serves as disseminator of PAR research • Awards PAR research	http://antipodefoundation .org/
The International Development Research Centre	• Digital Library of PAR research	http://www.idrc.ca/EN/ Pages/default.aspx
Post Growth Institute	• Online community of researchers who support holistic human development not contingent on economic growth through PAR research methods	http://postgrowth.org/
International Institute for Environment and Development	• Conducts and supports PAR research on climate change, human settlements, natural resource management, and sustainable markets	http://www.iied.org/
Center for Participatory Research and Development Partnership With the Climate Action Network	• Conducts and supports PAR research that promotes people-centered sustainable development that limits human-induced climate change	http://www.climatenetwork. org/profile/member/center-participatory-research-and-development-cprd
Consultative Group on International Agricultural Research, Research Program on Climate Change, Agriculture, and Food Security	• Conducts PAR research on sustainable agriculture and collects climate change data	http://ccafs.cgiar.org/how-we-work#.U54byfldUpp

Body Maps as Tools for Reflection on PDR

Participant-driven ideologies and theoretical orientations call for research approaches that bring participants' embodied experiences, lived lives, senses, emotions, thoughts, beliefs, and so on to the forefront. For example, body maps have been traditionally used in the field of occupational health, where employees and employers raised awareness of occupational hazards in the workplace. Since then, body maps have been used in educational contexts and clinical practice to map experiences, pain, and symptoms, and in therapeutic sessions to help clients better explore certain aspects of their lives (Galstado, 2012). More specifically, body maps are life-sized human body images that are created through drawing, painting, or other art-based techniques that represent people's bodies, aspects of their lives, and on a larger scale, the world they live in through creative means without chronological order or decontextualization. This visual data collection method goes beyond the interview, and can help bring understanding and increased self-awareness and reflection to a person's contextualized experiences (Galstado, 2012).

Figure 8.2   Jasmine's Body Map

PAR
ACTION
RESEARC
ER RESEAR
ED. PRACTITI
HER, RESEARCH
RE MY POLICY SH
SHOES FOR THE PAR
CPANT-RESEARCHER
ED-PRACTITIONER PAR
TICIPANT, RESEARCHER,
SEARCHED. PRACTITIONE
SEARCHER, RESEARCHED
PARTICIPANT, RESEARCHE
PRACTITIONER AND ALSO
TEACHER LEADER IN EDU
CATIONAL POLICY. SHOES
ICY SHOES WHEN I AM A
ICIPANT-RESEARCHER
ED-PRACTITIONER
IN POLICY

SHOE
PAR
ED

Source: Jasmine Ulmer.

In the following pages, we share body maps of student collaborators. We asked students to create a body map about their experiences with participant-driven research in their personal contexts. We use these maps to illustrate contextualized connections to participant-driven research and to show how context shapes the ways in which scholars react and respond to inquiries and research prompts coming from the individuals and communities outside academia.

Figure 8.3 Becky's Body Map

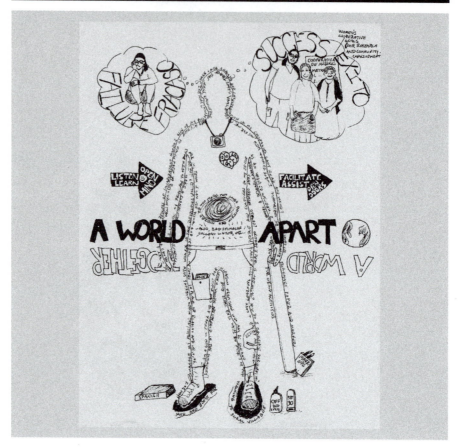

Source: Rebecca Williams.

GLOSSARY

Activism. "Collective action to exert pressure on centers of power in order to remedy grievances and felt injustices" (Program for the Advancement of Research on Conflict and Collaboration, n.d.).

Activism. Produces emancipatory knowledge (Hale, 2006).

Community-based research. Takes a holistic view of the problem, and can be initiated by either researchers or community members (Panel of Research Ethics, 2013).

Participatory research. Systematic form of inquiry where researchers collaborate with those affected by the issue. The primary purpose is to educate *and* take action to effect change through a shared purpose (Green et al., 2003).

Participatory research. Prioritizes active involvement of all subjects of research.

Action oriented because subjects usually act on the results of the study (Panel of Research Ethics, 2013).

Action research. Deliberate inquiry process that is conducted by and for the people taking action. This type of research is conducted so that the actor can improve and/or refine his or her actions to reach a desirable goal (Sagor, 2000).

Action research. Generates personal and profound social change (Riel, 2010).

Action research. Contributes to the practical concerns of people involved in a problematic situation *and* furthers the goals of society (Gilmore, Krantz, & Ramirez, 1986).

Action research. Used to understand and alter policies of social systems (Troppe, 1994).

Action research. Learning by doing (O'Brien, 2001).

Action research. A natural component of teaching (National Council of Teachers of Mathematics, n.d.).

Participatory action research. Activist-like approach to research where the goal is to empower the local community. Works best when there is a thorough understanding of the local power structure and issues (International Institute for Sustainable Development, n.d.).

Community-based participatory research. Merges inquiry methods with community capacity-building strategies. Usually conducted to improve health and/or environmental outcomes. Designed to bridge the gap between the knowledge of academics and what is practical within a community (Viswanathan et al., 1994).

Community-based participatory action research. Collaboration between the people most affected by a community issue and individuals having formal research knowledge and skills to conduct research and analyze the issue, with the goal of developing strategies to solve the issue.

The different levels of community-based participatory action research include: Level 1: Outsiders gather information from the community members; Level 2: Outsiders have members of the affected population collect the data. These community members may or may not analyze the data; and Level 3: Outsiders and community members work together as partners in the research study (KU Work Group for Community Health and Development, n.d.).

Critical participatory action research. Draws on critical theories in the codevelopment of participatory action research to illuminate disparities in the distribution of opportunities, resources, and dignity; challenge ideological categories that are projected onto communities (e.g., delinquent, at risk, victim); and identify how "science" has been utilized as a tool to legitimize dominant policies and practices (Torre, Fine, Stoudt, & Fox, 2012).

Critical participatory action research. Addresses the *who* of research (i.e., who has the right to participate) as well as the *how* (i.e., how the research will be conducted to minimize hegemonic hierarchy). The critical tradition of research challenges the *why* of research (e.g., what are the components of the issue of inequality, poverty, poor literacy; Morrell, 2005).

Ethnomimesis. Methodology comprising participatory action research and participatory arts (O'Neill, 2007).

Ethnomimesis. Methodology that is both reflexive (phenomenoglcial and hermeneutical) and critical of realist ethnographic methodologies (O'Neill et al., 2002).

Ethnomimesis. Phenomenological hermeneutic methodology that expands ethnographic work by incorporating participatory action research and artistic expression into the retelling of life story interviews with the express purpose of effecting change (O'Neill et al., 2002).

Section key points:

- The new knowledge that research generates could be utilized to better meet the needs of those outside the academy

- PDR is messy and complex but also generative and empowering

- The paradoxes of PDR may help address and dismantle normativity of thinking, knowing, understanding, and interacting with others

- Novice and experienced researchers can incorporate PDR in their personal research programs and community relations

- Researchers have access to local, regional, national, and international resources that support PDR initiatives

PDR Exemplars From Student Researchers

Next we will share two very different examples of PDR that have been carried out in the classroom and dissertation contexts. The following examples and paradoxes are used to illustrate the complex, unfinished, and unexpected nature of scholarship that deliberately involves participants. Ideally, PDR projects become projects without predetermined, researcher-driven, and peer-reviewed or validated methodologies. However, as the following examples illustrate, projects without predetermined and validated methodologies are most likely always only partially successful in their PDR goals, since the methods, interactions, power, policy, practices, and so on are always changing and in flux. In addition, these examples illustrate how different PDR projects are likely to involve participants in different degrees and thorough various roles.

Working Together With the National Association on Mental Illness (NAMI): A Community-Based Classroom Project[1]

Background

This brief example comes from a classroom research activity designed to provide students experiences with participant-driven research and processes associated with it. During the introductory qualitative research class that Mirka teaches, students

---

1. This section authored by Mirka Koro-Ljungberg, Kristi Cheyney, and Chandra Bowden.

engage in a collaborative mini-study to promote experiences of conducting a qualitative study. Until a few years ago, students had been able to choose any topic and focus on it as long as democratically decided among the students. However, Mirka noted that too few student-selected projects had an actual impact on the lives of others; neither were these projects serving any larger communal or individual need outside the classroom. This was worrisome, and more research was needed that would illustrate to students the importance of participant-driven work and collaboration with communities and community members.

Pedagogical Paradox

The initiative to engage in participant-driven research activities came from the instructor. Even though students selected this topic, they did not initiate a PDR approach, and they did not have a clear understanding of what this type of work would entail. The instructor introduced her agenda and goals, attempting to raise students' consciousness about research that could serve others. Without a doubt this project was also meant to serve the instructor—her vision as a scholar and educator and her perception of students' needs. Since engaging in any PDR project initially also served the instructor's needs and vision, it wasn't purely egalitarian or completely participant driven, of course. Even though later in the process, the instructor's initial need to engage in this project was replaced by the needs of the National Alliance on Mental Illness (NAMI) and student researchers; once the design evolved, it was unclear whose needs and purposes the project best served.

Students in the class recommended various potential PDR topics, but they found collaboration with NAMI most interesting. Members of NAMI expressed interest in studying stigma, and they wanted to know more about the local community's perceptions and understandings. By "community," we refer to one university community situated in the southeast part of the country. NAMI's local chapter president was a student in our class, and she served as a liaison between the class and NAMI. Through different negotiations with NAMI in which we learned about their previous projects and goals, we decided on the study design, interview questions, and presentation format. The NAMI chapter president directed the talk and negotiations between our class and other NAMI members. The study and initial interactions with NAMI began by learning more about stigma and its impact on individuals with mental illness. We learned that stigma remains an impediment to seeking and receiving the requisite care for mental illness. Researchers have also differentiated among different types of stigma, including public, structural, and courtesy stigma, and self-stigma. Furthermore, we negotiated a purpose for our study: We wanted to better understand community members' perceptions of mental illness and the stigma associated with mental illness. More specifically, this study addressed the following research question: How do community members understand and experience the stigma associated with mental illness?

Ethical Paradox 1

What made students in the introductory class on qualitative research "qualify" to study stigma and become advocates for increased awareness related to mental illness? It was not clear what made them appropriate advocates for individuals with these serious conditions. We wondered whether advocacy, in this form, would be beneficial and for whom. Similarly, there was some uncertainty about whether students (most of them without any medical or counseling training) could generate sufficient understanding to study this topic in depth. If in-depth study or understanding was impossible or unlikely, the benefits of this study might stay at the level of students' methodological learnings (which on their own can be a desirable goal in other contexts). How would students with personal experiences with mental illness manage a study like this, which might be too private and potentially touchy or maybe hurtful? It was clear that there was no right or even appropriate answer. Maybe we were not even sure what the (research) question was.

The following story from the class illustrates this ethical paradox. Once the study had been designed and discussed in class, one student sent an anonymous note to the instructor (slipped under the instructor's door) stating that she or he had mental illness and that the instructor should be aware of that. Even though the note did not have a name and did not ask the instructor to do anything or take any action per se, it seemed to call for a response. The instructor felt that the content of this note had to be addressed and that this student would need to have the option to earn her or his grade some other way if she or he desired to withdraw from the study and not complete the assignment. Thus the instructor addressed the entire class by providing options for study participation, no further questions asked. As a result, every student had the choice of whether to participate or not, and how to participate if so desired. After the discussion, all students were willing to participate in this project, and they were able to choose their level of involvement.

Study Design

The study, originally framed as a hermeneutical study (focusing on the researchers' [i.e., students'] pre-understanding, understanding based on data, and new pre-understanding), was designed to meet the three primary goals of participatory research outlined by Schneider (2012). These goals were "to produce practical knowledge, to take action to make that knowledge available, and to be transformative both socially and for the individuals who take part" (p. 153). The project was divided into three phases—knowledge production, action, reflection—and transformation not only permeated each phase but also informed subsequent as well as past phases. Students and this project produced knowledge that assisted NAMI in understanding the needs of the community better. It also allowed NAMI to design additional and future education projects and select collaboration partners building from this knowledge and this study. Students interacted with the community members and collected data to make gained knowledge available, especially for NAMI members.

However, not all students found this type of research experience the most useful or helpful introduction to qualitative research. For example, some students felt that these interactions and this project were too time consuming and took away from learning "the foundations of qualitative research methods." One student stated the following in his/her class evaluations:

> I learned a lot from the independent project about the power of community research; however, I did not learn as much as I wanted to about the foundations of qualitative research methods. The project was powerful and the community aspect had unexpected benefits, but I feel like it took focus away from our learning and reflecting on the research process. It became more about meeting the needs of the community. I also wonder if it would be possible to find a way to make the project community based but also more relevant to the interests of everyone in the class. I was frustrated by the extra reading on a topic that, while interesting, had no alignment with my interests. Perhaps the community project would be better served in a more advanced class.

Yet students' overall reaction to the project and its usefulness were positive and supportive.

Working Through Data:
Wearing Mental-Illness-Labeled T-Shirts

During one week, 14 students and the instructor intermittently wore mental-illness-labeled T-shirts both on and off campus, and they recorded personal reflections and took observation notes of their experiences. T-shirts were worn everywhere students and the instructor went. Some students reported that they chose not to wear the shirts all the time, since they seemed "inappropriate." Each student printed his or her own T-shirt with a randomly selected mental illness label on it (i.e., schizophrenia, bipolar disorder, depression). All the labels were recommended and provided by NAMI. During the initial stages of the project's development, one participant-researcher wondered,

I wonder how people within and outside the NAMI participants involved in the research felt about the T-shirts. The organization spoke for the community of people with mental illness, but did they represent the community well? Especially with regard to participation in a study intended to describe stigma that also reinforced categorical labeling and potentially reinforced non-people-first language, which has a long tradition in disability studies.

—Darby

Do I even know what stigma means? So I did what any
other college student would do: I looked it up online.
[laughter] . . . The definition I found used the word *disgrace*
to describe a stigmatizing experience. I immediately thought
about people I knew that had a mental illness and the feeling
of disgrace that may be put upon them by others or that they
might feel themselves. I thought of my mom's youngest sister.
This is hard to admit but . . . I have always discounted her as
a part of my family. It occurred to me, I had been stigmatizing
her because of what she had and how she was. I had neglected
her existence. I had avoided her at family gatherings. I never
thought she could do anything on her own or that she could
have a family or that she was worth my time.

Many participant-researchers shared that they knew persons with symptoms of
mental illness who were affected by stigma. One participant-researcher admitted
that "having a parent with mental illness has been a mark of shame. I self-
stigmatize probably more than others would if they knew, so worried that others
will know my dirty little family secrets."

Along with reflections, the participant-researchers recorded their observations of
the community's reaction to seeing them in T-shirts with mental illness labels. One
community member told a participant-researcher who was wearing a T-shirt with
the words "bipolar disorder" that she was "too pretty to have bipolar disorder." In
her journal, the participant-researcher objected by writing, "That was to me a very
stigmatizing phrase. People with mental illness are not pretty? This guy obviously
has a preconceived idea about what people with mental illness look like."

Practical and Pedagogical Paradoxes

All students in the class and all participants in the study did not experience similar
processes. Some decided to participate as bystanders or observers, some wore
T-shirts but did not write many reflections, some reflected more than participated,
some focused on interviews and some more on the observations. Bystanders and
those who witnessed students wearing T-shirts had a choice to participate or not.
Potential study participants had a choice to ignore our students or interact with
them. Some students felt and reported that courtesy stigma (as experienced by
others and family members) turned into internalized stigma in this study. Only
being a part of the study was stigmatizing. T-shirts and note pads were no longer
signifiers of a researcher but of somebody associated with mental illness. Similarly,
being a researcher may have not been desirable for all students, since it required
them to wear stigmatizing shirts. Methodology and research became lived and
personalized in unexpected and sometimes even indescribable ways.

Working Through Data:
Interviewing Community Members

After IRB approval, community members who approached the students were invited to participate in individual interviews about their perceptions of mental illnesses. The 22 community members who volunteered to participate in interviews (5 men and 17 women) were between the ages of 18 and 46 years old. Since the students spent most of their time wearing the shirts at the university, all the interviewees except two were affiliated with the university. Eight interviewees were undergraduates, and the balance were graduate students or professionals. The interviewees identified their ethnicities as follows: White (16), Hispanic (2), Chinese (1), African American (1), Cuban (1), and Puerto Rican (1). When asked if participants knew anyone with a mental illness diagnosis, only three interviewees stated that they had no contact with persons affected by mental illnesses. Collectively, the interviewees stated that they knew eight persons with depression, six with bipolar disorder, and three with schizophrenia. Finally, two interviewees disclosed that they had the diagnoses of obsessive-compulsive disorder and generalized anxiety disorder. Semistructured interviews took place in a variety of settings, such as private study rooms at the university's library, classrooms that were not in use, and graduate student offices. No compensation was offered for participation. When necessary, time was spent to establish or increase rapport so the interviewees were comfortable speaking with researchers. The individual interviews were audio-recorded and transcribed. Identifiers were removed from the transcriptions and interviewees were assigned a pseudonym.

Typically, the initial questions probed to explore the interviewee's thoughts and feelings about seeing the mental illness labels on the T-shirts. Other questions focused on personal encounters with someone with a mental illness; on prejudice, stigma, and how depression (or other types of mental illness) enable or disable individuals in terms of engaging in typical or important life events; how individuals felt about living and working with someone with mental illness; and so on. Because the interviews were semistructured, some interviewers asked a follow-up question that related directly to the interviewee's remarks, and some integrated more of their own experiences in the follow-up questions. While most interviews lasted an average of about 45 minutes, four interviews exceeded 75 minutes and a few ended before 30 minutes lapsed.

Students read and "coded" their transcribed data, at first independently. The transcriptions and initial analyses were then shared with the data analysis team, which comprised seven self-selected participant-researchers who conducted a domain analysis by Spradley (1980). The transcriptions and preliminary analyses were divided among the data analysis team members, who carefully reread the interviews to explore and extend initial themes and search for more overarching ideas. These overarching ideas led to the development of cover terms. During brainstorming sessions, a domain analysis worksheet was utilized to highlight semantic relationships among the many included terms and the fewer cover terms. Preliminary findings were also shared with NAMI.

Theoretical Paradox

This project exemplified some interesting theoretical paradoxes. For example, students' individual pre-understandings were collapsed into a collective pre-understanding that represented everybody's and simultaneously nobody's personal experiences. In this way, our pre-understanding was a textual composite across researchers, and each individual understanding was contextually reduced and somewhat simplified to a point where many personal details and circumstances became unrecognizable. Heidegger's notion of being and time as a singular and situational event was no longer possible when conducting research as a group. However, at the same time, a singular event was felt and expressed collectively and in multiple ways. In other words, any singular being and sense of time were multiplied and repeated and at the same time way stripped from the contextual and situational elements of being-in-the-world. It was impossible to create singular understandings of mental illness, which led us to adopt a more collective notion of "being-in-the-world," thus extending and pushing Heidegger's original notions.

Another paradox that I struggle with in these instances is the use of marginalized populations for the benefit of the "norm." One can hope the encounter will lead to changed thoughts and beliefs, but it may also be threatening or discomforting to the person and family living with mental illness.

—Darby

We will not discuss the findings here in detail, but we note that domain analysis reflected community members' understandings of (1) sources of stigma, (2) impacts of stigma, (3) conceptualizations of stigma, and (4) pathways to change stigma. According to the participants, stigma is moderated most effectively by a combination of education and contact with people with a mental illness diagnoses. Contact helps others understand the reality of mental illness and begins the process of mitigating negative **stereotypes**. Education by itself does not reduce stigma. Rather, there needs to be a conversation with the individuals and families directly affected.

Sharing the Results: Community Forum

We were especially interested to know how we could share our findings in meaningful and communal ways. Preliminary findings were also reviewed by NAMI. The results were compiled into PowerPoint and Prezi presentations for the members of the local NAMI affiliate and the community at large. Held at the university, the forum was attended by approximately 40 community members in addition to the 22 participant-researchers. The forum began with socializing and refreshments provided by the students. After students had presented the literature review, their observations and reflections about wearing the T-shirts, and findings from the domain analysis, community members shared their experiences and understandings of mental illness stigma. Wearing the T-shirts labeled with mental illness diagnoses was a catalyst for observation and reflection by the participant-researchers as well as the community members. The analysis suggested that many parts of the project were transformative for those involved. Not only did the attendees of the culminating forum note the well-organized, thoughtful, and informative presentations, but also the personal transformations of the participant-researchers were evident to community members, who stated that this project idea clearly not only impacted their colleagues emotionally, but also raised their awareness about stigma. In addition, one NAMI member wrote an e-mail thanking the participant-researchers: "It's moving to hear of the process the researchers experienced, affirming that there are people who care and experienced a shift themselves." We concluded that future studies should consider community-based **participatory action research as a powerful tool for understanding mental illness stigma**.

In your own research, you could:

- Have individual and group reflection sessions to address the paradoxes that impact your study

- Acknowledge the paradox that is most challenging for you as a researcher, and chronicle the story of that paradox as it unfolds throughout your study

Voice, Diversity, and Literacy Leadership With Young Children at Risk: Learning From and With Childcare Workers[2]

Another example of PDR in doctoral research involved one student's inquiry into the atypical success of a large subsidized childcare center that serves children at risk. Student researcher Kristi, in designing her study, accounted for the previously documented reluctance of workers employed in these settings. Through photovoice methods (Gubrium & Harper, 2013); open-ended, semistructured interviews; extensive participant observation; and modified narrative analysis procedures, Kristi

---

2. This section authored by Mirka Koro-Ljungberg, Kristi Cheyney, and Chandra Bowden.

It strikes me that the structure of the university schedule inhibits such projects and may even serve as a response to the student who sought additional "foundational" methods. What if the course was extended? Can this process be authentically carried out within the semester? If not, what is lost by not participating through the sharing-back process? Is it effective to collect and analyze the data without presenting it to the community?

—Darby

This is such an interesting study. I think I would want to "shadow" a person living with mental illness for several days in order to understand not only the stigma associated with their diagnosis but also their experiences with others and themselves. Writing a journal and making notes of daily conversations would provide many insights.

—Cheryl

could both leverage candor with those she wanted to research and create a space for her participants to carve out their own path toward reenfranchisement in an educational community that had previously disregarded their critical contributions. Inherent in this line of inquiry were multiple paradoxes—relational, theoretical, ethical, practical, and pedagogical. Because inequities in early literacy experiences form one concern in the documented disparities in school readiness, Kristi examined the early literacy practices of the target center from the perception of the administrators who had created and sustained atypically high-quality early literacy practices for these very-high-risk children. The guiding purpose was to better understand the elements that contributed to the target center's better-than-expected success.

Unfolding Methods

To identify a subsidized child-care center that effectively addressed language and literacy for an at-risk population, Kristi relied on extreme case sampling (Flick, 2009). She approached the local early learning coalition and elicited nominations for community programs that were notable for overall program quality and high literacy assessments, and yet were known to serve an economically-, culturally-, linguistically-, and ability- diverse population of young children.

Kristi's collaborators are referred to here by their chosen pseudonyms: Sofia (the school's executive director) and Maria (the "onsite director" of the three- to five-year-old program).

Over the course of the study (from December 2012 through June 2013), Kristi spent over 100 hours at DCC functioning as a participant observer. After a four-week period of establishing rapport, Kristi sat with her informants to develop collaborative goals for the study (McIntyre, 2008). They discussed her goals and theirs. Kristi also asked them to go back to their teachers and engage in informal discourse about goals that their teachers might have in the process, although she did not study the teachers directly. These collaborative goals became the backbone of their collaborative relationship. They returned to them often throughout the process and allowed the goals to guide their inquiry.

Ethical Paradox 1

Developing collaborative goals was not an easy process, and in fact created some ethical paradoxes Kristi would need to finesse. Whose goals would lead the process? For example, one of the informant's goals for participation in the study was to deconstruct the popular stereotype of child-care workers as "babysitters." Both informants flatly rejected the title of "caregiver," prompting Kristi to change the way she referred to them and their staff. In one sense, this goal stood in opposition to one of Kristi's own goals, which had shaped her research "planning." Kristi had been interested in investigating the feminist standpoint regarding women and caregiving roles. Kristi expected her informants to embrace their roles as caregivers and to be concerned with expressing the importance of these caregiving skills for the broader society. The rejection of this role was clear not only in the participatory goals but also in their interviews and meetings. Kristi reports having to shift her thinking in order to remain truly open to the data and to what would later emerge in her analysis. Kristi's goal of illuminating the importance of "women's work" to the greater good of society shifted to the collaborative goal of "empowering other women working in the child-care profession, as participants share their own experiences and invite continuing dialogue with other practitioners."

During Kristi's time at the center, she took photographs and participated in school activities, interacting with the teachers and children. Maria and Sofia were also asked to take photographs of literacy interactions throughout the day, and both collections of photographs played a critical role in semistructured, open-ended interviews about literacy praxis within their setting. In addition to documenting daily literacy practices, images were used for narrative elicitation or as entry points for beginning interview conversations. This process also allowed participants to identify subjects that were meaningful to them rather than beginning interviews with a list of questions that had been established beforehand. Tables of exemplar photos were presented. Kristi encouraged participants to talk about them. Photographs were also used to guide follow-up interviews. The final dataset consisted of over five hours of interviews, Kristi's participant observation notes, and 4,338 photographs (479 taken by Maria and Sofia).

Relational Paradox

This use of images both created and resolved a key relational paradox. Kristi wondered how to establish a relationship with participants that would result in candid dialogue and yet where she could maintain an objective separation as called for by her dissertation committee. The time spent in participant observation allowed an important rapport to develop, but Kristi also reported that a sense of separation evoked a viewing of events through a camera lens and not her own eyes. The camera lens keeps no appraisals of its own. It simply documents. The camera facilitated Kristi's efforts to be a "conscious observer," that is, someone who could be fully present in the moment and yet withhold judgment. Likewise, using photos for elicitation in interviews allowed participants to direct the discourse, but it also provided a similar boundary, where the images absorbed the possible interrogatory nature of interviews. The paradox of remaining objective and yet fully relationally invested became attainable through the use photovoice methods. But how important were complete presence, objectivity, and relational investment?

After audio recordings of interviews were transcribed in detail, Kristi prepared the transcripts for analysis by embedding the photographs used during the interviews within the text documents. This made it possible to analyze crucial images as organic complements to the women's words. Because this research included visual and participatory elements, Kristi added a unique iteration to the basic listening guide, which she called "Collaborative Visual Voice." This involved (1) reviewing the extant photo archive for images that exemplified, contradicted, or further illuminated the preliminary findings and revising findings as needed; and then (2) meeting with participants to review findings and to revise them again as needed. Last, Maria and Sofia helped create a photographic installation to communicate results to their communities. Images were used to represent findings for the participants' own community in a photographic installation. In this way, Kristi's iteration of Gilligan's listening guide provided a pathway for recurrent individual and collaborative reflection on the paradoxes that would unfold as the research progressed. Though the participants would later consult with Kristi on the manuscript she submitted for publication to a scholarly journal (Kristi included them as co-authors), collectively they viewed the installation as a more socially significant format for dissemination in light of their collaborative research goals.

Elicitation

The images allowed Kristi to capitalize on important aspects of PDR. The photographs created a type of a connection zone between the women and supported Kristi in leveraging deeper levels of transparency. Moreover, these distinct functions of the images ran together and merged as the study progressed.

Kristi took photographs daily, and Maria and Sofia took photographs in her absence. Kristi asked participants to share language and literacy activities as they took place naturally during the day. Later she downloaded the photographs.

Theoretical Paradox 1

Using photos for elicitation created a theoretical paradox around how to share situated knowledges. Each of the three women brought different knowledges—and ways of knowing—to the research experience. Kristi brought to the table extensive content knowledge of early language and literacy and child development, but also background and direct experiential knowledge of child care as a distinct early childhood setting and child-care workers as unique professionals. However, Maria and Sofia each had their own distinctive content and experiential knowledges. How could these distinct knowledges be shared? Whose theory/practice would take precedence? Would they merge at some point? Kristi wanted to allow her participants to guide interviews, but she also felt apprehensive about letting go of her own questions. Kristi was able to settle into this tension and uncertainty by trusting the process she had laid out in her research design. On the day of each individual interview, Kristi presented Maria and Sofia with a table of their own photographs *first* and invited them to talk about an image of their choosing. For example, Figure 8.4 shows Sofia's image of a teacher engaging in language interactions with toddlers during a stroller excursion.

Figure 8.4   Sofia's Image of a Teacher Engaging in Language Interactions With Toddlers

Kristi Cheyney

Sofia selected this image in order to talk about how her teachers were able to weave language interactions throughout the day and not just during designated story times. This is a well-established best practice in early childhood, and it was important to Sofia that Kristi understand her teachers' extensive pedagogical and content knowledge. From this interaction, Kristi gained an understanding of the teachers' knowledge as well as Sofia's. Perhaps more important, Sofia's selection of this image and her meaning making helped Kristi understand Sofia's internal discourses around knowledge in the context of her school, and the value she placed on teacher-established "best practice" *alongside* teachers' own folk knowledge. These types of opportunities, however uncomfortable for a student researcher, could not have happened in the absence of Kristi's willingness to trust the process and her participants.

There were also times where Kristi introduced photos of her own choosing, often images she had captured herself. During individual interviews with both Maria and Sofia, Kristi inquired about a sequence of photographs she took of a child with Down syndrome playing with mulch on the playground (see Figure 8.5). One of the themes generated during the analysis involved the way teachers were able to effectively meet the needs of children with disabilities, and Kristi selected these images in order to open the discussion about one particular teacher–child interaction that progressed over a few minutes' time. She showed each photograph, one at a time, as she explained what the teacher was doing off camera as an example of an effective teaching moment.

Figure 8.5 Kristi's Images of a Child With Down Syndrome Playing With Mulch

Though the photographs are both humorous and adorable, Kristi chose the sequence because the teacher handled the situation well, and she was able to ask more detailed questions about the way teachers address children with special needs and the difficulties they face in these situations (i.e., inadequate teacher training in special needs, prohibitively long processes in accessing support from external agencies).

Ethical Paradox 2

When does one fully participate, and when does one step back and observe? Kristi worked with this paradox within a PDR framework by inviting the teacher participants of one study to participate in professional development activities after the data collection had ended. The teachers in this study worked *with* Kristi to plan the content of the workshops Kristi would facilitate. Kristi was also able to contribute her expertise more strategically, as her months of participant observation informed her approach to the teacher's perceived professional needs as well as the way she introduced new knowledge, strategies, and inquiries. The arrows of power (think back to Image 11.2) flowed in a truly reciprocal fashion.

Representation

The final part of the project was to share study findings with a larger audience. Kristi and her participants used the collaborative research goals agreed upon at the beginning of the project as a constant guide to designing and planning the installation. The installation was shown at a university gallery in April 2013 and at DCC in June 2013.

In this way, representation of the findings created another unanswerable question.

Theoretical Paradox 2

Whose meaning making would be represented and in what format? All three women agreed to work toward consensus for each photograph that would be included in the installation. Consensus proved complicated. For example, one discussion over representation arose about a series of images that depicted "Mrs. Wishy-Washy Day," where Maria dressed up as the beloved children's literature character and conducted a shared storybook reading for the children and teachers. Kristi felt the images were important to her understanding of the literacy interactions she observed at the school. Sophia, who can be seen holding the big book in many of the photographs (see photo), was reluctant to use the images in the installation because she wanted this section to highlight Maria.

The Mrs. Wishy-Washy sequence was the first set of installation images we discussed as a group. During the course of the discourse, Sofia came to the

Figure 8.6 "The Best of Me" Photographic Installation

Kristi Cheyney

Kristi Cheyney

Figure 8.7 Mrs. Wishy-Washy Day

Kristi Cheyney

conclusion that her discomfort with this particular image was less about her wanting to highlight Maria's brilliant moments and more about her own discomfort with seeing herself in any photograph, on the walls of a gallery, or in her school, for all to see. She felt exposed. Kristi reports reiterating many times that Sofia could back out of the installation at any time. In the end it was Maria, even more painfully shy, who helped Sofia make the decision to trust the process and to sustain belief that their collective story needed to be told. Through the group dialogue over this one photograph and the narrative it elicited, the women found a collective need to share this powerful voice of interdependence with their community.

Another Understanding of PDR: Where to Go From Here[3]

Gainesville, June 25, 2014

Mirka: It seems to me that we now have more questions than earlier and very few answers. Where to go next?

Becky: I feel empowered yet powerless. I am interested in international work, and in this work you are always coming from the powerful position and you are working with people who are "oppressed." So to do participatory methods from the development perspective can be very effective but also hard. You are really tailoring your research to the people within the community but not always in successful ways.

Mirka: But are you really tailoring the research, or is it already almost prethought and somehow premeditated?

Becky: That's exactly where I get tied up. You are always coming from the position of power. Always. No matter how much of the research process you give up, you still have a privileged perspective in some ways.

Mirka: I agree. Yet at the same time I wonder why privilege is necessarily a bad thing. Can privilege be used to serve the other, or is "distribution of privilege" always an oxymoron?

Becky: Not sure, but it seems like you come full circle again. My privilege is providing collaborators and study participants an opportunity to have their voices be heard, but they are still being heard through my privilege—through the groups, journals, and spaces I have access to.

Mirka: What if privilege is not a position or something to be possessed, but privilege is something that can be distributed or shared like social capital?

Becky: Yes, I am thinking in those lines. How can I release my privilege to somebody else or activate it in behalf

_____

3. This section authored by Mirka Koro-Ljungberg, Rebecca Williams, Justin Hendricks, and Darbianne Shannon.

of others? But right now (in my current work in Honduras) I get caught into this simple notion of literacy. I am working with groups with a very low level of literacy, so how do I involve them in research and data analysis, for example? It seems like no matter how I engage with them, I am taking away their voice and altering their message in some ways.

Justin: I think about what is being produced in the process and who it benefits. What is the usability of research for us? Research may not translate for us or other people involved in the project. How to make research mutually beneficial? You may lose your job doing this.

Darby: And yes, losing your job leads to losing your privilege. The thing I struggle with is how to make PDR manageable. And it seems that to make it manageable I have to choose. I am not sure I want to choose and take a side.

Becky: Am I facilitating a research process or manipulating the process? Sometimes the outside perspective of the researcher can enable different perspectives and experiences from the community to be brought forward, since the researcher is working outside the internal power structures. It is also possible that if you let the community completely drive a research project, it leads to silencing of some voices and promoting potentially liminal or even impairing perspectives.

Mirka: Yes, as a researcher, you might have a possibility to create space to intervene differently and potentially impact the power relations within that community. But then at the same time it can be ethically questionable for researchers to point or call out the silenced community members, their oppression, or to encourage and support the community to intervene and change things.

Becky: You might also run into situations where community members do not want certain discourses to be representative of the community's perspective.

Justin: I have been doing some research with Mormon feminists, and I have been wondering about my ethical obligation to this group. Do I have an obligation to stay with this oppressed community through the rest of my career? What kind of commitment do I make for them, and what does it mean if I just do one project? In some way I am using this community as a stepping-stone for my career, especially if after one project I move on to other projects and other communities. What is the best way of going about that, seeing as most likely I cannot commit my entire career to studying one community?

Darby: This seem a little problematic to me, because the quality of the conversations you have with those people depends on the relationship you establish with them. The level of trust may not be the same if you are just in and out.

Mirka: Justin is bringing up an interesting point related to "rejection" and feeling important and cared for. It is interesting to think about research and scholarly interests. For example, at some point a scholar sees the importance of studying with a specific group of people, and then later this group is no longer important or significant enough. Does this imply that the problems or dilemmas associated with this group or community are solved, or did the researcher lose her/his interest, change her/his research focus for one or another reason? What happens and why, when a scholar stops researching with a particular community?

Justin: I have also thought about community's desires and "wants" especially when the community is very heterogeneous and possibly without communal hierarchy or structure. How do you know what the community wants? What's a community?

Mirka:	I am not sure. I also wonder if participant-driven research needs to be community based. Can participant-driven research happen between two people? Can two people form a community? In some ways I would like to challenge the role of community in participant-driven research because I think there is a difference there. Participant-driven research is not always associated with a community or a group of people, and community-driven research might not be participatory. I think we need to be more careful and specific when using these terms. At the same time, as we have seen earlier in this section, the lines are blurred, and different practices blend. What is accomplished by these conceptual discussions anyway?
Justin:	What if there are multiple researchers and research projects active within one community? Do you have an ethical obligation to critique or support the other research being done? Do you need to collaborate with other research groups? And what if community interests change over the time of research? Who calls quits or initiates the changes?
Mirka:	Justin's comment makes me think about the evaluation of PDR. Who has the authority to carry out an evaluation or critique of PDR? Instead of traditional notions of validity and reliability (i.e., drawing from quantitative research), maybe the utilization of research and its findings is a sign of validity or trustworthiness. But it is not so simple— utilization of research also implies a particular beneficiary.
Darby:	Maybe PDR is impossible to evaluate and one cannot say whether it is good or bad. Where to go from here?
Becky:	In the context of my research in Honduras, people from within the community have a political agenda

regarding land tenure rights, whereas outside researchers were able to give this discourse and conversation much more historical perspective. For example, "outsiders" noted how the existing discourse and perspective came about and what its role in the history of Honduras is. In this case, the community was representing themselves in a certain way for a particular political purpose. More specifically, this group has been presenting themselves in a specific way to get indigenous land rights while still trying to maintain their Afro-descendants' heritage. These people are trying to work all discourses that might forward and benefit their political agenda.

Darby: Why did the community identify or recognize that this particular political agenda was what they were going to go after? And how did that influence the researcher? Even when research comes from within, what are some external elements that influence the type of research and questions the communities choose to address?

Becky: It has been somewhat difficult for me to figure out what is going on in the community, since there are two groups that basically fight over this within the community. One of them is taking an "I wanna play nice with the government" approach, and the other one has taken a very anti-establishment approach, since the establishment has been the oppressor. Within the community, you see this division every day.

Mirka: Darby's question also prompts a question from another perspective. Can research and researchers be used to perpetuate and (potentially unwillingly) support certain types of community agendas that might be oppressive on their own? One can think about community goals, purposes, and activities that are desirable from the community perspective, but they may violate some rights of minorities or those oppressed, or these purposes and agendas might position minorities in a continuously negative and oppressive light. A meaningful community goal can turn into or continue to highlight other oppressive structures.

Darby: Yes, and what research is not being done, since this is the research we decided to do.

Becky: It is also interesting to think about this from the member-checking perspective. I would like to go back to the community and ask if everybody participated in the project and who were those whose opinions and perspectives were not taken into account. Who were selected to represent the community? Who are the community?

Mirka: What are researchers' ethical responsibilities in these situations?

Becky: What about research agendas that are benefiting "my" community but hurting the communities next door? I saw that a lot in Honduras. This is something that keeps me up at night.

Darby: Do you bring these questions to the community? Do you ask about their ethical responsibilities as a partner and co-creator of this knowledge? I understand that this is your position, but these are my concerns—let's talk about this. Or do you lose trust by raising those questions? I wonder.

We just wonder

   But we also need to move and

Take a stance

Despite the uncertainty and possible fear

We wonder while moving . . .

READING LIST OF LIFE

Coetzee, J. M. (2000). *Disgrace*. Penguin Books.

Sijie, D. (2001). *Balzac and the little Chinese seamstress*. Anchor Books.

Oksanen, S. (2012). *Kun kyyhkyset katosivat* (When the doves disappeared). Like Kustannus Oy.

Robert Ulmer

Irruption 3: Living Uncertainty

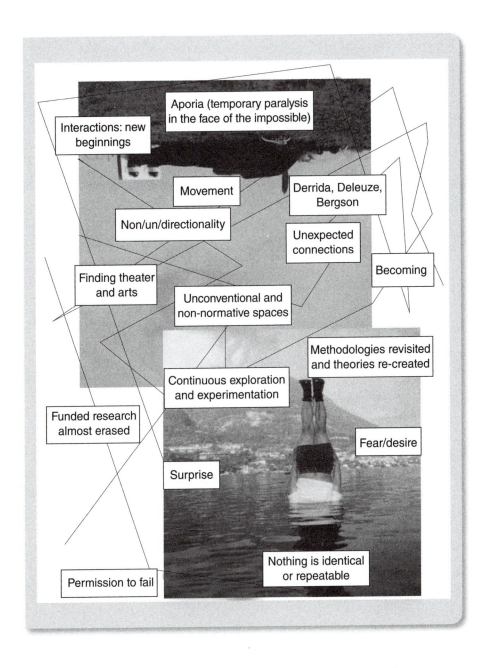

Aporia (temporary paralysis in the face of the impossible)

Interactions: new beginnings

Movement

Derrida, Deleuze, Bergson

Non/un/directionality

Unexpected connections

Becoming

Finding theater and arts

Unconventional and non-normative spaces

Methodologies revisited and theories re-created

Continuous exploration and experimentation

Funded research almost erased

Fear/desire

Surprise

Permission to fail

Nothing is identical or repeatable

REFERENCES

Academy of Management. (2006). *Academy of Management code of ethics.* Retrieved from http://aom.org/uploadedFiles/About_AOM/Governance/AOM_Code_of_Ethics.pdf

Ammenwerth, E., Iller, C., & Mansmann, U. (2003). Can evaluation studies benefit from triangulation? A case study. *International Journal of Medical Informatics, 70*(2–3), 237–248. doi: http://dx.doi.org/10.1016/S1386-5056(03)00059-5

Banner, J., & Cannon, H. (1997). *The elements of teaching.* New Haven, CT: Yale University Press.

Barad, K. (2007). *Meeting the universe halfway.* Durham, NC: Duke University Press.

Baudrillard, J. (1983). *Simulations* (P. Foss, P. Patton, & P. Beitchman, Trans.). New York, NY: Semiotext[x].

Baudrillard, J. (1990). *Revenge of the crystal: Selected writings on the modern object and its destiny, 1968-1983* (P. Foss & J. Pefanis, Eds. & Trans.). London, UK: Pluto Press.

Baudrillard, J. (2000). *The vital illusion.* New York, NY: Columbia University Press.

Baudrillard, J. (2003). *Cool memories IV, 1995–2000.* London, UK: Verso.

Baudrillard, J. (2010). *Jean Baudrillard: Carnival and cannibal, ventriloquous evil* (C. Turner, Trans.). London, UK: Seagull Books.

Baudrillard, J., & Witwer, J. (2000). *The vital illusion.* New York, NY: Columbia University Press.

Baumrind, D. (1964). Some thoughts on the ethics of research: After reading Milgram's "Behavioral Study of Obedience." *American Psychologist, 19,* 421–423.

Beardsworth, R. (1996). *Derrida and the political.* London, UK: Routledge.

Behar, R. (1996). *The vulnerable observer: Anthropology that breaks your heart.* Boston, MA: Beacon.

Benton, A., Androff, D., Barr, B.-D., & Taylor, S. (2012). Of quant jocks and qual outsiders: Doctoral student narratives on the quest for training in qualitative research. *Qualitative Social Work, 11*(3), 232–248.

Bernard, R., & Ryan, G. (2010). Introduction to text: Qualitative data analysis. *Analyzing qualitative data: Systematic approaches.* Thousand Oaks, CA: Sage.

Bernauer, J., Semich, G., Klentzin, J., & Holden, E. (2013). Themes of tension surrounding research methodologies education in an accelerated cohort-based doctoral program. *International Journal of Doctoral Studies, 8,* 173–193.

Biesta, G. (1998). Say you want a revolution . . . suggestions for the impossible future of critical pedagogy. *Educational Theory, 48*(3), 499–510.

Bloome, D., & Egan-Robertson, A. (1993). The social construction of intertextuality in classroom reading and writing lessons. *Reading Research Quarterly, 28*(4), 304–333.

Bogdan, R., & Biklen, S. (2006). *Qualitative research for education: An introduction to theories and methods* (5th ed.). Boston, MA: Pearson.

Bogue, R. (2005). The minor. In C. Stivale (Ed.), *Gilles Deleuze: Key concepts* (pp. 110–120). Montreal, Quebec: McGill-Queen's University Press.

Braidotti, R. (2006). Posthuman, all too human: Towards a new process ontology. *Theory, Culture and Society, 23*(7–8), 197–208.

Bridges, G. S., Gillmore, G. M., Pershing, J. L., & Bates, K. A. (1998). Teaching quantitative research methods: A quasi-experimental analysis. *Teaching Sociology, 26,* 14–28.

British Educational Research Association. (2010). *The processes of commissioning research report. Retrieved from* http://www.bera .ac.uk/commissioning-and-consuming-research-in-education/the-processes-of-commissioning-research/#2

Britzman, D. (1997). The tangles of implication. *Qualitative Studies in Education, 10*(1), 31–37.

Brown, S., & Stenner, P. (2009). *Psychology without foundations.* London, UK: Sage.

Browning, G. (2000). *Lyotard and the end of grand narratives.* Cardiff: University of Wales Press.

Burkhardt, H., & Schoenfeld, A. (2003). Improving educational research: Toward a more useful, more influential, and better-funded enterprise. *Educational Researcher, 32*(9), 3–14.

Cannella, G., & Lincoln, Y. S. (2011). Ethics, research regulations, and critical social science. In N. Denzin & Y. S. Lincoln (Eds.), *The SAGE handbook of qualitative research* (pp. 81-89). Thousand Oaks, CA: Sage.

Carter, S., & Little, M. (2007). Justifying knowledge, justifying method, taking action: Epistemologies, methodologies, and methods in qualitative research. *Qualitative Health Research, 17*(10), 1316–1328.

Cartwright, W. (2006). Reasons and selves: Two accounts of responsibility in theory and practice. *Philosophy, Psychiatry, and Psychology, 13*(2), 143–155.

Charmaz, K. (2010). Grounded theory: Objectivist and constructivist methods. In W. Luttrell (Ed.), *Qualitative educational research* (pp. 183–207). New York, NY: Routledge.

Cheek, J. (2010). Human rights, social justice, and qualitative research: Questions and hesitations about what we say about what we do. In N. Denzin & M. Giardina (Eds.), *Qualitative inquiry and human rights* (pp. 100-111). Walnut Creek, CA: Left Coast Press.

Childers, S., Rhee, J.-E., & Daza, S. (2013). Promiscuous (use of) feminist methodologies: The dirty theory and messy practice of educational research beyond gender. *International Journal of Qualitative Studies in Education, 26*(5), 507–523.

Chomsky, N. (1967). "The Responsibility of Intellectuals". The New York Review of Books 8 (3). http://www .chomsky.info/ articles/19670223.htm

Christians, C. (2011). Ethics and politics in qualitative research. In N. Denzin & Y. S. Lincoln (Eds.), *The SAGE handbook of qualitative research* (4th ed., pp. 61-80). Thousand Oaks, CA: Sage.

Coleman, R., & Ringrose, J. (2013). Introduction. In *Deleuze and research methodologies.* Edinburgh, UK: Edinburgh University Press.

Cook, S., & Gordon, M. F. (2004). Teaching qualitative research: A metaphorical approach. *Journal of Advanced Nursing, 47*(6), 649–655.

Cooper, K., & McNab, S. L. (2009). Questioning as a pedagogical tool in teaching and research. In S. Kouritzin, N. Piquemal, & R. Norman (Eds.), *Qualitative research: Challenging the orthodoxies in standard academic discourse(s)* (pp. 199–215). New York, NY: Routledge.

Crabtree, B., & Miller, W. (Eds.). (1992). *Doing qualitative research: Multiple strategies.* Newbury Park, CA: Sage.

Creswell, J. (2007). *Qualitative inquiry and research design: Choosing among five approaches* (2nd ed.). Thousand Oaks, CA: Sage.

Crotty, M. (1998). *The foundations of social research.* London, UK: Sage.

Davis, W. (2001). Introduction: The dimensions and dilemmas of a modern virtue. In W. Davis (Ed.), *Taking responsibility: Comparative perspectives* (pp. 1–27). Charlottesville: University Press of Virginia.

Deleuze, G. (1990). *The logic of sense* (M. Lester, Trans.). New York, NY: Columbia University Press.

Deleuze, G. (1991). *Bergsonims* (H. Tomlinson & B. Habberjam, Trans.). New York, NY: Zone Books.

Deleuze, G. (1995). *Negotiations, 1972–1990.* New York, NY: Columbia University Press.

Deleuze, G., & Guattari, F. (1987). *A thousand plateaus: Capitalism and schizophrenia.*

(B. Massumi, Trans.). Minneapolis: University of Minnesota Press.

Deleuze, G., & Guattari, F. (1994). *What is philosophy?* (H. Tomlinson & G. Burchell, Trans.). New York, NY: Columbia University Press.

DeLyser, D., Potter, A., Chaney, J., Crider, S., Debnam, I., Hanks, G., . . . Early, M. (2014). A synthesis of the literature on research methods education. *Teaching in Higher Education, 19*(3), 242–253.

Denzin, N., & Giardina, M. (2014). Introduction: Qualitative inquiry "outside" the academy. In N. Denzin & M. Giardina (Eds.), *Qualitative inquiry outside the academy* (pp. 9–31). Walnut Creek, CA: Left Coast Press.

Denzin, N., & Lincoln, Y. (Eds.). (2011). *The SAGE handbook of qualitative research* (4th ed.).Thousand Oaks, CA: Sage.

Denzin N. & Giardina, M (2010) (Eds.), *Qualitative inquiry and human rights* Walnut Creek, CA: Left Coast Press.

Derrida, J. (1982). *Margins of philosophy* (A. Bass, Trans.). Chicago, IL: University of Chicago Press.

Derrida, J. (1992). *The other heading: Reflections on*

today's Europe (P. A. Brault & M. P. Naas, Trans.). Indianapolis: Indiana University Press.

Derrida, J. (1993). *Aporias* (T. Dutoit, Trans.). Stanford, CA: Stanford University Press.

Derrida, J. (1995). *The gift of death: Religion and postmodernism* (D. Wills, Trans.). Chicago, IL: University of Chicago Press.

Derrida, J. (1997). *Of grammatology.* (G. Spivak, Trans.). Baltimore, MD: Johns Hopkins University Press.

Derrida, J. (1999). Hospitality, justice, and responsibility: A dialogue with Jacques Derrida. In R. Kearney & M. Dooley (Eds.), *Questioning ethics: Contemporary debates in philosophy* (pp. 65–83). London, UK: Routledge.

Derrida, J. (2001a). "A certain 'madness' must watch over thinking": Refusing to build a philosophical system, Derrida privileges experience and writes out of "compulsion." A dialogue around trace and deconstructions. Jacques Derrida's interview with François Ewald. In G. Biesta & D. Egéa-Kuehne (Eds.), *Derrida and education* (pp. 55–76). London, UK: Routledge.

Derrida, J. (2001b). "I have a taste for the secret" (G. Donis, Trans.). In G. Donis & D. Webb (Eds.), *A taste for the secret* (pp. 1–92). Cambridge, UK: Polity Press.

Derrida, J. (2002). *Negotiations: Interventions and interviews, 1971–2001* (E. Rottenberg, Trans.). Stanford, CA: Stanford University Press.

Derrida, J. (2005). *Paper machine* (R. Bowlby, Trans.). Stanford, CA: Stanford University Press.

Derrida, J. (2006). *Specters of Marx* (P. Kamuf, Trans.). New York, NY: Routledge.

Derrida, J. (2007). A certain impossible possibility of saying the event. *Critical Inquiry, 33*(2), 441–461.

Dewey, J. (1939). Experience, knowledge, and value: A rejoinder. In J. A. Boydston (Ed.), *The later works* (1925–1953): Vol. 14. *1939–1941 Essays and miscellany* (pp. 3–90). Carbondale, IL: Southern Illinois University Press.

Doyle, S. (2013). Reflexivity and the capacity to think. *Qualitative Health Research, 23*(2), 248–255. doi: 10.1177/104973 2312467854

Early, M. (2014). A synthesis of the literature on research methods education. *Teaching in Higher Education, 19*(3), 242–253.

Edelsky, C. (Ed). (1999). *Making justice our project: Teachers working toward critical whole language practice.* Urbana, IL: National Council of Teachers of English.

Edgoose, J. (2001). Just decide! Derrida and the ethical aporias of education. In G. Biesta & D. Egea-Kuehne (Eds.), *Derrida and education* (pp. 119–133). London, UK: Routledge.

Egéa-Kuehne, D. (2003). The teaching of philosophy: Renewed rights and responsibilities. *Educational Philosophy and Theory, 35*(3), 271–284.

Eisenhart, M. (2001). Educational ethnography past, present, and future: Ideas to think with. *Educational Researcher, 30*(8), 16–27.

Eisenhart, M., & DeHann, R. (2005). Doctoral preparation of scientifically based education researchers. *Educational Researcher, 34*(4), 3–13.

Evink, E. (2009). (In)finite responsibility: How to avoid the contrary effects of Derrida's ethics. *Philosophy & Social Criticism, 35*(4), 467–481.

Farmer, T., Robinson, K., Elliott, S. J., & Eyles, J. (2006). Developing and implementing a triangulation protocol for qualitative health research.

Qualitative Health Research, 16(3), 377–394. doi: 10.1177/104973 2305285708

Feinberg, J., & Shafer-Landau, R. (2008). *Reason and responsibility: Readings in some basic problems of philosophy* (13th ed.). Belmont, CA: Thomson Wadsworth.

Flick, U. (2009). *An introduction to qualitative research* (4th ed.). Thousand Oaks, CA: Sage.

Flick, U., & Bauer, M. (2004). Teaching qualitative research. In U. Flick, E. von Kardorff, & I. Steinke (Eds.), *A companion to qualitative research* (pp. 340–348). Thousand Oaks, CA: Sage.

Fosnot, C. (Ed.). (2005). *Constructivism: Theory, perspectives, and practice* (2nd ed.). New York, NY: Teachers College Press.

Foucault, M. (1972). *The archaeology of knowledge and the discourse on language* (A. M. S. Smith, Trans.). New York, NY: Pantheon Books.

Foucault, M. (1986). *The history of sexuality*: Vol. 3. *The care of the self* (R. Hurley, Trans.). New York, NY: Vintage Books.

Foucault, M. (1995). *Discipline and punish* (A. Sheridan, Trans.). New York, NY: Vintage Books.

Foucault, M., Burchell, G., Gordon, C., & Miller, P. (1991). *The Foucault effect: Studies in governmentality with two lectures by and an interview with Michel Foucault.* Chicago, IL: University of Chicago Press.

Foucault, M., & Faubion, J. D. (1998). *Aesthetics, method, and epistemology.* New York, NY: New Press.

Freeman, M., deMarrais, K., Preissle, J., Roulston, K., & Elizabeth, S. P. (2007). Standards of evidence in qualitative research: An incitement to discourse. *Educational Researcher, 36*(1), 25–32.

Freiherr von der Goltz, W. M. (2011). Functions of intertextuality and intermediality in *The Simpsons.* Retrieved from http://duepublico. uni-duisburg-essen.de/ servlets/DocumentServlet? id=26560&lang=en

Freire, P. (1998). *Pedagogy of the heart.* New York, NY: Continuum.

Frost, P. (1999). Why compassion counts! *Journal of Management Inquiry, 8,* 127–133.

Galstado, D. (2012, September 26). *Body-map storytelling as research: Documenting physical, emotional and social health as a journey.* Presentation at the Centre for Critical Qualitative Health Research Seminar, University of Toronto. Retrieved from http:// www.ccqhr.utoronto.ca/ sites/default/files/CQ_ Body_Map_Storytelling_ Presentation.pdf

Gee, J. (2005). *An introduction to discourse analysis: Theory and method* (2nd ed.). New York, NY: Routledge.

Gilmore, T., Krantz, J., & Ramirez, R. (1986). Action based modes of inquiry and the host-researcher relationship. *Consultation, 5*(3), 160–176.

Gobo, G. (2004). Sampling, representativeness and generalizability. In C. Seale, G. Gobo, J. Gubrium, & D. Silverman (Eds.), *Qualitative research practice* (pp. 435–456). London, UK: Sage.

Gochman, D. (1982). Labels, systems, and motives: Some perspectives for future research and programs. *Health Education and Behavior, 9,* 167–174.

Green, L. W., George, M. A., Daniel, M., Frankish, C. J., Herbert, C. P., Bowie, W. R., & O'Neill, M. (2003). Appendix C: Guidelines for participatory research in health promotion. In M. Minkler & N. Wallerstein (Eds.), *Community-based participatory research for health.* San Francisco, CA: Jossey-Bass.

Gubrium, A., & Harper, K. (2013). *Participatory visual and digital methods.* Walnut Creek, CA: Left Coast Press.

Gubrium, J. F., & Holstein, J. A. (1997). *The new language of qualitative method.* New York, NY: Oxford University Press.

Gürtler, L., & Huber, G. L. (2006). The ambiguous use of language in the paradigms of QUAN and QUAL. *Qualitative Research in Psychology, 3*(4), 313–328.

Habermas, J. (1971). *Knowledge and human interests* (J. J. Shapiro, Trans.). Boston, MA: Beacon Press.

Habermas, J. (1990). *Moral consciousness and communicative action* (C. Lenhardt & S. Weber Nicholson, Trans.). Cambridge, UK: Polity Press.

Hale, C. (2006). Activist research v. cultural critique: Indigenous land rights and the contradictions of politically engaged anthropology. *Cultural Anthropology, 21*(1), 96–120.

Hammersley, M., & Atkinson, P. (1995). *Ethnography: Principles in practice.* London, UK: Routledge.

Hayes, S., & Koro-Ljungberg, M. (2011). Dialogic

exchanges and the negotiation of differences: Female graduate students' experiences of obstacles related to academic mentoring. *Qualitative Report, 16*(3), 682–710.

Heidegger, M. (1996). *Being and time* (J. Stambaugh, Trans.). Albany, NY: State University of New York Press.

Heidegger, M. (2010). *Phenomenology of intuition and expression: Theory of philosophical concept formation.* London, UK: Continuum.

Hein, S. (2004). "I don't like ambiguity": An exploration of students' experiences during a qualitative methods course. *Alberta Journal of Educational Research, 50*(1), 22–38.

Hunt, M. (2010). "Active waiting": Habits and the practice of conducting qualitative research. *International Journal of Qualitative Methods, 9*(1), 69–76.

Hurworth, R. (2008). *Teaching qualitative research.* Rotterdam: SensePublishers.

International Institute for Sustainable Development. (n.d.). *Participatory research for sustainable livelihoods: A guide for field projects on adaptive strategies.* Retrieved June 5, 2014, from http://www.iisd.org/casl/caslguide/par.htm

Jackson, A., & Mazzei, L. (2012). *Thinking with theory in qualitative research: Viewing data across multiple perspectives.* London, UK: Routledge.

Jacques, R. S. (2010). Signifier and signified. In A. J. Mills, G. Durepos, & E. Wiebe (Eds.), *Encyclopedia of case study research* (pp. 862–863. Thousand Oaks, CA: Sage.

Kincheloe, J. L. (2001). Describing the bricolage: Conceptualizing a new rigor in qualitative research. *Qualitative Inquiry, 7*(6), 679.

Koro-Ljungberg, M. (2007). "Democracy to come": A personal narrative of pedagogical practices and "Othering" within a context of higher education and research training. *Teaching in Higher Education, 12*(5–6), 735–747.

Koro-Ljungberg, M. (2012). Researchers of the world, create! *Qualitative Inquiry, 18*(9), 806–816.

Koro-Ljungberg, M., Cavalleri, D., Covert, H., & Bustam, T. (2012). Documents of learning: Graduate students' experiences of tension when studying qualitative data analysis approaches. *Reflective Practice, 13*(2), 195–207.

Koro-Ljungberg, M., & Hayes, S. (2006). The relational selves of female graduate students during academic mentoring: From dialogue to transformation. *Mentoring and Tutoring, 14*(4), 389–407.

Koro-Ljungberg, M., & Hayes, S. (2010). Proposing an argument for research questions that could create permeable boundaries within qualitative research. *Journal of Ethnographic and Qualitative Research, 4*(3), 114–124.

Koro-Ljungberg, M., & MacLure, M. (2013). Provocations, re-un-visions, death and other possibilities of 'data.' *Cultural Studies ↔ Critical Methodologies, 13*(4), 219–222.

Koro-Ljungberg, M., & Mazzei, L. (2012). Problematizing methodological simplicity in qualitative research: Editors' introduction. *Qualitative Inquiry, 18*(9), 726–729.

Koro-Ljungberg, M., Yendol-Hoppey, D., Smith, J. J., & Hayes, S. B. (2009). (E)pistemological awareness, instantiation of methods, and uninformed methodological ambiguity in qualitative research projects. *Educational Researcher, 38*(9), 687–699.

KU (University of Kansas) Work Group for Community Health and Development. (n.d.). Introduction to evaluation: Intervention research with communities: A gateway to tools. In *The community tool box.* Retrieved May 22, 2014, from http://ctb.ku.edu/en/table-of-contents/evaluate/evaluation/intervention-research/main

Kuhn, T. (1996). *The structure of scientific revolutions* (3rd ed.). Chicago, IL: University of Chicago Press.

Laroche, L., & Roth, W. M. (2009). Teaching and learning qualitative research: Educational space as a fluid. In S. Kouritzin, N. Piquemal, & R. Norman (Eds.), *Qualitative research: Challenging the orthodoxies in standard academic discourse(s)* (pp. 229–246). New York, NY: Routledge.

Lather, P. (1993). Fertile obsession: Validity after poststructuralism. *Sociological Quarterly, 34*(4), 673–693.

Lather, P. (2001). Validity as an incitement to discourse: Qualitative research and the crisis of legitimation. In V. Richardson (Ed.),

Handbook of research on teaching (4th ed., pp. 241–250). Washington, DC: AERA.

Lather, P. (2007a). *Getting lost: Feminist efforts toward a double(d) science.* Albany: State University of New York Press.

Lather, P. (2007b). Validity, qualitative. In G. Ritzer (Ed.), *The Blackwell encyclopedia of sociology* (pp. 5161–5165). Oxford, UK: Blackwell.

Lather, P. (2008). Getting lost: Critiquing across difference as methodological practice. In K. Gallagher (Ed.), *The methodological dilemma: Creative, critical, and collaborative approaches to qualitative research* (pp. 219–231). Abingdon, UK: Routledge.

Lather, P. (2010). *Engaging science policy: From the side of the messy.* New York, NY: Peter Lang.

Lather, P. (2013). Methodology-21: What do we do in the afterward? *International Journal of Qualitative Studies in Education, 26*(6), 634–645.

Lather, P., & St. Pierre, E. A. (2013). Introduction: Post-qualitative research. *International Journal of Qualitative Studies in Education, 26*(6), 629–633.

Law, J. (2004). *After method.* London, UK: Routledge.

Lemert, C. (2007). *Thinking the unthinkable: The riddles of classical social theories.* Boulder, CO: Paradigm.

Levin, C. (1996). *Jean Baudrillard: A study in cultural metaphysics.* Hertfordshire, UK: Prentice Hall.

Lévi-Strauss, C. (1966). *The savage mind.* Chicago, IL: University of Chicago Press.

Linn, R. (2003). Accountability: Responsibility and reasonable expectations. *Educational Researcher, 32*(7), 3–13.

Llamas, J., & Boza, Á. (2011). Teaching research methods for doctoral students in education: Learning to enquire in the university. *International Journal of Social Research Methodology, 14*(1), 77–90.

Lorenz, W. (2003). European experiences in teaching social work research. *Social Work Education, 22*(1), 7–18.

Luttrell, W. (2010). Interactive and reflexive models of qualitative research design. In W. Luttrell (Ed.), *Qualitative educational research: Readings in reflexive methodology and transformative practice* (pp. 159–163). New York, NY: Routledge.

Lyotard, J.-F. (1997). *Postmodern fables* (G. V. D. Abbeele, Trans.). Minneapolis: University of Minnesota Press.

Lyotard, J.-F. (1999). *The postmodern condition: A report on knowledge* (G. Bennington & B. Massumi, Trans.). Minneapolis: University of Minnesota Press.

MacLure, M. (2006). The bone in the throat: Some uncertain thoughts on baroque method. *International Journal of Qualitative Studies in Education, 19*(6), 729–745.

MacLure, M. (2010). The offence of theory. *Journal of Education Policy, 25*(2), 277–286.

MacLure, M. (2013). Researching without representation? Language and materiality in post-qualitative research. *International Journal of Qualitative Studies in Education, 26*(6), 658–667.

Marshall, C., & Rossman, G. (2006). *Designing qualitative research* (4th ed.). Thousand Oaks, CA: Sage.

Mason, J. (2002). *Qualitative researching* (2nd ed.). London, UK: Sage.

Massumi, B. (1987). Translator's foreword: Pleasures of philosophy (B. Massumi, Trans.). In G. Deleuze & F. Guattari (Eds.), *A thousand plateaus: Capitalism and schizophrenia* (pp. ix–xv). Minneapolis: University of Minnesota Press.

Massumi, B. (1998). Sensing the virtual, building the insensible. *Architectural Design, 68*(5/6), 16–24.

Massumi, B. (2002). *Parables for the virtual.* Durham, NC: Duke University Press.

Mauthner, N. S., & Doucet, A. (2003). Reflexive accounts and accounts of reflexivity in qualitative data analysis. *Sociology, 37*(3), 413–431. doi: 10.1177/0038038 5030373002

Maxwell, J. (1996). *Qualitative research design: An interactive approach.* Thousand Oaks, CA: Sage.

Mayan, M., & Daum, C. (2014). Politics and public policy, social justice, and qualitative research. In N. Denzin & M. Giardina (Eds.), *Qualitative inquiry outside the academy* (pp. 73–91). Walnut Creek, CA: Left Coast Press.

McAllister, M. (2003). Blackbirds singing in the dead of night? Advancing the craft of teaching qualitative research. *Journal of Nursing Education, 42*(7), 296–303.

McIntyre, A. (2008). *Participatory action research.* Thousand Oaks, CA: Sage.

McCabe, J. L., & Holmes, D. (2009). Reflexivity, critical qualitative research and emancipation: A Foucauldian perspective. *Journal of Advanced Nursing, 65*(7), 1518–1526. doi: 10.1111/j.1365-2648.2009.04978.x

Merleau-Ponty, M. (1974). *Phenomenology of perception.* New York, NY: Routledge & K. Paul; Humanities Press.

Merleau-Ponty, M. (2004). *The world of perception.* New York, NY: Routledge.

Mitchell, W. (2001). Romanticism and the life of things: Fossils, totems, and images. *Critical Inquiry, 28*(1), 167–184.

Mitchell, W. (2005). *What do pictures want?* Chicago, IL: University of Chicago Press.

Mol, A. (2002). *The body multiple: Ontology in medical practice.* Durham, NC: Duke University Press.

Mol, A., & Law, J. (1994). Regions, networks and fluids: Anaemia and social topology. *Social Studies of Science, 24*(4), 641–671.

Mol, A., & Law, J. (2002). Complexities: An introduction. In

J. Law & A. Mol (Eds.), *Complexities: Social studies of knowledge practices* (pp. 1–22). Durham, NC: Duke University Press.

Morrell, E. (2005, November 30–December 3). Critical participatory action research and the literacy achievement of ethnic minority groups. In National Reading Conference, *55th yearbook of the National Reading Conference*, Miami, Florida.

Morse, J. (2005). Qualitative research is not a modification of quantitative research. *Qualitative Health Research, 15*(8), 1003–1005.

National Council of Teachers of Mathematics. (n.d.). *How is action research defined?* Retrieved May 22, 2014, from https://www.nctm.org/uploadedFiles/Lessons_and_Resources/Grants_and_Awards/How%20is%20Action%20Research%20Defined%281%29.pdf

Nietzsche, F. (1999). *The birth of tragedy and other writings* (R. Speirs, Trans.). Cambridge, UK: Cambridge University Press.

Nola, R., & Irzik, G. (2003). Incredulity towards Lyotard: A critique of a postmodernist account of science and knowledge. *Studies in History and Philosophy of Science, Part A, 34*(2), 391–421.

Novikov, A., & Novikov, D. (2013). Foundations of research methodology. *Research methodology: From philosophy of science to research design*. Boca Raton: CRC Press.

O'Brien, R. (2001). Um exame da abordagem metodológica da pesquisa ação [An overview of the methodological approach of action research]. In R. Richardson (Ed.), *Teoria e prática da pesquisa ação [Theory and practice of action research]*. João Pessoa, Brazil: Universidade Federal da Paraíba. (English version) Retrieved June 5, 2014, from http://www.web.ca/~robrien/papers/arfinal.html

O'Byrne, A. (2005). Pedagogy without a project: Arendt and Derrida on teaching, responsibility and revolution. *Studies in Philosophy and Education, 24*(5), 389–409.

O'Connor, D., & O'Neill, B. (2004). Toward social justice: Teaching qualitative research. *Journal of Teaching in Social Work, 23*(3–4), 19–33.

O'Donnell, A. (2014). Another relationship to failure: Reflections on Beckett and education. *Journal of Philosophy of Education, 48*(2), 260–275.

O'Neill, M. (2007). Re-imagining diaspora through ethno-mimesis: Humiliation, human dignity, and belonging. In O. Guedes-Bailey, M. Georgiou, & R. Harindranath (Eds.), *Transnational lives and the media: Re-imagining diasporas* (pp. 72–96). New York, NY: Palgrave.

O'Neill, M. (2012). Ethno-mimesis and participatory arts. In S. Pink (Ed.), *Advances in visual methodology* (pp. 153–172). Thousand Oaks, CA: Sage.

O'Neill, M., Giddens, S., Breatnach, P., Bagley, C., Bourne, D., & Judge, T. (2002). Renewed methodologies for social research: Ethno-mimesis as performative practice. *Sociological Review, 50*(1), 69–88.

Panel of Research Ethics. (2013). Government of Canada. Retrieved May 19, 2014, from http://www.pre.ethics.gc.ca/eng/policy-politique/initiatives/tcps2-eptc2/glossary-glossaire/.http://www.pre.ethics.gc.ca/eng/policy-politique/initiatives/tcps2-eptc2/glossary-glossaire/

Patrick, M. (1997). *Derrida, responsibility and politics*. Aldershot, UK: Ashgate.

Perlesz, A., & Lindsay, J. (2003). Methodological triangulation in researching families: Making sense of dissonant data. *International Journal of Social Research Methodology, 6*(1), 25–40.

Polkinghorne, D. E. (2005). Language and meaning: Data collection in qualitative research. *Journal of Counseling Psychology, 52*(2), 137–145. doi: 10.1037/0022-0167.52.2.137

Preissle, J., & Roulston, K. (2009). Trends in teaching qualitative research: A 30-year perspective. In M. Garner, C. Wagner, & B. Kawulich (Eds.), *Teaching research methods in the social sciences* (pp. 13–21). Surrey, UK: Ashgate.

Program for the Advancement of Research on Conflict and Collaboration. (n.d.). Retrieved June 5, 2014, from http://www.maxwell.syr.edu/parcc/Research/advocacy/Advocacy_and_Activism_Overview/

Raddon, M., Raby, R., & Sharpe, E. (2009). The challenges of teaching qualitative coding: Can a learning object help? *International Journal of Teaching and Learning in Higher Education, 21*(3), 336–350.

Raingruber, B. (2009). Assigning poetry reading as a way of introducing students to qualitative data analysis. *Journal of Advanced Nursing, 65*(8), 1753–1761.

Reinertsen, A., & Otterstad, A. (2012). Being data and datadream/ing pedagogies with Pinter: A dream/dialogue/data/play about being ruthlessly honest about own motives eventually Max Stirner. *Cultural Studies ↔ Critical Methodologies, 13*(4), 233–239.

Rice, C. (2010). The space-time of pre-emption: An interview with Brian Massumi. *Architectural Design, 80*(5), 32–37.

Richardson, L. (2000). Writing: A method of inquiry. In N. Denzin & Y. Lincoln (Eds.), *Handbook of qualitative research* (2nd ed., pp. 923–948). Thousand Oaks, CA: Sage.

Riel, M. (2010). *Understanding action research.* Center for Collaborative Action Research, Pepperdine University. Retrieved May 22, 2014, from http://cadres.pepperdine.edu/ccar/define.html

Rilke, R. M. (1993). *Letters to a young poet.* New York, NY: Norton.

Roulston, K, deMarrais, K., & Lewis, J. (2003). Learning to interview in the social sciences. *Qualitative Inquiry, 9*(4), 643–648.

Sagor, R. (2000). What is action research? In *Guiding school improvement with action research.* Retrieved June 5, 2014, from http://www.ascd.org/publications/books/100047/chapters/What-Is-Action-Research%C2%A2.aspx

Sanchez, C., & Barbour, J. A. D. (2012). A critical approach to the teaching and learning of critical social science at the college level. In S. Steinberg & G. Cannella (Eds.), *Critical qualitative research reader* (pp. 429–440). New York, NY: Peter Lang.

Schneider, B. (2012). Participatory action research, mental health service user research, and the hearing (our) voices projects. *International Journal of Qualitative Methods, 11*(2), 152–165.

Schostak, J., & Schostak, J. (2008). *Radical research: Designing, developing and writing research to make a difference.* London, UK: Routledge.

Schwandt, T. (2007). *The SAGE dictionary of qualitative inquiry* (3rd ed.). Thousand Oaks, CA: Sage.

Shawver, L. (2001). If Wittgenstein and Lyotard could talk with Jack and Jill: Towards postmodern family therapy. *Journal of Family Therapy, 23,* 232–252.

Shor, I. (1992). *Empowering education: Critical teaching for social change*. Chicago, IL: University of Chicago Press.

Silverman, D., & Marvasti, A. (2008). *Doing qualitative research*. Thousand Oaks, CA: Sage.

Spivak, G. (1993). *Outside in the teaching machine*. New York, NY: Routledge.

Spivak, G. (1997). Translator's preface (G. Spivak, Trans.). In J. Derrida (Ed.), *Of grammatology* (Corrected ed., pp. ix–lxxxvii). Baltimore, MD: John Hopkins University Press.

Spradley, J. P. (1980). *Participant observation*. New York, NY: Holt, Rinehart and Winston.

St. Pierre, E. (1997). Methodology in the fold and the irruption of transgressive data. *International Journal of Qualitative Studies in Education, 10*(2), 175–189.

St. Pierre, E. (2002). "Science" rejects post-modernism. *Educational Researcher, 31*(8), 25–27.

St. Pierre, E. (2009). Afterword: Decentering voice in qualitative inquiry. In A. Jackson & L. A. Mazzei (Eds.), *Voice in qualitative inquiry* (pp. 221–236). London, UK: Routledge.

St. Pierre, E., & Roulston, K. (2006). The state of qualitative inquiry: A contested science. *International Journal of Qualitative Studies in Education, 19*(6), 673–684.

Strauss, A., & Corbin, J. (1998). *Basics of qualitative research: Techniques and procedures for developing grounded theory* (2nd ed.). Thousand Oaks, CA: Sage.

Sullivan, P. (2012). *Qualitative data analysis: Using a dialogical approach*. London, UK: Sage.

Tate, W. (2007). Linking education research and civic responsibility: Why Now? *Educational Researcher, 36*(7), 408–409.

Taylor, B., Anderson, R., Au, K., & Raphael, T. (2000). Discretion in the translation of research to policy: A case from beginning reading. *Educational Researcher, 29*(6), 16–26.

Tikly, L. (2004). Education and the new imperialism. *Comparative Education, 40*(2), 173–198.

Todd, S. (2003). *Learning from the Other: Levinas, psychoanalysis, and ethical possibilities in education*. Albany: State University of New York Press.

Torrance, H. (2011). Qualitative research, science, and government. In N. Denzin & Y. Lincoln (Eds.), *The SAGE handbook of qualitative research* (4th ed.). Thousand Oaks, CA: Sage.

Torre, M., Fine, M., Stoudt, B., & Fox, M. (2012). *Critical participatory action research as public science*. Retrieved June 5, 2014, from https://archive.org/stream/TorreEtAl.2012Critical PARAsPublicScience/Torre%20et%20al.%20%282012%29%20Critical%20PAR%20as%20Public%20Science#page/n1/mode/2up

Troppe, M. (1994). *Participatory action research: Merging the community and scholarly agendas*. Providence, RI: Campus Compact.

Tuhiwai Smith, L. (2001). *Decolonizing methodologies: Research and indigenous peoples* (4th impression ed.). London, UK: Zed Books.

U.S. Institute of Education Sciences. (2010). *Request for applications: Statistical and research methodology in education*. Retrieved from http://ies.ed.gov/funding/pdf/2011_84305D.pdf

Vikström, L. (2010). Identifying dissonant and complementary data on women through the triangulation of historical sources. *International Journal of Social Research Methodology, 13*(3), 211-221. doi: 10.1080/13645579.2010.482257

Viswanathan, M., Ammerman, A., Eng, E., Gartlehner, G., Lohr, K. N., Griffith, D., . . . Whitener, L. (1994). *Community-based participatory research: Assessing the evidence* (Evidence Report/Technology Assessment No. 99). Rockville, MD: Agency for Healthcare Research and Quality.

Wagner, C., Garner, M., & Kawulich, B. (2011). The state of the art of teaching research methods in the social sciences: Towards a pedagogical culture. *Studies in Higher Education, 36*(1), 75–88.

Waite, D. (2011). A simple card trick: Teaching qualitative data analysis using a deck of playing cards. *Qualitative Inquiry, 17*(10), 982–985.

Waite, D. (2014) Teaching the unteachable: Some issues of qualitative research pedagogy. *Qualitative Inquiry, 20*(3), 267–281.

Wang, H. (2005). Aporias, responsibility, and the im/possibility of teaching multicultural education. *Educational Theory, 55*(1), 45–59.

Weinbrot, J. (2012). The Baudrillardean object. *International Journal of Baudrillard Studies, 9*(2). Retrieved from http://www.ubishops.ca/baudrillardstudies/vol9_2/v9-2-TofCfinal.html

Welch, R., & Panelli, R. (2003). Teaching research methodology to geography undergraduates: Rationale and practice in a human geography programme. *Journal of Geography in Higher Education, 27*(30), 255–277.

Williams, J. (2011). Event. In C. Stivale (Ed.), *Gilles Deleuze: Key concepts* (2nd ed., pp. 80–90). Montreal, Quebec: McGill-Queen's University Press.

Wolcott, H. (1994). *Transforming qualitative data: Description, analysis, and interpretation.* Thousand Oaks, CA: Sage.

Wright, T., & Wright, V. (1999). Ethical responsibility and the organizational researcher: A committed-to-participant research perspective. *Journal of Organizational Behavior, 20*, 1107–1112.

Wright, T., & Wright, V. (2002, June). Organizational researcher values, ethical responsibility, and the committed-to-participant research perspective. *Journal of Management Inquiry, 11*(2), 173–185.

INDEX

Figures and tables are indicated by f or t following the page number.

as object, 54–55
  paradox of, 74–75
  resistance to, 52–54
  responses to, 51–52
Data analysis, 58–60. *See also* Data-wants
Data contamination, reflexivity and, 24
Data games, 55–56
Data volume, analysis approach and, 58–59
Data-wants
  analysis and, 58–60
  coding, 63–65, 64–65t
  counting, 61–62
  defined, 48
  dialoging with itself, 67–69
  dilemma of, 50–51, 52f
  filling and extending, 65–67
  listening to data, 60–61
  multiplying, 70–71, 72–73f
Davis, W., 124
Dead ends, 168–169
Decision making, 172
Decontextualization, 20–21
Deletions, 157
Deleuze, G., 8, 35–36, 37, 40, 42, 43,
      87, 164–165, 176
Denzin, N. K., 180
Derrida, J.
  community without community, 6
  decision making and, 128, 132
  erasure and, 157
  ghosts and, 138, 148–149
  on meaning, 18
  pedagogy without a project and, 133
  on questions and answers, 104
  responsibility and, 117–119, 124, 126–127,
      130–131
Differentiating, 31–32
Directionality
  of data, 48–49, 54–55, 58–60, 77–78
  of knowledge, 180–181, 181f
Discomfort, 114
Dog walking, 169–170
Doucet, A., 26
Doyle, S., 27
Duam, C., 180–181

Economic pressures and responsibility, 115
Edelsky, C., 144

Eisenhart, M., 120
Elliott, S. J., 31
Empty space, 4
Endings, 101
Epistemological diversity, 6–7
Erasure, 138–139, 157–160, 160–163t
Ethical paradoxes, 179
Ethics. *See* Responsibility
Ethnomimesis, 180, 189
Events, 138
Evink, E., 126, 133
Examples, use of, 146
Eyles, J., 31

Facilitation versus manipulation, 207–208
Failure. *See* Productive failures
Farmer, T., 31
Fermentation process, 88
Flow. *See* Fluid methodologies
Fluid methodologies
  Baudrillard and, 89
  benefits of, 97–98
  Deleuze and, 87
  implementation, 98–99
  Law and, 89–90
  Massumi and, 87–88
  Mol and, 89–94, 93f
  multiple parts conceptual illustration
      of, 94–97, 96f
  outcomes with, 84–86
Foucault, M., 13, 147
Foundations of Social Research
      (Crotty), 154–155

Gee, J., 13
Generative research, 103–104
Ghosts, 138, 148–156
Giardina, M., 180
Gordon, C., 147
Gordon, M., 144
Guattari, F., 40, 42, 43, 176
Gubrium, J. F., 13

Habermas, J., 35
Heidegger, M., 196
Hein, S., 141–142
Holmes, D., 27
Holstein, J. A., 13

⑤SAGE video

We are delighted to announce the launch of a streaming video program at SAGE!

SAGE Video online collections are developed in partnership with leading academics, societies and practitioners, including many of SAGE's own authors and academic partners, to deliver cutting-edge pedagogical collections mapped to curricular needs.

Available alongside our book and reference collections on the *SAGE Knowledge* platform, content is delivered with critical online functionality designed to support scholarly use.

SAGE Video combines originally commissioned and produced material with licensed videos to provide a complete resource for students, faculty, and researchers.

NEW IN 2015!

- Counseling and Psychotherapy
- Education
- Media and Communication

sagepub.com/video
#sagevideo